American
Avatar

Related Titles from Potomac Books

The Al Jazeera Effect:
How the New Global Media Are Reshaping World Politics
—Philip Seib

Public Opinion and International Intervention:
Lessons from the Iraq War
—Richard Sobel, Peter Furia, and Bethany Barrett, eds.

The "Ugly American" in the Arab Mind:
Why Do Arabs Resent America?
—Mohamed El-Bendary

American
Avatar

The **UNITED STATES** in the
GLOBAL IMAGINATION

Barry A. Sanders

To Julie & Peter, with warmest regards

[signature: Barry Sanders]

Potomac Books
Washington, D.C.

Library of Congress Cataloging-in-Publication Data
Sanders, Barry A.
    American avatar : the United States in the global imagination / Barry A. Sanders. — 1st ed.
        p. cm.
    Includes bibliographical references and index.
    ISBN 978-1-59797-681-7 (hardcover : alk. paper)
    ISBN 978-1-59797-774-6 (electronic edition)
    1. United States—Foreign public opinion. 2. United States—Foreign relations—2001-2009. 3. United States—Foreign relations—2009- 4. Anti-Americanism. I. Title.
    E895.S26 2011
    327.730090'5—dc23

                                                    2011019989

Printed in the United States of America on acid-free paper that meets the American National Standards Institute Z39-48 Standard.

Potomac Books
22841 Quicksilver Drive
Dulles, Virginia 20166

First Edition

10 9 8 7 6 5 4 3 2 1

To Nancy

Contents

No one likes us—I don't know why
We may not be perfect, but heaven knows we try
But all around, even our old friends put us down
Let's drop the big one and see what happens.
—*Randy Newman, "Political Science," 1972*

Preface

On September 12, 2001, while Ground Zero in Manhattan still glowed and smoked, Americans awoke to find themselves bathed in expressions of sympathy and affection across the globe. Jean-Marie Colombani, editor of the French daily *Le Monde*, headlined, "We Are All Americans." He asked rhetorically, "How can we not feel profound solidarity with those people, that country, the United States, to whom we are so close and to whom we owe our freedom?"[1] Flowers were strewn before American embassies from Germany to Japan. Crowds poured into the streets of foreign capitals to express their grief over the murders and destruction in New York, Pennsylvania, and Virginia.

A little more than two and a half years later, the same Jean-Marie Colombani wrote a story for *Le Monde* entitled, "We Are All Un-American?"[2] In the time between global polls of public opinion in 1999 and 2000 and similar polls in spring 2004, the percentages of people expressing a favorable view of the United States went from 83 percent to 58 percent in Britain; from 78 percent to 38 percent in Germany; from 62 percent to 37 percent in France; and from 77 percent to 27 percent in Morocco.[3] Similar drops in public favor were reflected in many other countries around the world. By mid-2004 the percentage of Jordanians expressing approval of their ally and major cash benefactor, the United States, dropped to 5 percent. What happened? What does it mean?

The United States was not universally loved even before September 11, 2001. Arabs celebrated the attacks in large public demonstrations in Cairo and Nablus, while people elsewhere expressed quiet satisfaction at the blow to the United States. Even where the pre-attack measurements of United States popularity were high, they were never 100 percent. At the deepest level, some of the expressions of disapproval of the United States reflect the same emotions that motivated the perpetrators of the attacks, who took their own lives in the process of striking out at the symbols of American economic and military power. In his sympathetic article on September 12, 2001, Colombani wrote, "America, in the solitude of its power . . . in certain parts of the globe . . . seems to draw nothing but hate."

For some it must be hate. For many others it may be too much love—unrequited love, disappointed love. The United States bears the world's hopes and dreams as no other nation in history. In its "solitude of power," the United States evokes expectations and longings among foreigners in their version of the "American Dream." This is true American exceptionalism, and it is unique in history. In his first visit to Europe as president, in April 2009, Barack Obama answered a question from a *Financial Times* reporter about whether he believed in American exceptionalism. He said, "I believe in American exceptionalism, just as I suspect that the Brits believe in British exceptionalism and the Greeks believe in Greek exceptionalism."[4] His suspicion ignores the anomaly of American exceptionalism. There is no discussion of British or Greek exceptionalism among the citizens of those nations, and certainly no such concept among foreigners. And this difference is not about relative power. We know of no concept of Roman exceptionalism believed by the people on the edges of the Roman Empire or Mongol exceptionalism by the outside observers of Genghis Khan's hordes. The world outside its borders has high expectations for America. Those expectations are a mixed blessing.

We must proceed with caution in analyzing attitudes based on opinion polling. The rapid decline in American popularity between 2000 and 2004 partly reflects the fickle and superficial nature of public opinion and the unreliability of global polling. Despite the absence of any real change in the United States or its policies between 2004 and 2005, Jordanian approval of the United States more than quadrupled to 21 percent in that time. French and German approval also rose, and British opinion dropped even further than in 2004. By May 2009, following the inauguration of President Obama and before he had implemented any significant changes in foreign policies, favorability ratings for the United States were once again at or above the levels from 2000 in most countries.[5] One year later, in May 2010, Pew showed favorable views of the United States had leapt another 13 percent in Russia and 11 percent in China while dropping 10 percent in Egypt and India and declining 13 percent in Mexico.[6] By March 2011, Pew found favorable views of the United States in China and India had dropped by 14 percent and 25 percent, respectively, from the 2010 figures.[7] This volatility in polling hints at a more fundamental problem in interpreting such results: public opinion is a superficial phenomenon, like surface eddies in the sea. The images on which they draw are deeper currents that change more slowly and, over time, more consistently influence people's conception of the world around them, including their pictures of the United States. This book examines both that fundamental visualization of America and the dynamic process of its expression.

Surveying the imagery people express about the United States exposes their consistent undercurrents of thought. People change their views rapidly, leaning toward more negative or positive opinions, but the imagery they use to articulate their concepts draws from a pool of old ideas. This pool changes, but only gradually. The United States is seen as rich, powerful, hypocritical, racist, imperialist, and democratic, among a host of other qualities. All of these and many others date back at least one hundred years in the popular imagination. All have some basis in fact, yet all are stereotypes, and none can be completely true. They are the data in people's minds, the components that people assemble to articulate their attitudes.

The attitudes that rule the selection of images from the pool are controlled by a set of predispositions. Some are fleeting—a mood, a temper. Some are deeper rooted—a fear, a hope. Some are quite permanent—a religion, an ideology. Many people can harbor conflicting predispositions, making predicting or changing their attitudes a confounding process. These biases guide the formation of opinions on any subject. They are the filters that sift through and select among the stored images. We must look at both the nature and process of image collection and the biases that determine which images are selected, in order to understand the views people express on America, whether changeable or permanent, pro-American or anti-American.

At the heart of this analysis is a question of how people's minds work. Certainly, the real-life United States, the nature of its existence and its policies, plays a role in the formation of people's views. Facts matter. Actions matter. But all images and opinions are ideas, with more or less attachment to reality. Ideas are in *their* heads. This is an inquiry about *them*. The slender connection between America and views about America underscores the difficulty facing American policymakers, diplomats, and citizens in seeking to understand and, perhaps, to change those attitudes.

Whatever light this book sheds does not come from me alone. I am much indebted to all those around the world with whom I have discussed this interesting topic, my students at UCLA who have explored many of these ideas with me over the years, and especially my friends who have plowed through drafts of this manuscript and offered valuable suggestions on both the substance and the process of finishing this project. The guidance I received on bringing this to publication came from many people, but particularly from Nicholas Cull and Philip Seib of the University of Southern California, Daniel Caldwell of Pepperdine University, Thomas Plate of Loyola Marymount University, and Leslie Breed McLean. I also appreciate the excellent work of Erin Auerbach, Jennifer Patton, Mark Finster, and Ellen Caldwell in helping make this a book that is worthy of your attention.

PART I
Collecting Images

1

INTRODUCTION

It will always be something else, a world unto itself, a Western
Heavenly Empire, a China of our imagination, a place to admire,
To be grateful to, and to be baffled by forever.
—*Hans Magnus Enzensberger, German poet*[1]

In his allegory of the cave, Plato portrayed people in a cave seeing the
world as shadows cast on the wall by all that passed the entrance. Their
perceptions were not reality; they were an indirect effect of reality. Sometimes, images are pure inventions of the mind and lack even this tenu-
ous link to substance. They are a fluid mix of matters seen, remembered,
forgotten, and invented. "America," as imagined around the world, is just
such an imperfect reflection of reality and of people's hopes, dreams, and
fears. It is a complex, evanescent, contradictory collection of ideas.

America is fertile ground for the study of images because it is unique
among places in the world as an idea.[2] It occupies a part of the mental
landscape of almost every person on the globe. If you ask a Chilean about
his image of Finland, he may have none. He may never have heard of Finland or Belgium or the Czech Republic. America, however, is among the
world's few universally recognized terms—even if the concept of it is radically different from one mind to another. The unique idea of the "American Dream," a rich and loaded concept, is nearly as pervasive. Everyone
has an opinion about America filled with imagery from the obvious to the

3

bizarre. The opinions seem to change like quicksilver, but the imagery fits recurrent themes.

Images of America in minds in the remotest parts of the world arise from its revolutionary history, its current power and wealth, its evangelical devotion to democratic liberalism, and its global commercial, cultural, and political interactions. Each of these elements relates to the others. Paradoxically, one of the most persistent negative images of America is that it is inward looking, self-absorbed, and ignorant of the outside world. It is considered diplomatically immature and inept. Yet the omnipresence of America in the minds of others reflects, in part, America's deep engagement with other cultures and places. The United States is one of the top three trading partners in either imports or exports (or both) with more than half of the sixty-seven major trading nations of the world and with all the most populous nations.[3] In the competitive world of business, this sort of trading success cannot come to those who are ignorant of other cultures and peoples. Further, the United States has diplomatic missions in 160 nations.[4] It has citizens living abroad in virtually every nation. More than half of Americans in the eighteen to twenty-nine age group report that they have friends or family living abroad.[5] The United States founded the United Nations and is its single largest source of financial support as well as its home. In the short span of two and a quarter centuries since its founding, the United States has gone from a fringe of colonial settlements on the eastern seaboard adjoining a wilderness, to a global position of unsurpassed economic, political, military, and cultural influence. How ignorant and incompetent can Americans be?

Yes, many Americans have less knowledge of foreign countries, foreign cultures, and foreign languages than people of similar backgrounds abroad. Part of this is geography. Even in this era of the European Union, a person traveling in Europe, the 850-mile distance equal to that which separates Chicago and New York, will cross six or seven national boundaries and the lands of six or seven languages and cultures. By this closeness, a normal traveler in Europe naturally takes on the sophistication of a cosmopolitan. It comes with the territory.

It is not only geography. What the United States does matters to every other country in the world. It, and it alone, exercises economic and military power worldwide. Conversely, the actions of most of the world's nations have no perceptible impact on the lives of Americans. Japan, then the world's second largest economy, suffered more than a decade of economic stagnation in the 1990s with no apparent harmful impact on the American economy. The United States recently suffered a similar debacle, and national economies all over the world feel the financial pain.

Another part is philosophical. There has always been a strain of American political thinking that it would turn its back on the rest of the world and "have with them as little political connection as possible."[6] The United States doomed the League of Nations with its rejection of the Versailles Treaty in 1920, and it continues to guard its sovereignty jealously with respect to international treaties. In the same vein, the George W. Bush administration spurned the treaty that established the International Court of Justice and generally looked with a jaundiced eye on international treaties and conventions. During its first years in office, the Obama administration gave a cold shoulder to trade agreements and failed to seek ratification of pending treaties with Colombia, Pakistan, and South Korea.

In the face of this reputation for aloofness, there is an opposing image of the United States meddling in every event in the most obscure parts of the world. If a government falls in central Africa, it is certain that someone will blame the CIA. The United States, its intelligence services, and its corporations are considered so pervasive and so fiendishly clever and knowledgeable that one of them is assumed to be behind every mishap and catastrophe. Disastrous floods in Pakistan in 2010 and subsequent earthquakes and tsunamis are thought by many in the Muslim world to be the result of a secret United States military project called HAARP, based in Fairbanks, Alaska, which controls the world's weather through electromagnetic waves.[7]

Consider the contrast between the comment by an Arab League official in Cairo who said of Americans that "they can hardly find Egypt on the map" with the contemporaneous comment by a Cairo university lecturer that "I was never a supporter of Nasser or Saddam Hussein, but we stood with him [sic] because they became symbols of our identity. The West creates these people."[8]

Images of the United States are full of such contradictions. They have to be. America, the object being imagined, is complex and contradictory. Some are ideas of what America is or was, and some are ideas of what

America does or did. "America" is not a single thing. It is a place, a piece of geography; it is a political actor, a nation; it is a group of people, a nationality; it is a symbol, a representation of a set of ideas for the political and economic ordering of life; and for many people it is the ideal of the perfect place, the name attached to their dreams for a better life. Within each of these, it is not a single thing. As a stretch of land, is it the black water swamps of South Carolina; the endless, broad plains of Iowa; the gritty streets of the South Bronx; or the beaches of Southern California? As a political force, is it a nation that rescued the Allies in World War I, preserving democracy, or a nation that refused to ratify the peace; a nation (among others) that failed to confront Hitler's menace in the 1930s or a nation that again rescued the Allies in World War II; a nation that supported a long series of Latin American dictators or a nation that later championed a crop of democratically elected leaders? As a people, is it a society dominated by a white, Protestant middle class, or is it a society that is over 36 percent minority and in which Roman Catholicism is the single largest religious denomination? As the world's most powerful and modern nation, is it a reactionary defender of the status quo or a disruptive agent of change and destroyer of tradition? As a symbol, is "America" the democratic and egalitarian ideal of the Enlightenment, or is it a rapacious, commercial homogenizer destroying indigenous cultures around the world? Is it real or is it a fantasy? It is all these things and more.

Images are stereotypes. They reduce a complex reality to a simpler thought. They extend the particular to the general. They can never capture a full reality or be more than partly true. With something as complex as America, the problem is multiplied a million-fold. America is vast and intricately varied, with a population that exults in its diversity. English historian John Gray explained,

> America is too rich in contradictions for any definition of it to be possible. For every attitude that is supposed to be distinctively American one can find an opposite stance that is no less so. . . .
> In truth, there is no such thing as an essentially American world view—any more than there is an essentially American landscape. Anyone who thinks otherwise shows they have not grasped the most important fact about America, which is that it is unknowable.[9]

Images are not necessarily visual. They are the ideas received from the senses and the imagination. They can be expressed in words, visions, smells, tastes, or any other sensation or form of communication.

Even if America could be perfectly depicted as in a snapshot, images are formed from imperfect information. A visitor can only meet a small fraction of its 309 million people, cover only a small quantity of its 3.6 million square miles, experience only a few weeks or months of its history. What a visitor thinks he saw might be skewed by the problems of preexisting expectations, perceptual difficulties, moods, circumstances, and memory. The phenomenon of competing eyewitnesses is well known in courts of law, where dueling witnesses honestly swear to opposing versions of events. Three-quarters of the convicts in American prisons who later have been exonerated and released on the basis of DNA evidence had been convicted by eyewitness testimony.[10] Still, the visitor to America can justly claim to have developed authentic personal images of America, and these claims take on credence. From de Tocqueville to Bernard-Henri Lévy,[11] the personal travelogue has been a fertile source of imagery of America. People believe them.

For every person who visits the United States for a firsthand look, there are multitudes who never come. Their images of the United States are based only on what others tell them: accounts of travelers, parents, friends, journalists, novelists, teachers, religious leaders, politicians, or others. The clouds and distortion in these lenses are so thick that any accurate realities derived from these accounts would be by sheer luck. As the perception of America goes from the mind of the firsthand witness to his books, articles, and speeches, and then to the minds and interpretations of those who recount what they think they read or heard to others, the initial account of reality transforms as the rumor does in the game of telephone. It does not emerge in the same form as it went in—even assuming no intent to color or twist the facts. In the hands of a newspaper editor or, worse yet, a censor, reality gets a selective and a distorted rendering on its way to the reader. News can become propaganda. Religious leaders, politicians, friends, and relatives may all bring intentional or subliminal spins to the accounts they give.

Reality, in the hands of a filmmaker, is a victim of commercial or political motivations to sell entertainment or deliver a message. Scenes that never did and never would happen are filmed against the backdrop of putative American locales. The America in the eyes of the world on film over the years has mostly been painted backdrops and stock footage. Now, even with the advent of less costly location shoots that enable filming at the real place, American cities are being portrayed anywhere in the world. They often look more American than America. Consider the film *Cold Mountain's* depictions of the Great Smoky Mountains and the television show *Psych's* scenes of Santa Barbara; the former was filmed in Romania, and the latter is shot in Canada. Things happen in movies that did not happen and would not happen. For all the remarkable maneuvers a driver might really witness on American streets and highways, no one sees the sorts of flamboyant car chases that are staples of the action film genre, such as in *Bullitt, The Fast and the Furious,* and *The French Connection.* This flood of output on fictional film, on television, and in print, rather than in America itself, forms much of the raw material of images of America in people's minds.

All these influences separating images from reality shrink in importance when compared to what happens to information when it enters the minds of the people forming the image. As ideas, images have no existence outside people's minds. Even by assuming there is a reality of America outside people's minds, we are leaping over two hundred years of philosophical ruminations. Bishop George Berkeley, the early eighteenth-century British empiricist philosopher, considered what could be definitively proven about the world. He concluded that he could say with certainty only that there is the mind, which can imagine ideas and organize perceptions of the senses (which are also ideas), and beyond that no "corporeal substance" exists.[12]

> It is evident to anyone who takes a survey of the *objects of human knowledge,* that they are either *ideas* actually imprinted on the senses; or else such as are perceived by attending to the passions and operations of the mind; or lastly, *ideas* formed by help of memory and imaginations—either compounding, dividing, or barely representing those originally perceived in the aforesaid ways. . . .
>
> It is indeed an opinion strangely prevailing amongst men, that houses, mountains, rivers, and, in a word, all sensible objects, have an existence, natural or real, distinct from their being perceived by the understanding. . . . What are the forementioned objects but the things we perceive by sense? and what do we perceive besides

our own ideas or sensations? and is it not plainly repugnant that any one of these, or any combination of them, should exist unperceived?[13]

In answer to the question of whether a tree falling in the forest makes a noise if no one is there to hear it, Berkeley would have said there was no noise, and there was no tree. All that we know of the existence of a real world consists of our reactions to sensations that hit our eardrums, retinas, and other points of perception—beyond that we cannot prove that anything is really there. To Berkeley, the processes of knowing and imagining cannot be separated. In short, it is all in our minds.

René Descartes's conclusion "Cogito ergo sum" ("I think, therefore, I am") makes a similar point: I cannot prove I exist or that anything exists; I only know for certain that I am having these thoughts; therefore, I must exist. In the discipline of epistemology, these egocentric theories that reality is only in the eye of the beholder were gathered under the category of solipsism and were again debated throughout the nineteenth century. In a way, the philosophers anticipated the imperceptible reality of quantum physics and the virtual reality of video games. The lines between the real and the imagined are now more blurred than ever. Today, ordinary people not inclined to philosophical musings can fairly wonder whether there is any reality out there. However, this book does not need to settle the philosophical argument. It will assume that America is real, that there is such a place and such a nation. Nevertheless, the images, which this book examines, are entirely in the minds of the beholders. That makes the issue complex enough.

People's minds store images. From early childhood throughout life, images are being added, amended, and forgotten. The mind becomes a wall of shelves holding a large number of images as though they are all audiotapes or DVDs. Gradually, these recordings deteriorate as memories fade and are altered as the imagination amends them. At a given moment, people may access these shelves for one image or a few images and assert that they portray the idea they have on a subject. At another time, they may play entirely different recordings from their collections of images and appear to have changed their views. Their underlying impressions (the total collection of recordings) may have changed little, while the expression of their views may have altered radically. Which images they pull off the shelf will depend on their predispositions—their moods, some recent event, or the way a question is put to them. Something can trigger an old memory. Something can suppress an idea. Sometimes they can have so many conflicting images in their minds that there is no way to coherently express them all. Therefore, the expression of images by groups on a given day—public opinion—is volatile. The underlying views are deep seated and change slowly.

Harold Isaacs captured this in the 1950s in his study of American views of China and India.[14] Isaacs interviewed at length 181 American "leadership types," and he found in each of the interviewees a mix of favorable and unfavorable images on generally common themes but, in each case, in different proportions from the images held by the others. In the case of China, he identified six historical periods in American relations with China and images remembered by interviewees from the different periods. Isaacs classified the periods as ages of respect, contempt, benevolence, admiration, disenchantment, and finally (beginning with the revolution in 1949) hostility. Images of the Chinese people ranged from "delicate, subtle, restrained,"[15] to "shrewd, wily, crafty."[16] They were seen as "bearded sages, patriarchs, scholars"[17] and "a vast hungry people; millions dying; misery, disease, beggars."[18] The strongest imagery was rooted in the interviewees' childhoods; for many, memories of Sunday school discussions of Christian missionary work in China in the period Isaacs called "benevolence" created indelible pictures of the Chinese as (ungrateful) wards. Isaacs observed:

> All the images and experiences of the past have some part. They are not effaced but are absorbed and rearranged in some new design. Much is relegated to the museums and to the memory and to the contending history books, but the greater part remains to bedevil the process of change itself. All the sounds, old and new, go on in our hearing at the same time, making the great din in which we live. All the old and new images flicker around us, giving our world and every individual mind the quality it has of a kaleidoscope.[19]

Isaacs pursued his work in later editions, tracking Gallup polls taken of the American general public's opinions concerning China in 1942 when it was an American ally; in 1966 when it was an avowed enemy; and in 1972 when relations between the two countries had taken a dramatic turn for the better. In the polls, the image of the Chinese for being "hardworking" fluctuated from an idea shared by 69 percent of Americans in 1942 to 37 percent in 1966 and back to 74 percent in 1972. The figures for "brave" moved from 48 percent to 7 percent to 17 percent, and for "practical" moved from 23 percent to 8 percent to 27 percent in the same periods.[20] The measures of other traits—such as religious, intelligent, sly, and treacherous—were similarly volatile. The expressed images would appear to go away with external events and then be rediscovered in observers' views when called forth by a change in the atmosphere, clearly demonstrating the difference between opinion and imagery.

The tapes and videos remained in place in the brain. They contained the full set of images accumulated through a lifetime of perceptions and changed only slowly. When the Gallup pollster put his questions to the subjects, the answers he received were good for that day only. On another day, in other circumstances, he might have gotten totally different responses. All the answers would be true in that they would reflect images taken from the mental shelves of the subject. What they would not be is meaningful in understanding the totality of the subject's attitudes. That can be understood only with a much more comprehensive survey of the content of the shelves—those recordings that are chosen for play at this time as well as those withheld or temporarily forgotten and to be played at another moment.

Think of the litany of images that might simultaneously occupy anyone's mental shelf space on the subject of America: free, powerful, democratic, arrogant, peaceful, dominant, land of opportunity, warlike, wealthy, imperialistic, friendly, focused on its own interests, generous, stingy, selfish, full of choices, religious, heathen, atheistic, isolationist, oblivious, intrusive, pervasive, intelligent, sanctimonious, immoral, technological, ignorant, unreliable, unpredictable, practical, pragmatic, shallow minded, uncultured, innovative, rootless, open minded, bourgeois, glamorous, fat, health conscious, commercial, hard working, lazy, money obsessed, work obsessed, respectful of civil and human rights, supportive of oppressive regimes, respectful of the rule of law, racist, respectful of the individual, lacking in sense of community, cruel, lacking in compassion, paranoid, Caucasian, diverse, beautiful, hideous, turbulent, and an abundance of other adjectives.

The ability to retain conflicting images of America on the mental shelves is significant. F. Scott Fitzgerald said, "The test of a first-rate intelligence is the ability to hold two opposed ideas in the mind at the same time, and still retain the ability to function."[21] By this measure, truly first-rate intelligences are ubiquitous. The world's view of America may be its most comprehensive love-hate relationship.

This book first considers the collection of images about America in many people's minds and how and when they arose: the images constructed from direct observation of and experience with America; the products of pictures shown and stories told by others; and the images that are purely the result of imagination. But having a storehouse of images does not determine a person's views. Rather, it is there to coalesce, amplify, and illustrate opinions. Since they are often so contradictory, the images themselves cannot be the opinions. People need a selection process to choose among images. This book then examines these selection schemas (predispositions). Among others, conformity, xenophobia, nationalism, partisanship, fear of loss, resentment, grievance, hope, desire, self-pity, shame, and religious faith join with issues of political philosophy and simple contrariness to select from images in order to express opinions.

Of all of those selection schemas, hope and desire are the most intriguing. The imagery selected to express hope and desire is especially laden with ideas of pure invention.

> Everybody has their own America, and then they have the pieces of a fantasy America that they think is out there but they can't see. . . . So the fantasy corners of America . . . you've pieced them together from scenes in movies, and music and lines from books. And you live in your dream America that you've custom-made from art and schmaltz and emotions just as much as you live in your real one. [22]

America, or something called America, has a role in the dreams and aspirations of large numbers of people all over the world. It tantalizes and taunts them. It offers a refuge from their present existence or is an imagined reproach for their present existence. It is a paladin on which hopes for redemption or rescue are placed. No nation can meet all these admiring expectations. The risk and costs to the United States of disappointing these many friends far outweighs the risks and costs of conforming to the worst expectations of those who scorn America.

2

IMPRINTS FROM INSIDE AMERICA

America, in all its complex existence and behavior, provides a vast store of raw material for the creation of images. Some ideas frequently voiced today about the United States go back to the nineteenth century: America is a beacon of democracy, equality, and tolerance; an isolationist and self-centered nation; an arrogant imperialistic conqueror; a land of opportunity; a hypocritical exploiter of the environment and of people; a model of stable and advanced political institutions; a racist nation; a leader in innovation, progress, and rationality; a nation of failures and ill-bred, ignorant boors who only value money; a rich and powerful model of success and modernity. Others are twentieth century additions: America is imperialistic; an active protector of people against tyranny and occupation; a nation preoccupied with its self-interest; a builder (and destroyer) of multilateralism and international law and institutions; a reliable (and unreliable) guarantor of others' safety and independence; a hyperpower that has no interest in the views of others; a source of glamour and excitement; a source and exporter of mindless and godless crude popular culture. These and an abundance of other images surface daily concerning events happening today. However, they all have their roots in older realities. The ideas that are expressed today often parrot those expressed by others many years ago.

During the first 125 years of the Republic, the images generated about America derived almost entirely from events and conditions within the United States. In the next century, the new images were mostly the product of the interactions between the people of the United States and the rest of the world. Very few images that are cited by people today do not have roots in these prior periods.

Democratic and Egalitarian

Contemporary French intellectual Alain Minc has said, "America is synonymous with democracy."[1] The American Revolution and Constitution did enshrine in writing and in institutions a revolutionary application of republican government. In 1801, after triumphing in a bitterly contested and controversial election, President Thomas Jefferson addressed the new nation at his inauguration. He set about healing the divisions among Americans by reminding them of the experiment in which they, together, were engaged. With characteristic grace and pith, Jefferson described all the elements of the American model of self-government. He explained that this is a "chosen country"; the fundamental governmental unit is the individual's government of his own life; the states are united in a republican system of representative government; the nation shall expand across a vast land with enough room for "descendants to the thousandth and thousandth generation"; capitalism and free markets are the economic system of the nation; tolerance is shown to religious practices in "various forms"; and government limits its intrusions on individual freedom, whether by regulation or taxes. Running through his talk was one overarching theme: "the master assumption of American political thought . . . its social freedom, its social equality."[2]

The Americans did not just announce their new system. They set out to implement it, and the world watched, often with skepticism. François Jean de Beauvoir, Marquis de Chastellux, was a French nobleman, statesman, soldier, and scholar who served with the French Expeditionary Force that helped the American revolutionaries against the British in 1780–83. Despite his sympathies for the Enlightenment ideals of the U.S. Constitution, he looked on its prospects pessimistically:

> In establishing among themselves a purely democratic government, had the Americans a real love of democracy? And if they have wished all men to be equal, is this not solely because, from the very nature of things, they were in fact equal, or nearly so? . . . .

Now . . . suppose that the increase of population reduces your artisans to the status they have in France and England—do you then
believe that your principles are democratic enough so that the
landholders and the opulent would still continue to regard them
as their equals?[3]

For several decades after its birth, the United States was considered a
fragile, utopian experiment that likely would be unable to preserve its independent nationhood or its republican government. During the Napoleonic Wars, both the French and the British acted as though American ships
and sailors were theirs for the taking. Beginning in about 1806, the British
seized a thousand American ships, and the French seized five hundred.
In the period from 1803 to 1812, the British impressed over ten thousand
American sailors into the Royal Navy. In 1812 the United States declared
war on Great Britain and fought to an impasse. In 1814, two months after
the parties reached a signed settlement (and not having heard that the
war was over), Gen. Andrew Jackson engaged the British at New Orleans
and won an astounding victory: seven hundred British killed and fourteen
hundred wounded, eight Americans killed and thirteen wounded. These
events were of much greater importance than is now recalled. Jackson's
victory over the superpower of the day made it clear to the dominant European nations that the United States was here to stay, and that it would
remain standing as an image of democracy and social equality.

Sovereign and Self-Interested

The war and the European depredations that led to the war aroused in
Americans a particularly strong attachment to the concept of sovereignty.
That attachment remains a major theme of American foreign policy. Since
the Peace of Westphalia in 1648 that ended the Thirty Years' War, nation-
states have uniformly declared their adherence to the rules of sovereignty.
Under this system, each nation is entitled to equal dignity with all other
nations, has defined borders that are to be respected by all other nations,
and is free to act within its borders without interference from any other
nation. On this simple laissez-faire, live-and-let-live framework, the international law of the jungle has been constructed. Since some borders are
not so well defined and often are in dispute, and since national governments often lack the power to garrison and protect their declared borders,

there has been plenty of room for sovereign states to do battle. Further, because the system purports to impose equal dignity among states that are far from equal in size, wealth, and power, there is an inherent instability in the system deriving from this effort to exalt fiction over facts. Those with greater power are often in search of pretexts to excuse attack on weaker neighbors, and those with less power are in constant need of allies to balance their power with that of their neighbors. In the years since 1648, under the system of sovereign nations, the normal condition among neighboring states has been war or the anticipation of war.

The Americans sought to flee the threat of this cruel world with a strict enforcement of their own sovereignty, hugely assisted by their geographic isolation. As George Washington advised in his farewell address in 1796, "The great rule of conduct for us in regard to foreign nations is in extending our commercial relations, to have with them as little political connection as possible . . . It is our true policy to steer clear of permanent alliances with any portion of the foreign world."

A Beacon for Humanity

Washington's advice became ingrained in the American character. Throughout the nineteenth century, it formed the bedrock of America's posture toward the world outside the Western Hemisphere. The Americans had confidence bordering on arrogance in their republic but no need to go abroad looking for worlds to conquer or people to convert. Their focus was inward. America was to serve as an example to others. It did not need to evangelize. It had only to stand there and be admired and emulated. This tradition began in 1630 when Puritan governor John Winthrop paraphrased Jesus to say that America is a "city upon a hill, the eyes of all people are upon us."[4] It persisted as a strain of American thinking through Ronald Reagan, when he referred to the nation as a "shining city on a hill." Over the centuries, America has offered its example to those who long for personal and political freedom. Ivan Klíma, a writer who grew up under Soviet rule in Czechoslovakia, recalled in 2002, "It was a great encouragement to me to know that there existed an entire continent where one could live freely, where they didn't jail people because of their attitude to the regime, where they didn't confiscate books or ban authors and where they didn't expel professors from universities for rejecting totalitarian (or any other) ideology."[5]

Land of Opportunity—Nation of Failures

To create this beacon for mankind, there was much to do. Immigrants flocked to American shores. As German professor Berdt Ostendorf said, "Across the world popular fantasies have always seen America as an Eldorado of fulfilled middle-class wishes."[6] In 1800 about 5.3 million people lived in the United States. Between 1815 and 1860, five million immigrants settled in America, drawn there by the promise of a new life or in an effort to escape from hopelessness at home.[7] They were welcome additions to a vast country in need of labor. However, they accentuated a scorn for the United States as "the Promised Land of failures"[8] among the comfortable people left behind. German writer Friedrich Gerstäcker put it poetically in 1855:

> "To America!" Lightly and boldly does the hothead audaciously call this out in the first and difficult hour which ought to test his strength, harden his mettle.—"To America!" whispers the desperate man who, on the verge of ruin, was here being pushed slowly but surely toward the abyss.—"To America!" says the destitute man quietly and resolutely; he, who has fought again and again with manly power against the force of circumstances, but always in vain, and who has paid for his "daily bread" with bloody sweat—and yet has not received it, who sees no aid for himself or his loved ones here in the homeland, and yet will not beg, cannot steal.—"To America!" laughs the criminal after a successfully executed robbery, exulting jubilantly in sight of the distant shore which will provide him security from the arm of the thus injured law.—"To America!" rejoices the idealist, who is angry with the real world because it is in fact real, and who envisages there, across the ocean, a prospect which conforms more closely to the one conjured up in his own mad mind.—"To America!"[9]

Much later, Evelyn Waugh told Graham Greene, "Of course, the Americans are cowards. . . . They are almost all the descendants of wretches who deserted their legitimate monarchs for fear of military service."[10] Whatever Gerstäcker, Waugh, and their compatriots thought of the emigrants, they did not deny that America was the right place to go for a person who wanted to turn his life around. These failures and cowards were put to populating a newly expanded nation. The 1803 Louisiana Purchase made the United States a continental power. Exploring and filling that land became a great national project for the United States. For many Europeans watching from their side of the Atlantic, it looked like the opportunity of a lifetime. The desperation of the poorest Europeans coalesced with the dreams of grandeur and self-confidence of progressive, entrepreneurial Americans as both groups contemplated the vast continent.

Of all images, "opportunity" has the most universal acceptance, even by the most critical observers. "Opportunity" was the one word used to describe the United States in 2010 by Anné Kulonen, a young Finnish-born composer of experimental music. Living in London, she has never visited the United States and has a skeptical view of its culture, government, and foreign policy. Still, she identified it as the one place that would give her music and her career the chance to succeed.[11] Similarly, Guilherme Marchi, a Brazilian cowboy, moved to the United States in his late teens. By 2010, at age twenty-seven, he had earned the United States Professional Bull Riding World Championship and a total of over $1.9 million in prize money. With his wife and daughter, he settled into an eighty-two-acre ranch in Texas and opened a thriving restaurant. An enthusiastic bull-riding fan gave him a mounted deer head for his wall. He commented, "In Brazil we only kill deer to eat them. It's strange what people do in this country, but I think I'm staying. I like it here."[12] The United States remains the place where, in the words of the U.S. Army–recruiting slogan, you can "be all you can be."

Rationality, Progress, and Arrogance

In 1830 the young French aristocrat Alexis de Tocqueville came to America for nine months, ostensibly to report on the progressive American prison system. His larger project was to examine the functioning of democracy in the American climate of social equality. In 1835 and 1840, he published the two volumes of *Democracy in America*, which set the standard for insightful and broad-minded analysis of the American political system, social scene, and character. They achieved a vast readership and became fountainheads of imagery of the new nation. In his view, democracy and free enterprise in the American context functioned well, leading to the likelihood of future stability and enormous growth in prosperity and power.

Tocqueville observed the psychological and philosophical devotion of Americans to liberal Enlightenment thinking:

> The Anglo-Americans place moral authority in universal reason, as they do political power in the universality of citizens, and they reckon that one must rely on the sense of all to discern what is permitted or forbidden, what is true or false. Most of them think that the knowledge of one's self-interest, well understood is enough to lead man toward the just and the honest. They believe that at birth each has received the ability to govern himself, and that no one has the right to force one like himself to be happy. All have a lively faith in human perfectibility; they judge that the diffusion of enlightenment will necessarily produce useful results . . . all consider society as a body in progress; humanity as a changing picture . . . and they admit that what seems good to them today can be replaced tomorrow by the better that is still hidden.[13]

He took note of the American tendency to adopt the attitude of a "chosen" people:

> At the same time that the Anglo-Americans are united among themselves in this way by common ideas, they are separated from all other peoples by a sentiment of pride.
>
> For fifty years it has been constantly repeated to the inhabitants of the United States that they form the only religious, enlightened, and free people. They see that up to now, democratic institutions have prospered among them, while they have failed in the rest of the world; they therefore have an immense opinion of themselves, and they are not far from believing that they form a species apart in the human race.[14]

In this, Tocqueville was echoing the contemporary sentiments of the original expositor of the theory of America's Manifest Destiny. In an 1839 article that was a clarion call of self-confidence, Jacksonian Democrat John M. O'Sullivan laid out the foundations of American exceptionalism:

> Yes, we are the nation of progress, of individual freedom, of universal enfranchisement. . . . We must onward to the fulfilment of

our mission–to the entire development of the principle of our organization–freedom of conscience, freedom of person, freedom of trade and business pursuits, universality of freedom and equality. This is our high destiny, and in nature's eternal, inevitable decree of cause and effect we must accomplish it. All this will be our future history, to establish on earth the moral dignity and salvation of man—the immutable truth and beneficence of God. For this blessed mission to the nations of the world, which are shut out from the life-giving light of truth, has America been chosen; and her high example shall smite unto death the tyranny of kings, hierarchs, and oligarchs, and carry the glad tidings of peace and good will where myriads now endure an existence scarcely more enviable than that of beasts of the field. Who, then, can doubt that our country is destined to be *the great nation* of futurity?[15]

This sentiment has echoed ever since. Woodrow Wilson spoke to the Senate in 1919 in these terms: "The stage is set, the destiny disclosed. It has come about by no plan of our conceiving, but by the hand of God who led us into the way. We cannot turn back. . . . America shall in truth show the way. The light streams upon the path ahead and nowhere else."[16]

Robert Kennedy expressed the idea thusly: "At stake is not only the leadership of a party or the leadership of a country—at stake is our claim to the moral leadership of the world."[17] George W. Bush said, "Our nation is chosen by God and commissioned by history to be a model to the world."[18] The foreign reaction to this American conceit is as predictable as it has been consistent. Germans in 1954 commented, "For America to consider itself as 'God's own country' revealed an unbearably hypocritical chauvinism."[19] Yet while the bragging was always annoying, many foreign listeners accepted the idea of American exceptionalism—of a special place with a new and tempting kind of society.

Stability, Prosperity, and Crude Materialism

Tocqueville was mightily impressed with the formal legal architecture of American government. He observed that the structure of American institutions enabled the nation to maintain a democratic republic despite the tendency toward mob rule found in democracies from ancient Athens to the French revolution. In contrast to the French centralized system, he admired the American federal form of government "which permits the Union to enjoy the power of a great republic and the security of a small one."[20] He endorsed the local governments and commissions that covered the landscape, saying they "give the people the taste for freedom and the art of being free," and he applauded the judicial power that serves "to correct the aberrations of democracy."[21] Tocqueville spoke at length of the especially American tendency to form voluntary associations, lodges, clubs, and the like. In this he anticipated by almost 160 years the analyses that explain the success of the American economy based on its high level of "social capital"—the trust and reliance that strangers place on each other.[22]

America's stable social and institutional structure is still a feature of the United States that earns plaudits from outsiders.

> To most open-minded Europeans, and to Germans in particular, the real greatness and achievement of America lay in the spirit and technique of its social structure. The architecture of American society appeared in the eyes of thoughtful Germans more admirable, more exemplary, than the architecture of American skyscrapers and mansions; American freedom in everyday life seemed to them a greater work of art than, say, American symphonies.[23]

Americans' fascination with material wealth and consumption did not pass without Tocqueville's notice. "The care of satisfying the least needs of the body and of providing the smallest comforts of life preoccupies minds universally."[24] Observations of American pursuit of wealth and habits of consumption have become commonplaces in literature about the country from its founding to today. "Money is the American's deity; only his piety and the wealth of the country have until now sustained his morals," observed Russian writer and diplomat Pavel Svin'in in 1815.[25] In 2002 Belgian-American writer Luc Sante put it simply: "Of all the nations of the earth, the United States unquestionably has the most stuff."[26]

Svin'in's, Tocqueville's, and Sante's versions, and innumerable similar observations by others in between, describe reality. The behavior of most Americans has always been industrious and aimed toward material wealth. It was true when it was a young nation of small farmers, and the advent of the Industrial Revolution in the early nineteenth century accentuated it. The Industrial Revolution began in the last years of the eighteenth century in England, but it had its greatest impact in transforming the United States throughout the 1800s. By the end of the century, a triumphant Senator Chauncey Depew could write the following summary of the achievements of the nation:

> A little more than a hundred years ago the first cotton-mill was running with 250 spindles. Whitney invented the cotton-gin, which created the wealth of the Gulf States and made the cotton industry over all the world tributary to them. Other inventors improved the machinery, and the single mill of that period has expanded into 1,000, and the 250 spindles have increased to 21,000,000. In 1794 the first wool-carding machine was put in operation, mainly under the impulse of American invention. There were in 1895 2,500 wool manufactories. The production of textile fabrics in this country supports about 600,000 employees. At the beginning of the century a few thousand tons of iron were manufactured. In 1899 the United States produced over 13,000,000 tons of pig iron, being more than any other country; while in the manufactured products of iron and steel we are also in the advance of nations.[27]

Once a rural backwater, by 1870 America had become the source of almost a quarter of the world's manufacturing production, second only to the United Kingdom. On the eve of World War I, it was the world's leading manufacturing nation, with 35.8 percent of world production.[28] At war's end it had more than half of world industrial production.

Unrefined and Ignorant

After an extended stay in the United States, Fanny Trollope returned to England in 1832 and launched her career as a writer with a biting critique of what she had seen. She described "a vast continent, by far the greater part of which is still in the state in which nature left it, and a busy, bustling, industrious population, hacking and hewing their way through it."[29] She was describing reality—real geography and real behavior. She observed a materialism and lack of refined culture: "I very seldom during my whole stay in the country heard a sentence elegantly turned, and correctly pronounced from the lips of an American. There is always something either in the expression or the accent that jars the feelings and shocks the taste."[30] Again, she was describing reality. Most of America was a rough and tumble place. "From Dickens to Beerbohm to Waugh to Amis (Kingsley and Martin), English novelists have ridiculed the Americans for their vulgarity, pomposity and other traits."[31] Tocqueville saw it too: "One must recognize that among the civilized peoples of our day there are few in whom the advanced sciences have made less progress than in the United States, and who have furnished fewer great artists, illustrious poets, and celebrated writers."[32] In 1833 German poet Nikolaus Lenau expressed it with hyperbole: "The American knows nothing; he seeks nothing but money; he has no ideas."[33] A pronouncement attributed to twentieth-century French statesman Georges Clemenceau is that, "America is the only nation in history which, miraculously, has gone from barbarism to degeneration without the usual interval of civilization.[34]

Tocqueville and Trollope both attributed the American lack of refinement and high culture to the American "preoccupations of material life."[35] To Tocqueville it was clear that this was not a problem inherent in democracy and that the future could bring a change of this circumstance as comfort and wealth accumulated among some people and gave them the leisure for contemplation and sophistication.

Nevertheless, after the United States had closed the frontier and become an industrial power and a more cosmopolitan and sophisticated place, an afterimage stayed on mental screens. As the twentieth century dawned, Russian liberal political scientist Moiseide Ostrogorski, described Americans as uniquely vapid in their materialism: "Of all races in an advanced state of civilization, the American is the least accessible to long views. . . . Always and everywhere in a hurry to get rich, he does not give a thought to remote consequences; he sees only present advantages. . . . He does not remember, he does not feel, he lives in a materialist dream."[36]

In Germany in the 1920s and '30s, "From most German [leftist] books and reports on America published at the time there again emerged the stereotype of a country dominated by the dollar, sadly lacking in civilization, backward in terms of culture, social progress, and human decency. The same picture was portrayed again by the Nazis, whose propaganda depicted the plutocratic, racially contaminated, brutal and greedy American."[37]

Even today, despite America's preeminence in science, higher education, fine arts, and technology, the beetle-browed, loud-mouthed, shortsighted, greedy ignoramus persists as a condescending sketch of a typical American by people in other societies from the most advanced to the most benighted.

Isolationist and Self-Centered

A related image springs from America's physical isolation from the rest of the world and the population's inward focus. The nation, "kindly separated by nature and a wide ocean,"[38] began its existence under an admonition to avoid political entanglements with Europe. Its enormous size and resources allowed most Americans to avoid physical and social contact with Europe. Its single market and single language enabled Americans to limit their knowledge of geography and languages to those things that mattered in their lives. Immigrants retained family ties and emotional ties with the "old country" but concentrated on becoming "Americans." As American economic and political power grew, others around the world needed to learn about America, and, through American products and films, others were given unavoidable opportunities to learn about America. Americans lacked a corresponding need and opportunity to learn about the world outside. The result has been the inward-looking attitude that has been often observed and resented. In the 1930s, English writer Graham Greene wrote of "America seeing the world in its own image . . . the eternal adolescence of the American mind."[39] German novelist and essayist Peter Schneider recently commented that the United States is "a fantastically tolerant and flexible society that has absorbed the whole world, yet has difficulty comprehending the world beyond its borders."[40] In 2002 English writer James Hamilton-Paterson groused, "These days we may find . . . offensive the degree to which America remains staunchly ignorant and dismissive of the ninety per cent of the planet that is not the United States."[41]

Given America's power and influence over the lives of others elsewhere, these observations, with real bases in fact but often exaggerated, are felt painfully abroad and are not easily dispelled. In the Gobi Desert in 2009, Mongolian environmental crusader Tsetsegee Munkhbayar complained that on his one trip to the United States, in 2007, the people he met had no idea where Mongolia is. He found Americans "friendly and open, but ignorant."[42] Of course, the San Franciscans who run the Goldman Foundation, which had flown him to San Francisco to receive a fellowship to further his work, must have known of Mongolia, its location, and his activism. These facts did not affect his views.

Racist Exploiter

The great American political struggle of the nineteenth century centered on slavery. From before biblical times through to the Enlightenment, most societies, East and West, accepted slavery as an unquestioned practice. However, by the late eighteenth century, in Western Europe, and particularly in England and France, attitudes had shifted, and involuntary servitude was recognized as a paramount evil. Nevertheless, in America's Enlightenment Constitution, nothing was done to end the institution for existing slaves and their descendants.[43] Slavery in a nation dedicated to the proposition that all men are created equal is a glaring contradiction. The British and Irish gloated with palpable sanctimony, as in this 1804 verse by Irish poet Thomas Moore:

> To think that man, thou just and gentle God!
> Should stand before thee with a tyrant's rod,
> O'er creatures like himself, with soul from thee,
> Yet dare to boast of perfect liberty.[44]

Tocqueville called the racial laws of the southern states an "unheard-of atrocity" that "serves to reveal some profound perturbation in the laws of humanity."[45] He astutely observed that the servitude of blacks could not continue indefinitely, but the emancipation of blacks would arouse a regime of racial prejudice and racial separation that would rend the nation. In due course, the Civil War was the United States' great cataclysm, and the Jim Crow laws, lynchings, and discrimination that followed poisoned race relations thereafter.

The United States was not the only country practicing slavery into the mid-nineteenth century and thereafter. Brazil did not issue its emancipation proclamation until 1888. In the year 2000 the United Nations estimated that there were as many as 100 million people in bonded labor in India.[46] Further, the emancipation of the slaves in the United States was not the result of slave revolts or of intervention by outside powers. (Great Britain and France each came close to giving diplomatic recognition to the Confederacy.) Rather, it was the result of a catastrophic war in which the white population of the North lost hundreds of thousands of lives in pursuit of both saving the Union and ending slavery. Nevertheless, because of the prominence of the issue in American history, the obvious contradiction between human bondage and the ideas America professes to be its essence, and the racial divide between the masters and slaves in American society, slavery and racial discrimination put indelible marks on the United States in the eyes of people throughout the world—especially non-white people. The United States, now with a population that is more than one-third non-European descent, with persons of color in high elective and appointive office and in important positions of business, social, and cultural leadership, and whose sports and entertainment heroes are often African American, Latin American, and Asian American, retains its image around the world as a racist white nation—a negative image that resonates powerfully in countries formerly under European colonial rule. The recent service as secretaries of state by Colin Powell and Condoleezza Rice seem to have had no effect on the image of the United States a racist, white nation. The election of President Barack Obama has blunted (but not entirely eliminated) this view.

Personal Freedom and Success

Another principal narrative of nineteenth-century America was the conquest of the continent. Bringing to life the Manifest Destiny, the Americans of European descent continued and accelerated the move westward that had characterized American settlement since the Mayflower. The big push across the frontier began in earnest with canals in the early nineteenth century and culminated with the completion of the transcontinental railroad in 1869. A series of gold rushes and other mining strikes starting in California in 1848, simultaneous with the United States taking almost half of Mexico's territory, gave impetus to the enthusiasm for westward migration.

This excitement and unlimited opportunity—when added to midcentury European civil strife, wars and famine—beckoned new arrivals in ever-growing numbers. From 1815 to 1860, about five million European immigrants settled in the United States.[47] The pace quickened to about ten million between 1865 and 1890, and to about fifteen million between 1890 and 1914.[48] The migrant had much to run from, but he also had an idea of what he was running toward. With its plentiful space and resources, its usually expanding economy and labor shortages, and its philosophical devotion to personal freedom, the United States' reputation as the place of hope for a better life penetrated even the most isolated poor hamlet of Europe. France recognized this in its 1886 gift of the Statue of Liberty. America added Emma Lazarus's words at its base:

> Give me your tired, your poor,
> Your huddled masses yearning to breathe free,
> The wretched refuse of your teaming shore,
> Send these, the homeless tempest-tossed to me,
> I lift my lamp beside the golden door.

For many, even before the Statue of Liberty was built, the "golden door" opened to a life of squalor and violence in urban tenements. However, for most people there was enough reality in the image so that it was reaffirmed and reinforced, and more settlers poured in. The new people helped propel the economy forward, adding voices to those propagating the idea of the United States as a place with streets paved with gold.

As the centennials of the American and French revolutions came and went, the nations of Europe and Asia, with few exceptions, remained imperial despotisms. The contrast between life at home and opportunities in America made "America" a word spoken of reverently among the populations of the Old World. America was portrayed in more than five hundred formulaic boys' novels written in the United States in the late nineteenth century by Horatio Alger Jr. They taught that an honest, hard working, self-reliant young American man not only could succeed—he would succeed. This view of the American dream—the idea of self-actualization, that you can be whatever you want to be—stimulated immigration and energized the native born.

No one who visited failed to notice that not everyone ended up on top. The Yiddish playwright from Ukraine, Sholom Aleichem, sarcastically observed the sweatshops of early twentieth century New York City: "Everything is possible in America. . . . You can do whatever you please. Want a factory?—You can set up a factory. Feel like opening a little store?—You can do that too. Want a pushcart?—That's also permitted. Or you can become a peddler, or work in a shop. It's a free country. You can bloat up from hunger, drop dead on the street—no one will stop you."[49] Still, they came; and they still do. Ivan Klíma wrote in 2002, "For more than a century now there has existed a sort of American dream. For some it means boundless affluence, for others freedom. . . . I am convinced that America's wealth, which derives from the work of many generations, is chiefly the result of the creative activity of free citizens."[50]

America's wealth and personal freedoms are today the envy of the world. In the twentieth century, the United States emerged from World Wars I and II undamaged and economically stronger than ever. It succeeded Great Britain as the financial arbiter of international transactions—the issuer of the world's reserve currency. America's gross national income is still more than 23 percent of the world's total gross national income and is growing at a faster pace than those of any of its major competitors except China and, at times, Germany.[51] Immigrants seeking a better and freer life still come. The same critics who decry American culture and foreign policy are often most annoyed by the difficulties they face in getting visas and green cards to reside in the United States.[52] The old Chinese comment that "the full moon's fuller in America" captures the sentiments of most people in the world, friend or foe.[53]

Moreover, the America of which they dream may have only a thread of connection to the actual country. For many people it is a placeholder for their highest hopes, "more a creed than a race or even a nation."[54] If it did not exist, they would have to invent it, like Atlantis, Eldorado, or Glocca Morra. It is both the real and imagined image of personal success.

Conqueror, Cruel Exploiter, Champion of Freedom and Justice, and Intrepid Hero

There have been prices paid for America's achievements. The American land was not empty when Europeans arrived. Recent estimates of Native American population in North America at the time of Columbus's arrival are about twenty million. By the time of the establishment of the United States, that population was far smaller, due mostly to diseases brought over from Europe. Still, there was a significant Indian presence, and it stood in the way of westward expansion.

Over the early years of the Republic, white settlers aided by the government engaged in a series of disconnected actions that dispossessed the Indians from desirable land between the Appalachians and the Mississippi River. All this became a concerted program with passage of the Indian Removal Act of 1830 that mandated the resettlement of entire tribes across the Mississippi. Tocqueville captured the poignancy of this cruel policy in an account of the Choctaw eviction across the river:

> At the end of the year 1831, I found myself on the left bank of the Mississippi, at a place named Memphis by the Europeans. While I was at this place, a numerous troop of Choctaws came . . . the savages were leaving their country and sought to cross to the right bank of the Mississippi, where they flattered themselves they would find the refuge that the American government promised them. It was then in the heart of winter, and the cold ravaged that year with an unaccustomed violence; snow had hardened on the ground, and the river carried along enormous pieces of ice. The Indians brought along their families with them; they dragged behind them the wounded, the ill, infants who had just been born, and the old who were going to die. They had neither tents nor carts, but only some provisions and arms. I saw them embark to cross the great river, and this solemn spectacle will never leave my memory. One heard neither tears nor complaints among this assembled crowd; they were silent.[55]

For the Indians it did not get better. Once exiled to the Great Plains, and often on the edge of starvation, the Indians were repeatedly moved again as their new lands, which had been solemnly promised to them forever, took on increased value to the white men for farming or minerals. Finally, with the slaughter of the Great Sioux Nation by the U.S. Cavalry at Wounded Knee, South Dakota, in 1890, the Indian Wars ended with virtually all the surviving Indians relegated to remote reservations.

Along the way, this struggle by both whites and Indians with the land and with each other captured the imaginations of people everywhere. American authors such as Henry Wadsworth Longfellow, James Fenimore Cooper, Mark Twain, Bret Harte, and Zane Grey wrote about it. So did European writers. German author Karl May, who never visited America, sold more than a hundred million copies in German and at least thirty other languages of his tales of a fictional German-born adventurer in the Old West called Old Shatterhand and his blood brother, the Apache chief Winnetou. Wild West shows, like Buffalo Bill's, toured Europe at the turn of the century. With the advent of movies, the Western and its cowboys and Indians became staples of the medium. Worldwide audiences embraced them.

Now, if you go to the small town of St. Arnaud on New Zealand's South Island and stumble in to the shooting range of the local gun club on a Wednesday night, you will get to be part of Cowboy Night. The members are dressed up as American cowboys, or at least the Kiwi interpretation of them. They have a great, shoot-'em-up time. If that is not convenient, you can put on your ten-gallon hat and do the Texas two-step at the Pensuk Great Western resort in Nakhon Ratchasima, Thailand, a few hours northeast of Bangkok.[56] It is one among many salutes to the American cowboy that dot the Thai landscape. In France in July, be sure to dress up in your denim and boots and stop at Mirande near Toulouse to dance at the Old West Saloon.[57]

Of all the stereotypical Western heroes, from Tom Mix to Hopalong Cassidy, the most influential iconic figure throughout the world was John Wayne. He normally played a Western hero who stood for the values of the American rugged individual. He would often be the voice and arm of moral authority in an evil and lawless world. Faced with a wrongdoer, he would seek to assemble a posse. If no posse could be found, he would act alone. Right and wrong were clear; no nuances needed to be considered. In the ultimate confrontation, he would demand peaceful compliance, but, absent compliance, he would resort to force. Gen. George C. Marshall was true to this spirit when he predicted in 1942 that at the end of World War II, "Our flag will be recognized throughout the world as a symbol of freedom on the one hand and of overwhelming force on the other."[58] John Wayne always prevailed. He was honest, direct, and ethical, and his every effort was exerted to protect the community, not his own interests. Both in American minds and in the minds of friends and critics abroad, John Wayne's behavior typifies the American approach to the world. In a single issue of the *New York Times*, at the end of the Iraq War in 2003, there were these three separate John Wayne allusions: a daughter of a Seabee who died in action saying, "When he got sent over there, we figured, there goes John Wayne, doing what he loved. We didn't worry. We knew he was capable of taking care of himself"; a comment that "outside the Pacific Stock Exchange in San Francisco, conservative stock traders voice misgivings about what they call the country's John Wayne approach to geopolitics"; and a statement that "we have definitely sent a John Wayne message to the world. . . . How can anyone not see that we have sent a message straight out of the American West? We're the good guys. We're the big guns in town. We'll tell you how it is going to be. But do we have the ability to build relationships?"[59]

By about 1960, Hollywood had grown weary of Westerns and made fewer of them. However, the thirst abroad for Old West adventures had not been slaked. Between 1960 and 1975, over six hundred western movies, called spaghetti Westerns, were produced in Europe. Among the most famous of the type was an early 1960s film, *A Fistful of Dollars*, directed by Sergio Leone of Italy. It starred young Clint Eastwood, who played a lone gunman pursuing dollars to the exclusion of all else. This was a reversal of the old idea of an American Western star, and it reflected Vietnam War–era European opinion of the United States. Of course, in John Wayne's films there were scoundrels too—those are the people he fought, in addition to Indians and Mexicans. Placing the blackguard at the center of the story reflected a new choice of image for emphasis, not a new image.

The contrarian, dark view of the Western hero has not occupied the field. It coexists with the old positive impression. Action hero and recent California governor Arnold Schwarzenegger recalls his childhood in Austria when "I would sit there and watch, for hours, American movies, transfixed by my heroes, like John Wayne. Everything about America . . . seemed so big to me, so open, so possible."[60] Even now, in this age of no-smoking campaigns, outside the United States, big, brightly lit billboards of the Marlboro Man convey an attractive image that pushes cigarette sales by the millions. Without uttering a word, his American appearance of rugged masculinity connects cigarette consumption to ideas of health, strength, freedom, and independence that overcome the consumer's knowledge of the product's dangers. In the late 1980s, the Polish freedom movement Solidarity adopted Gary Cooper's silhouette as its symbol. Polish leader Lech Walesa explains:

> Under the headline "At High Noon" runs the red Solidarity banner and the date—June 4, 1989—of the poll. It was a simple but effective gimmick that, at the time, was misunderstood by the Communists. They, in fact, tried to ridicule the freedom movement in Poland as an invention of the "Wild" West, especially the U.S.

But the poster had the opposite impact: Cowboys in Western clothes had become a powerful symbol for Poles. Cowboys fight for justice, fight against evil, and fight for freedom, both physical and spiritual.[61]

The latest incarnation, the 2010 remake of John Wayne's classic *True Grit*, with Jeff Bridges as the lawman, shows a more complex figure—a man who has had a hard life and the bruises to show for it. But he is still the hero, the man on the horse roused from his sleep to do good and right wrongs.

Despoiler, Progressive, and Master of Technology

Another image of America fed by nineteenth-century expansion is one of profligacy. Thomas Jefferson's description of a land "with room enough for our descendants to the thousandth and thousandth generation" spoke the minds of all Americans in 1801. Who could imagine that it was not so? Americans cleared the forest, planted crops on the land again and again, depleted the soil, and moved on. Then they started over in virgin soil. Soon, industrialization spurred the pace of changing the scenery. Mills required dams for power and canals for transportation. Professor David Nye in Denmark speaks of painter and naturalist John James Audubon's dismay: "In 1832, John James Audubon found that the Ohio Valley was 'more or less covered with villages, farms, and towns, where the din of hammers and machinery is constantly heard.' The woods were 'fast disappearing,' and 'the greedy mills, told the sad tale, that in a century the noble forest . . . shall exist no more.'"[62]

Audubon's voice was a lonely one at that early date. Americans believed that the land was a canvas on which they were to paint. It was both their obligation and their opportunity to enhance the land with civilization's works: railroads, towns, roads, and dams. A stand of woods was something to be cleared, a swamp something to be drained, and a canyon something to be dammed. Even now, in American legal parlance, any structure, however ramshackle and regardless of what it replaced, is referred to as an "improvement." This attitude led to great things. The American concepts of progress and can-do showed the world the amazing rapidity in which the wilderness can be made habitable. Only later did the price of progress come due. By the end of the nineteenth century, John Muir and other

A painterly image of western America by one of its European trained masters, Albert Bierstadt. *Merced River, Yosemite Valley* (1866). *Image copyright © The Metropolitan Museum of Art/Art Resource, NY.*

naturalists and conservationists began to have an impact on the public mind with campaigns to preserve what remained of the wild. The frontier had closed, and a new sense of limits was voiced. The establishment of national parks in the Theodore Roosevelt administration was the beginning of recognition of the impending loss of the nation's natural patrimony.

Out of all of this came disparate images of the nation: one of industry and technological achievement; one of extraordinary natural beauty; and one of wastefulness. All have bases in fact, and all have stuck. Fredrika Bremer, a Swedish novelist, visited in 1850 and marveled at American innovation, from Benjamin Franklin's eighteenth-century electrical experiments to the invention of anesthesia by Dr. William T. G. Morton in Boston in 1846:

> America is the land of experiment. . . . One of its sons drew the lightning from the clouds; another created wings out of steam for all the people of the earth; so that they might fly round the world; a third has, oh the happy man! discovered the means of mitigating

Frederic Remington established the standard vision of cowboy and Indian life on the Western plains in his paintings. *An Incident in the Opening of a Cattle Country* (1887). *Courtesy of the Museum of the American West, Autry National Center of the American West, Los Angeles.*

life's bitter enemy, bodily suffering, and of extending the wings of the angel of sleep over the unfortunate one in the hour of his agony! And all this has been done in the early morning of the country's life. . . . What will not this people accomplish during the day?[63]

The answer to her question included the telegraph, the telephone, the electric light, the moving picture, the airplane, the atomic bomb, and the computer. American technology remade life everywhere.

The American landscape, despite the beaver-like efforts to develop and despoil it, remained, and still remains in most places, among the globe's most scenic terrains. Tocqueville observed, "The Mississippi Valley is, all in all, the most magnificent dwelling that God has ever prepared for the habitation of man. . . . "[64] He never saw the Rockies, the Grand Tetons, or the Sierras. By the mid-nineteenth century, portraying such western mountain scenes in oils was a painting genre all its own. A profusion of Western life depictions by masters such as Frederic Remington

Carleton Watkins pioneered photography in remote areas of the American west. He introduced the Sierras to the world in photographs such as *The Half Dome, Yosemite* (ca. 1865). *Courtesy of The New York Public Library/Art Resource, NY.*

helped imprint ideas of the American Western landscape and its people on the minds of millions. By the 1870s, pioneering photographers such as Carleton Watkins and Charles Weed introduced people everywhere to the majestic beauty of the mountains of California and particularly the Yosemite Valley. Photography made travelogues wildly popular in Europe, where images of the American West as well as such special Eastern seaboard features as Niagara Falls drew public attention alongside competing images from India, Egypt, and other exotic locales. America's reputation as a place of great physical beauty was secured for all time.

Nevertheless, the polluting and destructive effects of human habitation and exploitation did not escape notice, either. Among his first impressions of the United States, Charles Dickens wrote in 1842:

> It pains the eye to see the stumps of great trees thickly strewn in every field of wheat; and never to lose the eternal swamp and dull morass, with hundreds of rotten trunks, of elm and pine

and sycamore and log-wood, steeped in its unwholesome water; where the frogs so croak at night that after dark there is an incessant sound as if millions of phantom teams, with bells, were travelling through the upper air, at an enormous distance off. It is quite an oppressive circumstance, too, to come upon great tracks, where settlers have been burning down the trees; and where their wounded bodies lie about, like those of murdered creatures; while here and there some charred and blackened giant rears two bare arms aloft, and seems to curse his enemies.[65]

Now there is a complete library of books to the same effect. French novelist Georges Duhamel made the following comment in 1931:

By what frightful miracle does this land, which stretches from the tropics to the icebergs, this country, which may be without grace, but yet is not without nobility, find itself so degraded and made ugly? The people who inhabit it seem more anxious to plunder it than to love it and beautify it. These fields are not ugly, but despised, slaughtered, and squalid, for they are left in prey to "renters" who seek nothing except an ignoble profit.[66]

Since the 1970s the understanding that a large portion of the natural heritage of the nation has been squandered by avaricious development has been accepted universally in the United States and abroad. Legislation to clean and regulate more strictly the uses of the land and the waterways has been enacted with overwhelming support. Yet these tendencies must still compete with the demands of population growth and economic growth. The mental images of a despoiled America live alongside the images of America's physical beauty, as both of those do actually cohabit in the countryside.

3

AMERICAN FOOTPRINTS ABROAD

The turn of the century brought an entirely new set of facts that gave rise to entirely new images. By the last decade of the nineteenth century, the United States grew to boast the world's largest economy. It had settled the West. It looked for new challenges and found them abroad. For the first time, people elsewhere began to develop images of the United States based on its position as a growing force and as a competitor, and on its welcome or unwelcome interventions in their affairs. Starting in the early twentieth century, the newly created images of America chiefly derive from its economic and military power and how the United States exercised them in its dealings with foreign nations. It was no longer just a "light unto nations." It became an active player in the games of nations.

Imperialist

In its first century, America's main foray into foreign affairs was the Monroe Doctrine of 1823, which articulated a policy of opposition to any European power acquiring colonies or otherwise interfering in the Western Hemisphere. Originally, the Monroe Doctrine was a response to the fear that the South American nations that had just expelled their Spanish colonial overlords were vulnerable to being newly colonized by competing, stronger European powers. Americans despised European imperialism and saw the South American revolutions as outgrowths of its own revered revolution. Americans had a growing sense of destiny to exert a sphere of influence over the whole hemisphere. With the Monroe Doctrine, the

United States declared itself the policeman of North, Central, and South America.

Initially, America's reach exceeded its grasp. In the world of sovereign states, with no overarching system of international law or enforcement, any policy becomes effective only if the party adopting has the power to effect it. Spain reacquired the Dominican Republic in 1861, and the United States, preoccupied with the Civil War, did nothing. Similarly, France intervened in Mexico from 1862 to 1867, and the United States did nothing.

However, as America flourished, it took an interest in the Panama Canal, and flesh was added to the bones of the Monroe Doctrine. In pursuing the canal project, the United States intervened in Colombian affairs, precipitating, even conniving, independence for Panama. As the canal approached completion, the United States realized the stake it would then have in protecting the Caribbean approaches to the canal from ownership by hostile powers. In 1898 in Havana Harbor, the sinking of the USS *Maine* (now known to have been accidental) ignited the Spanish-American War. In this quick and effective fracas, the United States crossed into the world of imperial powers by snatching a modest empire from the diminished Spaniards. Cuba, Puerto Rico, the Philippines, and Guam were among the spoils. Having acquired these far-flung possessions, the United States assembled the Great White Fleet, worthy of an imperial power, and sent it around the world in 1908 to announce the nation's entry as a junior member into the society of international imperial powers. Suddenly, the views of America by others were not limited to the ways Americans behave at home. For the first time, foreigners were concerned about what America and Americans had in store for them in their homes. Philippe Roger, a prominent French scholar, spoke in 2003 about how many of the ideas in France of the United States date from this period:

> The idea of dangerous America, imperialist America, the mighty-jawed Yankee, ready to devour Europe—the idea of America obsessed with money and materialism, America as the steamroller that would crush all spiritual values, religious values, and cultural values combined, led in France to a kind of alliance between secular and religious parties—this was the only ground on which they agreed—and then, of course, the very material, very empirical

danger of a new technological and commercial power that scared them, both for the competition it represented and also for the new forms of work that it created. . . . All these patterns were already in place from the end of the nineteenth century.[1]

These views were especially powerful when linked to the prior European view of America as an anti-imperial nation. Having persuaded others that it was an exception to the rapacious rules of European international affairs, the American reversal of policy disappointed its greatest admirers in Europe. The disappointment stung and was remembered.[2]

Self-Interested

At first, the creation of an American empire was a purely self-interested commercial and strategic matter. Even though it was an abandonment of pretensions to special American anti-colonial virtue, it did not involve a new model of international relations. America was participating in time-honored realist politics among nations. Realism in international affairs antedates the nation-state. Its exposition can be traced to the Greek city-states. Classicist Victor Davis Hanson paraphrases Greek historian Thucydides:

> Power, not justice . . . is always the final arbiter of state relations; self-interest, not morality, is what guides and must guide the behavior of states. Appeals to mercy or hope for reprieve are misguided, not rooted in either logic or a realistic understanding of human behavior.[3]

As the new century dawned, the United States continued to act as a neutral and a realist, brokering peace in the Russo-Japanese war and in Venezuela. True to George Washington, it entered no alliances. True to Thomas Jefferson, it stood as an example to others of the obvious virtues of republican government but did not act to export its system. Like all the other nations of the world, it did business with foreign nations as it found them and had no intent to reform their internal systems and ideologies. The world was full of monarchies and petty tyrants of all stripes. The United States palavered with all of them on whatever basis served America's security and commercial advantage.

Evangelist for Democracy, Multilateral, and Hypocrital

World War I changed America's approach to the world. Woodrow Wilson took the United States into the war and helped take the world into the peace at Versailles with brand-new concepts of international relations. In place of the pure pursuit of self-interest, Wilson's policies elevated international affairs to a moral crusade. The United States went to war to make the *world* safe for *democracy*, not, as was traditionally done, exclusively to make the United States safe for its citizens or aggrandize the United States at another nation's expense. As the war drew to a close, Wilson's "Fourteen Points" proposal in 1918—illustrating the design of the post-war era and his policies pursued at the peace conference—embodied an approach to international affairs that honored self-determination of people. He advocated nations yielding sovereign independence of action to a "general association of nations," the League of Nations. These ideas were radical. They placed a number of inconsistencies into the American practice of foreign affairs. These contradictions have been the source of both high expectations and grave disappointments in the minds of observers of American policy ever since. They set the terms of an America of the imagination in contrast to an America of the real world. America simultaneously guards its national security but promotes liberal democracy abroad at the expense of its security; demands a conscientious respect for its sovereignty but calls for intervention in the affairs of others; promotes self-determination but seeks respect for sovereign borders and stability; urges free trade but engages in protectionism; and leads the world in establishing multilateral institutions and international law but arrogates to itself alone the sovereign prerogative to decide on the actions it will take in world affairs.

In the deepest sense, none of these apparent contradictions are in conflict with the traditional idea that policies should be designed to enhance the enlightened self-interest of the nation adopting them. That gives them a subliminal consistency. Henry John Temple, Viscount Palmerston, famously said that nations have no permanent friends, only permanent interests. In fact, even nations' interests are impermanent. When Saddam Hussein carried the American spear into battle against the Iranians in the 1980s, the United States supported and supplied him. When he invaded Kuwait in 1991 and threatened American and world oil supplies, the United States led a coalition into what Saddam referred to as the "Mother of All Battles" against him. Similarly, for over a hundred years, the American strategic need to protect the Panama Canal as the naval lifeline between the east and west coasts of the United States assured it would tolerate no unfriendly governments in Central America, even if that interest compelled a sacrifice of its commitment to democracy. This consistent policy gave rise to a long line of banana republics. By 2009, with the Canal too narrow to handle major ships, the United States took a hard line against an allegedly unconstitutional removal and exile of the president of Honduras and righteously demanded an end to Latin American military coups d'états. Different circumstances entail different interests and invite different policies and different "friends." After all, each competing nation is acting with similar calculations for its own benefit.

The Wilsonian movement of liberal internationalism did not create a single world government; it created a series of institutions made up of individual sovereign states pursuing their own interests. Whether acting alone, within multilateral institutions such as the United Nations or the World Trade Organization, or in international treaty negotiations, every nation is seeking to maximize its advantage. The problem for the United States has been that in each of the dualities within its stated foreign policies, one alternative is based on short-term strategic interest, such as protectionism or sovereignty, and the other alternative is based on frequently trumpeted statements of conviction and supposed principle that it hopes will coincide with its long-term strategic interests. Another problem is that its commitments to bring virtuous change to the world outside its borders are taken more seriously than when such commitments are made by others, because the United States is thought to have the power to make them come true. The charges of hypocrisy by its enemies and the feelings of disappointment among its friends are hard to avoid:

> In the United States, democratic principles are indeed honored and upheld; they are part of the warp and woof of American society. Americans are, in their own homes and towns, a truly free and democratic people. . . . American interests all too easily blur the standards of democracy as they are applied elsewhere. In Indonesia, and perhaps in other countries as well, I have surmised that there is a general view, particularly among people like myself who have suffered the loss of their civil rights, that democracy is something reserved for Americans only.[4]

Inconstant, Unreliable, and Naive

America must look after its own security and commercial interests, as must every other nation. This is the prerogative of sovereign states. No one expects China or Finland to do otherwise. But since Wilson, the United States, unlike China and Finland, has professed its intention to bring democracy to those who do not have it. Over the years, American evangelizing for democracy has expanded to include promotion of free markets and human rights, all under the panoply of liberal democracy. Policies that are designed to promote America's immediate national security and those designed to evangelize are often in direct conflict. Each American administration strikes the balance differently, but none eliminates the conflict. For example, the United States has long trumpeted a devotion to noninterference in the internal affairs of other nations. This, coupled with its pursuit of its strategic self-interest, will frequently dictate support for non-democratic leaders who, in other circumstances, the United States would be working to unseat. The list of monarchs and dictators who have had American support in its fights against communism or Islamic fundamentalism is a familiar one—Anastasio Samoza in Nicaragua; Alfredo Stroessner in Paraguay; Augusto Pinochet in Chile; Fulgencio Batista in Cuba; Hosni Mubarak in Egypt; Hussein and Abdullah II in Jordan; Ibn Saud and his successors in Saudi Arabia; Chiang Kai-shek in China; Nguyễn Văn Thiệu in South Vietnam; and Reza Pahlavi in Iran are just a sampling. The United States supported Saddam Hussein when his opposition to the Iranian regime advanced American strategic interests, and removed him militarily when his fascist ideology conflicted with the American pursuit of democracy in the Middle East and threatened American strategic interests. George W. Bush said, "The advance of freedom is the calling of our time; it is the calling of our country. From the Fourteen Points to the Four Freedoms, to the Speech at Westminster, America has put our power at the service of principle."[5] He linked this proselytizing for "the global expansion" of democracy to American national security, arguing that "lasting peace is gained as justice and democracy advance. In democratic and successful societies, men and women do not swear allegiance to malcontents and murderers. . . . "[6] Barack Obama continued this American tradition in his 2009 speech in Cairo, saying, "But I do have an unyielding belief that all people yearn for certain things: the ability to speak your mind and have a say in how you are governed . . . the freedom to live as you choose. Those are not just American ideas, they are human rights, and that is why we will support them everywhere."[7] He reiterated this commitment while addressing the graduating class at West Point in 2010, saying that "a fundamental part of our strategy for our security has to be America's support for those universal rights that formed the creed of our founding."[8] Still, as in prior administrations, where undemocratic regimes support American security interests, as Mubarak's did in Egypt, he remained silent until domestic Egyptian unrest brought Mubarak down in early 2011. Also, as a practical matter, where undemocratic regimes have the power to deter American intervention, as with Hu Jintao in China, the American government minimizes or omits any effort to democratize that country. Evangelism is balanced with realism.

The same applies to multilateralism. Even before Woodrow Wilson, the United States was a proponent of multilateral institutions in both international commercial dealings (such as the Paris Convention for the Protection of Industrial Property of 1883) and international political and military affairs (such as the Hague Convention for the Pacific Settlement of International Disputes of 1899 and various subsequent Hague conventions on the rules of war). Over the years, the United States has been a leading voice in creating a global network of thousands of treaties among nations on every subject from customs duty harmonization to the law of the sea. Yet one of history's most notorious about-faces on an issue in international affairs occurred when Woodrow Wilson failed to get Senate ratification for the Versailles Treaty's creation of the League of Nations. In 1919 and 1920 the ideas of surrendering America's freedom of action in foreign affairs and facing a recurrence of America's recent victorious but painful foray into the affairs of Europe were too much for the solons of the Senate. They remained attached to the competing American philosophies of preserving the sovereign power to act alone and unfettered, and avoiding entanglements with the sordid affairs of Europe. The Europeans, having bought into Wilson's internationalism, felt betrayed by America's renewed isolationism. The French were furious and uncomprehending when the United States forgave German war reparations in the 1920s. Perhaps they felt mostly confused when the United States did participate in the 1928 Kellogg-Briand Pact to renounce war as an instrument of national policy (a treaty that remains in force).

Through all of this, the United States began to be regarded in European eyes as inconstant and unreliable, as well as naive in international affairs. In the 1930s Franklin Roosevelt spoke of the "Four Freedoms" but took little action against Hitler and Mussolini until after they declared war on the United States following Pearl Harbor. The United States preached self-determination for people but occupied defeated Germany and Japan for eight years after World War II. Previously, the United States' commitment to self-determination most notably did not apply to the attempted secession of the Southern states from the Union in 1861. It did not and does not apply to secessionist forces in Quebec, secessionists in Abkhazia and South Ossetia in Georgia, Kurds in northern Iraq or eastern Turkey, Catholics in Northern Ireland, or Basques in Spain. It did apply to those demanding the dismantling of the nineteenth-century European empires; East Timorese in Indonesia; Bangladeshis in East Pakistan; Serbs, Croats, and Bosnians in Yugoslavia; and Czechs and Slovaks in Czechoslovakia. It might or might not apply to Tibetans and Taiwanese in China—no one knows for sure. When the decisions get made, the principle of self-determination yields to realism, and the prestige of America rises or falls depending on which way the viewer hoped it would come out. As the American armies advanced on Baghdad in 2003, Kurdish leader Jalal Talabani said, "Before we only had the mountains as our friends. And now, thanks to God, we have the United States of America."[9] If his interests or those of the United States had not coincided at that moment, the opinion voiced by Talabani would likely have focused on allegations of American treachery, rather than friendship.

So long as America is on a mission to change the world, its policies will always have a Janus-headed quality. Sometimes certain changes are in America's interest, and sometimes they are not. Each administration may judge differently where to strike the balance between principle and realism, but the balance must be struck. Some argue that the path of principle will always be in America's interest in the long term, as George W. Bush argued (but did not consistently practice) in promoting democracy. Still, the nation has to get through many short terms before the long term arrives. In addition, the striking of the balance is partly dependent on internal American politics. While the nation as a whole embodies conflicting drives toward such themes as free trade and protectionism, there are many separate constituencies within the United States that support one or the other side of the argument consistently. Each administration reacts to these separate pressures. The current American policy, expressing support for free trade and World Trade Organization membership on the one hand and defending domestic agricultural price supports and quotas on the other hand, is indicative of these opposing strands of policy. Another prominent example is the long-standing American support for the United Nations (as well as a welter of other international institutions from the International Monetary Fund to the Asia-Pacific Economic Cooperation), versus the decision of the Bush administration to flout the United Nations' disapproval in invading Iraq in 2003. In the Iraq case, the U.S. government decided that its principled devotion to multilateralism and international institutions was trumped by its requirement to deal with a particular risk to its national security and its need to show other potential adversaries its steadfastness and resolve. The United States could not allow its threat to apply its overwhelming military power to be subject to a veto by third countries for fear that its future threats to use force would be discounted. To the administration, submitting to multilateral veto authority would be tantamount to forfeiting its power advantage in international affairs.

These examples of protectionism, unilateralism, and the use of force do not mean that the principles in American foreign policy of free trade, multilateralism, or peaceful dispute resolution have been vitiated. Those principles will survive to be applied another day in another circumstance. An effective foreign policy is one that uses all the intellectual and tactical tools at its disposal. If free trade best enhances the broad purposes of the nation, free trade should be espoused. If protectionism is best, protectionism is what is needed. Similarly, in each situation the policymaker must decide between the application of multilateralism or unilateralism, self-determination or stability, isolationism or internationalism, and promotion of democracy or nonintervention. American traditions are behind each of these alternatives. Principles and realism should be in the service of each other rather than in opposition to each other in managing international relations. The price to be paid for intertwining conflicting themes in the same nation's policies (and a price that the policymaker must consider in making choices) is a charge by both friends and enemies of hypocrisy and unreliability. America has a rich trove of such accusations against it, and they began long before current events unfolded:

What seemed so hypocritical to many Germans [in 1953] was the apparent contradiction between the realities and the appeals made by America. It was indeed difficult for them to understand—and to accept—the underlying reasons, partly changes in American politics, partly changes in world politics, and partly fundamental beliefs as well as passing fallacies prevalent in American thinking.[10]

To many Germans, Americans appeared as a people sadly lost on the international scene, unable to perform their part in foreign politics, lacking either the power or the experienced understanding—or perhaps both—needed for world leadership.[11]

Despite its different circumstances, as a victor in World War II rather than a defeated and occupied nation, a simultaneous survey of French opinion yielded similar sentiments:

The Frenchman [in 1953] fears, then, "American economic imperialism." He fears "Americanization." Finally, he fears being victimized by the blunders of a nation which, for all its good intentions, seems to him politically maladroit and lacking in experience. . . . These questions occur to him almost simultaneously and reflect his deep fear of involvement beside an America whose policy, he thinks, vacillates incoherently between extremes of isolationism and aggressiveness.[12]

The observation that Americans lack "experienced understanding" and that American vacillation between competing policies is a token of American naiveté and incompetence in world affairs is a constant theme of European, and particularly French, views of the United States in the field of foreign policy. It is inseparable from French and other European feelings of cultural and intellectual superiority that date back to the days of American colonial wilderness. It provides the usual psychological satisfactions of snobbery. It does not accord with the record. Reflecting on the respective courses of economic and political success of the United States and France over the last two hundred years, the inescapable conclusion is that the United States has played a much better hand. France went from being a great imperial power that controlled most of western Europe and a vast empire of resources abroad to being a modern nation of modest size with an economy slightly greater than that of California and a population about one-quarter of that of the United States. In the course of those years, France was defeated or badly mauled in every war it fought. Its victories were won by virtue of the efforts of its allies, prominently including the United States. Germany has an even worse record of success in world affairs. The scorn heaped by them on the United States in its conduct of world affairs is at least partly an understandable salve to these wounds.

Guarantor of the Rights of Others and Arrogant Exporter of the "American Way"

America's inconsistency in pursuing its principles is not the only source of criticism of its policies. Often criticism comes from disagreement with those principles. America operates on the assumption, ingrained in its founding documents, that it holds to concepts that are both universal and self-evident. Universality is the core justification for American confidence in its post-Wilsonian evangelism of liberal democracy and capitalism. As President Obama said on accepting the Nobel Peace Prize, "America will always be a voice for those aspirations that are universal."[13] But not everyone agrees that our values are universal.

> What was often the root cause of the strong German resistance against American "re-education" [in 1953] and of the German acceptance of clichés and generalizations antagonistic to America was the underlying fear that America wanted to remodel the whole world, including and especially Germany, in its own image, with "God's own country" as the blueprint according to which all the other countries and cultures were to be shaped.[14]

These Germans correctly perceived the American policy. Their complaint was not inconsistency; it was the *consistent* application of a repellent universalist principle that threatened their distinctiveness and pride. The American export of its values inevitably puts it in the role of "teacher" with all the implications of superiority that go with that role. The resentment is exacerbated when the "pupil" despises the lesson. Contemporary German novelist Peter Schneider dispassionately itemizes some of the differences in principle between Europe and the United States:

The divisions are too deep, and Europe cannot meet the United States halfway on too many issues—the separation between church and state, the separation of powers, respect for international law, the abolition of the death penalty—without surrendering its version of its Enlightenment inheritance.

On other contentious issues the United States feels as strongly: the universality of human rights and the need to intervene—if the United Nations is unable to act—when there is genocide or ethnic cleansing or when states are failing.[15]

Horst Mahler, the German radical activist, states the case against American universalism and in defense of cultural and political particularism in more inflammatory terms:

[The September 11 attacks presage] the end of the American Century, the end of Global Capitalism, and thus the end of the secular Yahweh cult, of Mammonism. . . . It is not a war of material powers. It is a spiritual struggle: the war of Western civilization, which is barbarism, against the cultures of the national peoples. . . . The oncoming crisis in the World Economy—independent of the air attacks of 11 September 2001—is now taking the enchantment from "The American Way of Life." The absolute merchandisability of human existence—long felt as a sickness—is lost, along with the loss of external objects, in which human beings seek recognition and validation—but cannot find them.[16]

This view of America's export of liberal democracy and capitalism is even stronger in more distant cultures outside of Europe. Harvard professor Samuel Huntington warned in 1995, "In the emerging world of ethnic conflict and civilizational clash, Western belief in the universality of Western culture suffers three problems: it is false; it is immoral; and it is dangerous."[17] Among people around the world, there are those who hunger for liberal democracy and those who do not want it. Among the former, American inconsistency and impotence in pursuing the spread of its faith is a cause of worry and contempt. Among the latter, America's attempts, whether or not consistent or successful, are themselves a problem.

Where the United States has succeeded in fostering a region's transition to liberal democracy from a despised totalitarian state, as in Eastern Europe, some genuine admiration and gratitude for American policies and behavior pertains.

Protector, Benefactor, Liberator, Overbearing Presence, and Occupier

Even gratitude has its problems. Where American intervention has been indispensable to help people escape dire conditions, whether military defeat and occupation or natural catastrophe, the Americans are initially welcomed and soon resented. People tend to dislike the feelings of dependence and obligation that come with having a benefactor. This was the feeling in France only nine years after Americans liberated the country: "France savored only for a moment the full joy of liberation. Then, with almost tragic insistence, *fear* returned to plague the moral climate of a sorely tried people. The old fear of weakness confronted by strength, however, was now compounded with a new and more humiliating fear, that of the protected in face of his protector."[18]

At the same time, the defeated Japanese, beneficiaries of a benign occupation, had some of the same emotions:

> The occupation brought with it an intensification of several elements of the traditional images of America, namely, those concerned with America's power and strength. On the unfavorable side, Americans are seen as arrogant, demanding, pushing, disrespectful, high living, luxury loving, and corruptible. The more favorable obverse of this is that Americans are skillful, accomplished, generous, bighearted, and tolerant.[19]

Self-Absorbed Hyperpower

American power—whether as conqueror, competitor, trading partner, or benefactor—is behind much of the emotion that drives people to think about America in so many contexts and then choose only certain thoughts to express. America's power means that what America does in world affairs matters. American international behavior through the twentieth century filled a groaning shelf of specific images in foreign minds, from the gallant and generous America of World War II and its aftermath to the paranoid America of the early 1950s to the uncertain America of the post-Vietnam era. As American power grew steadily after World War II and it emerged as the only hyperpower after the fall of the Soviet Union, foreign reactions to America became fixated on this imbalance of influence. In disputes around the world, American support determines winners and losers. The winners are, at least momentarily, grateful. The losers are resentful. Gratitude, as in the Israeli case, is expressed quietly. Resentment, as in the Palestinian case, is expressed loudly and often violently.

Among the smaller nations of the world, the sense of powerlessness was increased by the fall of the Soviet Union. During the bipolar era of the Cold War, less powerful large nations like Mexico, Egypt, and India, and even small nations such as Thailand, Ghana, and Austria, parlayed their non-aligned position into greater influence by acting as the swing votes between the Western and the Eastern blocs. They played one side against the other. The United States acted to keep each nation in its orbit and solidly supportive of its positions. It took seriously any hint of defection. The Reagan administration invaded the tiny island of Grenada to displace a new regime that leaned toward the Soviet side. The same administration forfeited its prestige and credibility to prevent (successfully) the loss of Nicaragua. Successive Cold War–era administrations were focused on keeping the Soviets out of places like Angola and Mozambique. The United States supported a legion of unsavory regimes and spent a fortune in foreign aid in the cause of holding the loyalty of smaller nations. The end of the Cold War took away the deciding vote of the smaller nations—there was no longer a choice to be made.

In the 1990s the United States, feeling no threat from these nations, reduced its foreign aid and shut down the United States Information Agency that reached out to the third world with radio programming and facilities such as American libraries. In the world of one great power, the disempowered nations of the world began to worry that the United States was paying no attention to them. After September 11, 2001, Pakistani foreign minister Mian Khursheed Mehmood Kasuri issued this plaintive appeal:

> We are a small country, and many Pakistanis feel that the U.S. government needs us and then forgets us. Secretary of State Colin Powell has told me personally that this time America's commitment to Pakistan is not focused on one issue. But the United States tends to forget because on its radar screen we may appear

as a blip and then we disappear. Something else appears on the screen. We would definitely welcome a long-term commitment by the United States.[20]

A world in which the small nations have to cry for attention is a dangerous one for the great power. The states and non-state actors who feel neglected, who cannot get redress for their real and imagined grievances, search for ways to be heard. They turn to the great equalizers among world powers. For many nations committed to liberal internationalism, such as the European sovereignties, the equalizers are the demands that all matters be dealt with in forums, such as the United Nations, where the old fiction of the equality of sovereign states still prevails under a rule of one nation/one vote, and the formation of countervailing alliances who hope that their power as a group can match American power.[21] For renegade regimes and non-state actors, who would not prevail at the United Nations, the equalizers are weapons of mass destruction and terrorism. Both weapons of mass destruction and terrorism are low-cost versions of the Colt .45 of the Old West cowboy or the Mac-10 of the urban gang-banger—they gain respect and compliance from the otherwise more powerful victim who is in their sights. Therefore, it is the unique strength of America among nations that creates an incentive for the proliferation of weapons of mass destruction and terrorist tactics among its weakest opponents.[22]

Dangerous Policeman of the World and Fiduciary

To the one great power, this situation presents policy challenges that cannot be answered by reference to the old tradition of sovereign states acting for themselves. It also cannot be found in the Wilsonian theory of liberal internationalism that seeks to associate sovereign states in international organizations that expect member nations to sacrifice some immediate self-interest for the long-term security of having acted together for higher (peaceful) goals. In its position as the overwhelming power, the United States is increasingly called upon to exercise its worldwide influence in ways that advance the interests of constituencies in other countries, whether or not Americans have an interest in the matter. The people of the world know that America's actions affect them, and, even though they do not vote in American elections, they expect America's government to consider their views and their welfare. They see America as a fiduciary, a trustee, on account of its power over them. They put America in the role of the policeman who acts to protect others without regard to his own safety, as he is employed by and is responsible to the entire community. American leaders have often spoken of missions to bring benefits to the world as a whole, but they have seen it exclusively as something to be done as a moral mission or for America's long-term best interests, and something to be put aside if America's short-term best interests dictate otherwise. This idea of trusteeship is a new expectation, one that is not applied to other, less-powerful nations, and one that is not often fulfilled by American behavior.

This view comes from the perception of American power. Pakistani novelist Tariq Ali said in 2002, "It is the imposition of [American] hegemony, the forms it assumes as well as the resistance it generates, that will mark the politics of the present century."[23] To many, America's unlimited ability to act, particularly in ways that affect their lives, adds up to a feeling that the United States is dangerous. "The heart of the problem is that many people here [in England] feel their destiny is in the hands of an untrammeled U.S. . . . . The sense of being swept along by an alien force that we cannot control is unsettling and causes resentment."[24] A South African flight attendant was heard saying, "They act like the big guy riding roughshod over everyone else."[25] In Islamic countries, with their cultural predilection toward finding outside forces at work, professor Edward Said explained,

> For at least three generations, Arab leaders, politicians, and more-often-than-not U.S.-trained advisers have formulated policies for their countries with, at basis, a near-fictional, fanciful idea of what the U.S. is. The basic idea, far from coherent, is about how Americans run everything; the idea's details encompass a wide, jumbled range of opinions, from seeing the U.S. as a conspiracy of Jews, to believing that it is a bottomless well of benign help for the downtrodden, or that it is utterly ruled by an unchallenged white man sitting, Olympian-like, in the White House.[26]

Toward the end of the Clinton administration, before the Bush administration and the war on terror, a leading Pakistani militant complained, "America should reconsider its policy of interfering in other countries' business. The whole world is beginning to hate your country. America has become a negative symbol. Its name has become a curse. China, on the other hand, is also a big power. But no one hates China because it leaves other countries alone."[27]

While the militant sees the United States everywhere, others see it ignoring Pakistan and turning inward. While he wants the United States to leave him alone, others want it to bring them democracy and human rights. When the United States pursues vigorous, costly engagements in the Middle East, which it says are in the cause of liberal democracy, others say it is to pursue America's selfish interests. In 2004 the Pew Research Center's survey found that "solid majorities in France and Germany believe the U.S. is conducting the war on terrorism in order to control Mideast oil and dominate the world. People in Muslim nations who doubt the sincerity of American antiterror efforts see a wider range of ulterior motives, including helping Israel and targeting unfriendly Muslim governments and groups."[28] A *New York Times* reporter, John Burns, quoted his Baghdad driver, who had been interned in Saddam Hussein's prisons, as saying, "It was God who finished Saddam, not the Americans. The Americans broke all their promises to us. They have brought their infidel beliefs to Iraq. We hate them and they are worse than Saddam."[29] In Islamic lands powerful America is dealing with a society in which all good things come from God and all bad things must come from whoever else has power. The issue is America's power. It is a challenge to every frustrated person. With the unprecedented power comes an unprecedented duty in the minds of many people. The charge that the United States is in the time-honored process of pursuing its own interests (true or not) is a serious indictment in these minds, and, in view of American rhetoric about its higher purposes, a serious disappointment to them.

As much as people clamor for America to share its responsibilities, and as much as it may want to do so, the problems of the perception of American unilateral power cannot be avoided. "The U.S. is so powerful and the U.N. is so weak," said Mishary Nuaim, a political analyst at Saudi Arabia's King Saud University. "Nobody can do anything to stop the U.S."[30] After the bombing of UN headquarters in Iraq, Farouk Mohsen, a Cairo carpenter said, "It was just a matter of time. . . . The U.N. is just a puppet of the U.S., and anyone who is angry with the U.S. is likely to consider the U.N. a target."[31] When a Danish cartoonist drew a mocking cartoon of the prophet Mohammed, which was published in many western nations other than the United States and with which there was no American involvement, the Pakistani foreign minister accurately warned that it would fuel the level of anti-American anger in the Islamic world.[32] Anti–United States demonstrations ensued throughout the Middle East. Almost all people have long forgotten that the Korean War pitted the United Nations against the North Koreans, and the 1991 Gulf War and the sanctions that followed were acts of the United Nations against Iraq. The actions against Colonel Muammar al-Gaddafi of Libya in 2011 began with American imposition of a no-fly zone, but were promptly turned over to NATO. All those are seen as American actions. Bringing in the United Nations, NATO, or any other international coalition may help the United States in its international operations and may clothe American actions in a sense of legitimacy, but it will not do much to help the United States shed its image as the one great actor on the world scene.

It is not surprising that the citizens of the world have reacted by seeing the United States as an awesome power (the "Colossus of the North" in Latin American parlance), a nation to be dreamed of and longed for, a nation to be resented for its arrogant interventions in others' affairs and its hypocrisy in fostering tyrannies while preaching democracy, a disappointing leader that fails to pay attention to them, and the source of their failures and inadequacies.

For those who interpret American actions as insufficiently caring and overly self-interested, contrary evidence goes unnoticed. A 2010 poll of 395 Pakistani journalists found that 37 percent of them rejected the idea that the millions of dollars of aid given by the United States following the 2005 Kashmir earthquake was motivated by a "sincere desire to help."[33] On January 12, 2010, the earth shook in Haiti. Port-au-Prince fell down on and around its residents, killing or maiming hundreds of thousands. More than a million were rendered homeless and without food or water. In the ensuing days and weeks, the United States, its government, and its people mounted one of history's most comprehensive and generous international relief efforts. It was not perfect. It took a few days to get through to the people. But, under the difficult circumstances, it was phenomenal. At first, especially as there were start-up delays, it attracted the world's attention. However, by early February, as the relief effort continued to gain effectiveness, only one story on Haiti could be found on newspaper front pages around the world—an alleged baby abduction plot by an American Baptist orphanage group that was taking children across the border to the Dominican Republic without formal Haitian government paperwork. In the aftermath of weeks of looting, rape, and murder by hoodlums preying on the devastated city, it was these defendants who merited the filing of the first criminal case in Port-au-Prince following the quake—a case that was later quietly dropped.

Diabolical Manipulator

Although the image of overwhelming American power is based on a reality that is unique in world history, the image often exaggerates America's genuine ability to influence events. With respect to September 11, a young German was quoted to express a commonly held view: "We can't imagine that the C.I.A. didn't know something about this." Then he asked rhetorically, "Did you think that Americans were really on the moon?"[34] These suspicions are based on certain facts and certain American behavior—but the facts are just the starting point. The images are invented ones of supernatural and sinister control of events, of devilish manipulation of everyone's lives. They lead to farfetched expectations that the United States should manipulate all events to everyone's satisfaction regardless of who they are and where they live. They lead to disappointment.

4

IMAGES FROM THE
IMAGE MACHINES

Many images of America have their roots in America's way of life and its self-portrayal. They need no connection to any event. They are more a matter of what America is and how it appears than what it has done.

Purveyor of Crude and Godless Culture and Technical Prowess

American power has another pervasive impact on people's lives and their images of America. It propels the diffusion of American culture—American "cultural imperialism." Professor Samuel Huntington saw that power spreads culture: "A universal civilization requires universal power. Roman power created a near-universal civilization within the limited confines of the Classical world. Western power in the form of European colonialism in the nineteenth century and American hegemony in the twentieth century extended Western culture throughout much of the contemporary world."[1]

American power extends its culture in a number of ways. The evident success of America in every measure leads to a desire to investigate and emulate it. The Japanese of the late nineteenth-century Meiji restoration period sent delegations to the United States and to Western Europe to copy the best both had to offer. After World War II, the Japanese were apt and active students of the American system, from constitutional law to the Deming system of manufacturing quality control. In the 1990s Russia and the other former Iron Curtain countries mimicked the American economic and legal model, with mixed success. Others around the world have admired and adopted American ways less formally. Consider the transformation of the financial markets of Europe over the last thirty years, from cozy clubs to aggressive and competitive marketplaces for major transactions. Typically, the American models that are imported elsewhere are adapted to meet local conditions and styles, but the American influence remains recognizable.

American power also leads to the spread of its culture because its individualistic and capitalistic way of life is wrapped up in the liberal democratic ethos that the United States proselytizes. When the United States related to the rest of the world solely as an example, as a "city on a hill," its power and its culture were not as closely connected. But in confronting Nazism and communism, promotion of the individualistic and democratic values of American culture as well as its consumer capitalism were the very things for which American power was deployed. With the end of the Cold War, the United States worked actively to introduce market economies and all their accoutrements to Russia, China, and every other corner of the globe. The American government used its power to leverage diplomatic efforts, enter a myriad of trade conventions and treaties, and open international markets for American companies. It insisted that foreign countries be open to American products, even products discouraged at home, such as tobacco.

American power is not only deployed by example and by diplomacy. The United States demonstrates its high technology with foreign military sales and frequent active military applications. The technology embedded in our modern form of warfare is one type of cultural export that impresses intensely interested observers from Baghdad to Benghazi. The United States' military cultural effect extends beyond ordnance. The United States has been demanding deep cultural changes among the Iraqis, Afghans, and Pakistanis. It calls for rights for women. In response, the new Iraqi and Afghan constitutions guarantee that at least 25 percent of parliamentarians must be women, a higher percentage than in the United States Congress. The United States demands a secular education system that educates both boys and girls, and pressures the Pakistanis to limit its Islamic madrassas. The latest American anti-insurgency military doctrine requires an accommodation to a certain level of Western norms as an important element of military victory, while at the same time it accommodates the American military objectives to elements of tribal culture that it finds on the ground.

In addition to political and military power, the nature of America's market economy means that the power of its economic engine automatically sells American culture abroad. American culture is a consumer culture. American businesses sell their products and services, and, as they grow, they increasingly sell them in other nations as well as at home. The first American internationalists, in addition to diplomats and missionaries, were bankers, tobacco salesmen, and oil men. Over time, representatives of the automobile, steel, arms and aerospace, agricultural, and entertainment industries joined them. Therefore, more than in classical antiquity or in the British Empire, the growth of American power meant the extension of American culture. When American companies sell their products and services, they sell the "American Way of Life." Also, when American consumer products companies move their manufacturing abroad to reduce labor costs, they assure that the host nation will develop a taste for the goods they have begun to produce.

In 1959, during a brief moment of U.S.-Soviet détente, American vice president Richard Nixon and Soviet general secretary Nikita Khrushchev engaged in their famous Kitchen Debate at an American trade pavilion in Moscow. The Soviets had just bested the United States in space with their launch of the Sputnik satellite. Nixon laid his claim to American superiority on the basis of its cameras, dishwashers, and washing machines on display at the fair. To many observers it may have seemed a superficial if not vacuous argument, but to the Soviet people who saw and heard this conversation, the freedom, prosperity, and comforts represented by these appliances were of the essence. Modern Western consumer culture sells well to many people who live without it and without the choices and personal freedom it represents.

A developing nation's first connection to advanced Western technology is likely to have been the acquisition of American commercial jets for its national airline. When its citizens enter those planes, they enter a different world, one that cannot fail to impress them. American medical and pharmaceutical technology is another point of contact. "Large majorities around the world, including those who are critical of the United States in other areas, admire the U.S. for its technological and scientific advances."[2] They want what America sells.

Glamour, Excitement, Beauty, Sex, Superficiality, and Inauthenticity
Power and selling do not tell the whole story. In the embrace of American culture, there is as much pull as there is push. Even though many people deny it when interviewed by pollsters,[3] the economic facts demonstrate

that most people like American culture and want more of it. "There can be no doubt that the United States has produced the world's most varied and integrative culture, and it is no accident that it is the only one to have a worldwide appeal."[4] The widespread images of American culture as crass and materialistic are more than matched by the image of a life free of want and oppression, of free expression, and of individual fulfillment. At the Nixon-Khrushchev Kitchen Debate, an American, George Feifer, was stationed beside a Ford Thunderbird to promote the virtues of the car to the Russian crowd. He reported getting far more questions about the American way of life and the American school system than the car. Tatanya Steponova, who attended, said, "I just somehow sensed how free that country was. . . . Through the way they behaved, through the way they were dressed. You just could see that these were free people and we were not." She later married Feifer.[5]

People everywhere want to patronize American fast food chains, buy American jeans, flock to American theme parks, and enjoy American music and movies. Traditionalists decry it, but the vast majority of people demand it. A report from Brno, Czech Republic, related how the people lamented the loss of their traditional milk bar in the center of town that was replaced by a McDonald's but observed that they patronized the McDonald's and that the town council actively wooed it to Brno. The reporter continued, "One neighbor [in Brno] told us that she would send her child to a different nursery because our son's school didn't have enough Barbie dolls and other western toys."[6] The Opening Ceremonies of the Olympic Winter Games in Torino, Italy, in 2006 were an opportunity to showcase Italian culture—from Ferraris to Sophia Loren. Nevertheless, the Italian directors arranged for the world's athletes to march into the stadium to the strains of "Funkytown," "Celebration," and similar American disco and pop songs. The crowd (and the athletes) loved it.

Nothing signals the foreign demand for American culture more than the commercial popularity abroad of American movies, television, and popular music. They are condemned by the local cultural elites, for whom any popular culture, whether imported or homegrown, threatens their personal and professional positions as arbiters of taste. Often the general public will express ambivalence toward the notion of an invasion of alien culture. Nevertheless, the market proves that ordinary people want it and insist on getting it. In 2007 five billion people outside of the United States and Canada paid to see Hollywood movies.[7] *Avatar*, which opened in

2009, earned almost three-quarters of its $2.7 billion in box office revenue abroad.[8] Disney's *High School Musical* and its sequels presented its attractive, non-threatening picture of American life to over 200 million mostly 9- to 14-year-old females in 100 countries.[9] In 2007 United States film and television industries showed a $13.6 billion trade surplus.[10] In 2008 worldwide, American film exports were ten times the amount of film imports to the United States.[11]

Whatever people may say about liking American movies and television, the fact that they see so much of it is vital in understanding the sources of images of the United States. Australian writer David Malouf talked about the glamorous image he associated with the United States from boyhood trips to the local cinema:

> America was what I lost myself in at the Lyric Pictures every Saturday afternoon. A world sufficiently like our own as to be entirely familiar, but so unlike, with its skyscrapers, its freeways and flyovers, its limousines, its fast-talking "babes," its uniformed cabbies and bellboys and gangsters, as to be explicable only as a vision of a more sophisticated and glamorous future that we had not yet caught up with.[12]

English writer Jenny Diski said of her childhood in the 1950s, "America . . . was light. It beamed above my head from the cinema projection booth, particles dancing in its rays, ungraspable as a ghost, but resolving finally on the screen into gigantic images of a world I longed for, yet only half believed in."[13]

The impact of films, television, and other theatrical or literary material on image formation is multilayered. Typically, a movie has a story, a set of characterizations of various people, and a visual representation of a series of locales. The film itself presents an image of its technical sophistication, its production values. Film scripts, even when they are not "message films," convey imagery. In the American tradition of free speech, the Hollywood scripts frequently focus a jaundiced eye on American society. In telling larger truths, they shine light in the duality of good and evil in the individuals and societies they depict. The 1940 John Ford film version of John Steinbeck's *The Grapes of Wrath* showed the world an America afflicted with Depression poverty, desperation, and cruelty; so much so that the Motion Picture Export Association briefly withdrew it from export to France under State Department prodding. Ironically, Stalin banned it in 1948 because it showed that even the poorest of America's proletariat could afford a car.[14] Harper Lee's *To Kill a Mockingbird* told the story of both Jim Crow racial prejudice and the presence and actions of righteous people. Stephen Spielberg's *Saving Private Ryan*, written by Robert Rodat, was an account of American bravery and camaraderie in rescuing Europe from Nazi occupation. Stephen Gaghan's *Syriana* was a tale of Americans and the American government meddling murderously in the Middle East in service to a greedy and sinister oil industry. For decades, Hollywood cranked out cowboy stories for audiences with underlying themes of American individuality, bravery, morality, and resourcefulness. Now, action films are a particularly powerful vehicle in the international market because of their freedom from reliance on dialogue, so they are comprehensible across the language barrier. Innumerable action movies are stories of American heroism against American criminal evil or alien evil of some kind set in American locales with plenty of gunfire, car chases, death, and destruction. Consider everything from *Beverly Hills Cop, Terminator*, and *Men in Black* to *Spider Man* and *Iron Man*. All these stories fix images in the viewers' minds. Many of these images have been conveyed by films and television to a world public that does not visit the United States, does not read much or at all, and has little or no contact with Americans. Their storehouse of images is almost entirely the product of word of mouth and films and television.

But is it primarily the story that conveys the imagery people retain? The plot may appeal to or reinforce the predispositions people have with respect to the United States, as discussed in the following paragraphs. It may attract them to see the film. But what is remembered is more likely to come from the characterizations and the settings. People do not remember *Casablanca* for its narrative about Vichy-controlled Morocco. It is a love story, and the retained images, among others, are of smoldering American Humphrey Bogart as Rick, the cynical tough guy with the melting heart of gold, and beautiful Ingrid Bergman as Ilsa, the inscrutable pivot of the love triangle. It is these characters, their appearance, their natures, and their behaviors, that stick in the mind. The scenes in the saloon, in the bedroom, and at the airport are what people retain.

Moving from the sublime to the ridiculous, *The Simpsons* is one of the world's most-watched televisions shows. Its plots are amusing but beneath recall. What is remembered and considered typically American are the characters and the settings. The town of Springfield, similar to the towns described in *American Beauty* and *Back to the Future*, is a pretty, well-ordered, clean, middle-American small city, like Springfield, Massachusetts; Springfield, Missouri; or Springfield, Illinois. The characters are surprisingly diverse in both ethnicity and personality. The American family composed of the Simpsons is a stand-in for a normal American family in the minds of people everywhere. Homer is a well-meaning, ignorant, self-centered, bumbling dolt. Marge is a long-suffering wife. Bart is a wise guy. Lisa is a know-it-all. Maggie sucks her pacifier. And so on. The situation forms one key image of America as a place where there is modern, ordinary, working-class/middle-class Western life. Problems arise, and problems are solved, not much differently from what used to happen in television series of the 1950s like *Father Knows Best* or *The Adventures of Ozzie and Harriet*. However funny and stupid the behavior of the players seems, the picture of normality and innocence is an attractive one in much of the world. Nick King, a fishing guide in a remote New Zealand town, saved his money to buy his own power boat and named it *Santa's Little Helper*, in honor of the Simpsons' dog.[15]

The other element that is transmitted abroad by *The Simpsons* is the relative wealth of the United States. Even Homer, this uneducated working man with his job at the power plant, has a house that would be considered large in the wealthy societies of Japan or Hong Kong. He has a car; he has his beers. In action films of murder and mayhem and disaster films featuring earthquakes and floods, the audience looks behind the action to see the skyscrapers of New York and Chicago, the palm trees and beaches of Miami, the cars, the clothes, the way of life. People do not remember *Gone with the Wind* as an anti-Yankee screed; they remember a love story, and they remember the scenes behind the action: Tara, the finely dressed aristocrats, the fancy dress balls, the slaves, the horse near death from exhaustion. As David Malouf said above, it is the freeways and the babes he remembers. Therefore, counterintuitively, the many Hollywood generated films like *The Big Sleep, Blade Runner, L.A. Confidential, Chinatown,* and *Crash* that have a storyline depicting Los Angeles as a dystopia of evil, hatred, corruption, and intrigue leave the foreign viewer with alluring impressions of sunshine, wealth, sex, and glamour. They sell the Southern California region almost as well as the Rose Parade in its New Year's Day sunny glory. This is a lesson for any budding propagandist: do not worry about the script—emphasize the background. Richard Nixon was on to something trumpeting the washing machine in the Soviet Union.

Beyond the scenes and the personalities, the movies and television offer a world in which the people are beautiful and talented. America has an obesity epidemic, but its actors do not. The United States has no monopoly on beautiful people and talented entertainers, but it has plenty of both and has the most developed industry for the worldwide promulgation of images of these people. Celebrity, glamour, and beauty are attractive. Why else would we find Mongolia in 2008 issuing a set of commemorative postage stamps of Hollywood stars such as Marilyn Monroe? Their faces sell stamps. Mongolians want them on their letters. Stamp collectors want them in their albums.

The artists as well as the audiences see the United States as the place to succeed. From Charlie Chaplin to Johnny Depp, some actors have critiqued the nation's bourgeois ethos and have moved abroad, but they knew that success as a performer came to them by being in the United States. Artists and entertainers everywhere agree with Anné Kulonen, the Finnish-born London composer, who said that in the performing arts, the United States is synonymous with opportunity.[16] When the alluring actress is not American, as in the case of Nicole Kidman or Penelope Cruz, Hollywood makes her career, and her glamour rubs off on America in people's imaginations.

Finally, there is the role played by the enjoyment of the entertainment medium, itself. Increasingly, the development of low cost digital equipment is enabling film and television production industries to grow in all countries, and the American dominance over all genres is a thing of the past. The small, elegant film has been a staple of French filmmaking. Now the production of such films has spread to Brazil, Spain, Mexico, Canada, and Australia. However, the American lead in big-budget, high-gloss, technically amazing movies is the preserve of Hollywood, as it has always been. These are the films that get the big audiences globally. Hollywood depends on foreign sales for two-thirds of its box office revenue.[17] In this era of enhanced 3-D and IMAX films, there is no sign Hollywood will be displaced. *Avatar* was made in New Zealand by a Canadian, but it is a 3-D Hollywood film in the eyes of the world. What Pixar can do in computer animation is so special that even Walt Disney Studios had to buy them rather than try to replicate them. Except for anime from Japan, the United States has no major competitors in animated films. You leave the theater asking, "How did they do it?"

As we think of how images of America are made, Marshall McLuhan's bon mot, "The medium is the message," rings true. Whatever is on the screen, the moviegoer comes away impressed with the technical skill of the United States. It is a taste of a more modern and more advanced world. When Anné in Finland watched *Little House on the Prairie* in the 1970s, she saw a story of a family and a uniquely American situation. But she also experienced a lifelike reproduction of the story that was beyond the production qualities of anything then made for Finnish television. She adopted the view that Americans and American things are "glossier," and in a related idea, they are less real. Things can be too glossy. It is a subtle fact that the method by which an enormous variety of images of America are transmitted, electronic media, is responsible itself for leaving the viewer with two of the most oft-repeated images of America: superficiality and inauthenticity. The movies and television programs are creations of the mind and technology; they *are* inauthentic.

Amid the countless images delivered by the entertainment industry, both by its success in the global marketplace and in the content of its output, are the same leading images that American industry and government policies convey: America is overwhelming in size, strength, and influence, and epitomizes Western modernity. There is fundamental truth in those images, and, to the extent such things are capable of objective statistical measurement, the data confirm their truth.

5

THE UNITED STATES LOOMS: MEASURING REALITY

America's current place in the world is built on the facts of the past. Contemporary imagery borrows from past imagery because images fade slowly as reality evolves. A statistical look at the cold facts that define the United States relative to other nations confirms the accuracy of many of the often-conflicting images found in the preceding historical review. Joseph S. Nye Jr., dean of the Kennedy School at Harvard, says, "Not since Rome has one nation loomed so large above the others."[1] He understates the case. Rome had to compete with the Persian Empire and had no impact on the contemporaneous Chinese Empire of the Qin and Han Dynasties. In contrast, the United States stands unrivalled above the entire world in a large number of objective economic, political, military, and cultural measures.

Wealthy and Successful

How big is the gulf between the United States and the rest of the world? It is very big. The United States does not have the largest territory, or the biggest population, or the highest mountain, or the longest river, but it does have the largest economy—by far. In 2010 American gross domestic product totaled almost $15 trillion,[2] while the second largest economy, China, totaled about $5.8 trillion.[3] When understood in the terms of purchasing power, taking into account costs of living and population size, the purchasing power of Americans in 2008 exceeded that of the rest of the world's citizens, except those who live in oil-rich Norway or the handful of tiny oil or banking enclaves of Luxembourg, Kuwait, Bermuda, and the like.[4] By this measure, the average American income bested the average income in the other major modern, diversified Western economies by 15 to 30 percent and were several times that of the typical non-Western economies.[5] For comparison's sake, assume the average purchasing power of an American in 2008 was one hundred dollars, that of a Pole was thirty seven dollars, and that of a Russian was thirty four dollars. According to this scale, the purchasing power of a Nigerian was less than four dollars, despite the enormous oil revenues of Nigeria. A citizen of Niger had purchasing power of $1.50.

In raw per capita income, the American economy generates about $127 dollars per day for the average American.[6] Looking at daily income for the entire world, about 35 percent of the world's population lives on less than two dollars per day, and about one-eighth of the world's population lives on less than one dollar per day.[7]

Since the dollar replaced the pound sterling as the world's reserve currency at the Bretton Woods Conference in New Hampshire in 1944, the image of the "Almighty Dollar" has been enshrined in the minds of people. The price of gold is quoted in dollars; the price of oil is quoted in dollars. The value of the Chinese currency, the yuan, is allowed to float, but only within a range measured in dollars. If the value of the dollar rises or falls, the value of the yuan rises or falls with it, and the Chinese economy feels the reverberations. This helps perpetuate the nineteenth-century Chinese image of America, derived from the remittances home from the Chinese laborers toiling on the transcontinental railroad, as the Gold Mountain.

The economic crisis that began in 2008 will result in some adjustments to these figures and relationships. The continuing growth of China has had and will have an impact. But it is unlikely that the relative positions of the United States and the rest of the world will radically change anytime soon. Those who project that the Chinese economy will overtake the American economy put their expected date somewhere between 2027 and 2040, if it ever happens.[8] The short- and long-term economic prospects of the European and Japanese economies are diminished by their aging populations. The interrelationship of the world's economies with the United States' economy assures that when, as in 2008 and 2009, there is an economic downturn in the United States, most of the rest of the globe suffers proportionally to, if not more than, the United States. Further, as has been true throughout history, the prospects for American long-term economic resilience are enhanced by its uniquely open, creative, and entrepreneurial culture. Just as it did during and after the Great Depression, the United States should remain at the forefront of the world economy for a long time.

Thus, the image throughout the world that the Americans are rich begs no elaborate explanation. As early as 1844, the Hungarian Ágoston Mokcsai Haraszthy said of Americans, "There is one single point to which all are driving, and this is 'wealth.'"[9] The statistics support this image. We do not need to delve into subtle psychological processes to find its root. But the statistics tell only a slice of the truth. They are totals and averages. There are too many poor Americans (over 47.8 million as of 2009),[10] and there are more than a few rich Russians. In the vast American economy, there are uncounted thousands of homeless, millions of low-income inner-city dwellers, and millions of rural poor. Russian plutocrats and their Mexican counterparts can be found in their villas on the Riviera. In many countries, people can live well on less money than those living in the United States. The weather may be better or worse than in America. A fulfilling rural life may not require much cash. People's expectations may be lower. Any image of a complex object, even one based on objective data, suffers from being an incomplete picture, a simplification, a stereotype. Statisticians have tried to account for some of this complexity. The United Nations adds measures of life expectancy, years of schooling, and adult literacy to the income tabulation of gross domestic product to assemble its "Human Development Index" to try to give a more accurate picture of the relative quality of life of the people of the world. By this measure the United States stands near the middle of the list of leading Western nations, Japan, and South Korea. This position accords with what any traveler finds in comparing life in the United States with that encountered in the European capitals. Who would say that life in Zurich or Paris is less prosperous on average than life in Chicago or New York? In this contest among the top twenty-four nations, the only nations scoring over ninety-two on the scale are in the West (including Japan and South Korea).[11] Comparing the Western-style prosperity of Tokyo with Manila makes the point obvious. A great distance separates the lives of typical Westerners from those of the common citizens of the major nations of Africa, Asia, Central Europe, the Middle East, and South America.

The World Bank approaches it differently, by devising a measure of per capita wealth that is calculated by aggregating its estimates of each nation's natural capital (the value of its agricultural land and natural resources), produced capital (the value of its structures, plants, and equipment), and intangible capital (the value of its human and social capital inherent in the skills of its population and in its social structure). Nevertheless, it gets the same conclusion. In the World Bank's most recent estimate, for the year 2005, Americans, with per capita wealth of $734,195, were not the very richest but they were among them. The United States trailed only Denmark, Iceland (before its banking crisis of 2008), Luxembourg, Norway, and Switzerland.[12] The high-income (mostly Western) nations of the Organisation for Economic Co-operation and Development (OECD) held 82 percent of the world's wealth.[13]

In view of these figures, it is the entire West that leads the world economically, and the United States is not head and shoulders above the competition in all measures. No matter. In the minds of people everywhere, the United States stands astride the global economy in all respects, because the United States is the avatar of the Western juggernaut. America is the symbol of individual freedom, free market economic prosperity, technological progress, and the whole structure of modern Western society wherever it is employed. For more than a hundred years, America has been "seen as a process or a worldview capable of being separated from its physical home and transferred elsewhere."[14] The entire syndrome of modernization became "Americanization." "America" entered "the realm of the spirit."[15] As a disembodied presence, America is seen to lead even in ways it does not lead. At the end of World War II, with Europe again prostrate, the United States' economy accounted for 50 percent of the world's GDP. Many explained mid-century American leadership as a temporary aberration resulting from Europe's fratricidal wars and expected America to be overtaken by a resurgent Europe and Japan in due course. Their surprise was the durability of American leadership and the fact that the lead kept growing, not shrinking. In 2000 Japan's GDP was 49 percent of the American figure; by 2005 it shrank to 34.5 percent. The interdependence of the world economy tends to prevent smaller economies from gaining on the United States'economy. Formerly, when the United States,

Germany, Great Britain, and France competed for economic leadership, one country would gain at the expense of the others. If one weakened, the others gained. Today's interdependence mutes that effect. If Airbus makes a sale, it does so at the expense of Boeing but to the benefit of a battalion of American Airbus subcontractors. In general, economic growth abroad benefits American suppliers, investors, and consumers. American economic growth has become a necessary condition for foreign prosperity. As a visit to home furnishing stores like Pottery Barn or Crate & Barrel or to general merchandise stores like Target or Wal-Mart will show, very little that the American consumer buys comes entirely from the United States. If the United States economy slows a little, the Malaysian economy slows more. Even China is invested in the success of the American economy—America is the leading destination of China's exports and the fourth-largest source of its imports;[16] as of 2010 China held over $750 billion of American sovereign debt.[17] The 2008 economic crisis in the United States brought growth projections for China in 2009 to single digits for the first time in over a decade. China survived the downturn well and recovered its growth rate in 2010, but only by a massive return to government investment in the Chinese economy. This stimulus spending reversed years of disinvestment from state-owned enterprises. Privatization of state-owned enterprises had been a great boon to the Chinese economy before 2009. The return to state ownership raises questions about future Chinese growth.

Similarly, the United States is the leading source of imports to countries as diverse as Brazil, Canada, Chile, Colombia, Egypt, Israel, Mexico, Peru, Saudi Arabia, and Venezuela, and the leading destination of exports from Algeria, Bangladesh, Brazil, Canada, China, Colombia, Ireland, Israel, Japan, Mexico, Nigeria, Pakistan, Peru, the Philippines, Saudi Arabia, the United Kingdom, Venezuela, and Vietnam. The United States ranks among the top four trading partners for nations whose combined population constitutes at least 90 percent of the world's population.[18] On total, about one-eighth of all exports by the other nations of the globe are for the American market. The American economy is not only the world's largest—it is the single strongest engine pulling the train of the others.

Omnipresent and Economically Dominant

The trade figures underscore another objective fact that relates to imagery abroad: Americans and American interests are present everywhere. The economic penetration into foreign societies implicit in the breadth and depth of the trade in goods and services is reinforced by globalized investment patterns centered in the financial markets of the United States. Far and away the leading center of capital investment and entrepreneurship, the United States is the home of most of the world's largest multinational companies, from ExxonMobil to Johnson & Johnson. Six of the world's ten largest businesses by market value are American companies that do business globally.[19] Investments by investors throughout the world originate in or pass through the United States. Total United States market capitalization on the New York Stock Exchange and NASDAQ at January 1, 2010, was about $17.3 trillion, compared to Japan's second-place position at about $3.8 trillion.[20] The conventional idea of Americans as self-absorbed, inwardly focused, and isolationist collides with this reality of a nation of multitudinous global interests and involvements. However, this worldwide impact generates another negative impression among some observers, who decry this influence, saying, "'Free Markets' is simply a euphemism for free mobility of American capital, unrestrained expansion of American corporations, and free (uni-directional) movement of goods and services from America to the rest of the world."[21]

Generous and Parsimonious

Economic power and economic presence are not the only measures of a nation. They are not the only sources of images. Americans consider themselves a generous people and are quick to cite the Marshall Plan that reconstructed post–World War II Europe. As of 2008 the United States leads the world in total government grants of foreign aid, giving about twice as much as second place Germany and well over twice the amounts from each of third, fourth, and fifth place United Kingdom, France, and Japan, respectively.[22] This understates American donations. Unique in the world, about half of American charitable donations are by individuals, directly or through a constellation of American nongovernmental organizations. Save the Children, CARE, Catholic Relief Services, the International Rescue Committee, World Vision, and a multitude of others represent Americans giving to foreign recipients. If you visit Siem Riep, Cambodia, to see Angkor Wat, you will see restorations of the different temples each being carried out by a different foreign nation. All the sites bear signs acknowledging the governmental donor except the American-financed site, which acknowledges the many individual donors. The worldwide reach of the American military, especially its navy, often makes the United States the first on the scene to respond with emergency relief, as in recent devastating earthquakes in Haiti, Pakistan, and Japan. To many abroad, this leadership gives an image of generosity. When earthquake victims open a food package marked "A Gift from the USA," it does have an effect. On the other hand, when calculated as a per capita expenditure, the United States falls lower on the list of givers. When calculated as a percentage of GDP, the United States' governmental giving ranks twenty-fourth in the world, tied with Kuwait.[23] Despite the forgoing facts, these metrics give rise to an image at home and abroad of the United States as "the stingiest nation in the world."[24]

Profligate, Efficient, and Fat

A related image is one of wastefulness—the America that gorges on energy and raw materials while the rest of the world is relatively abstemious. This is the image of the America that refused to ratify the Kyoto Accord on global warming. It was heard often in the discussions surrounding the 2009 follow-up meeting in Copenhagen. However, here too the numbers lead to contradictory conclusions. In energy consumption, Americans, who are only 4.6 percent of the world's population, consume more than 20 percent of world energy production—a seemingly clear case of extravagant wastefulness. On the other hand, that 20 percent of energy consumption powers the American economy to create more than 23 percent of world GDP—a clear case of efficient resource use.[25] To put the same facts a third way, on a per capita basis, Americans rank tenth among world energy consuming nations, somewhat more efficient than the Canadians—not a performance that merits accolades for conservation, but not a case of stark piggishness. Even the American reputation for gluttony, justified by the epidemic of obesity afflicting the nation, does not put the United States at a pinnacle in the world of overweight—only near it. Figures recorded in 2008 list American men as third in the world (behind Lebanon and Qatar) and American women as sixth among the globe's fattest.[26] Even though the United States is justly considered to be among the carb-loading leaders, the obesity epidemic has become a worldwide affliction, and the rest of the globe is catching up quickly. Where, as in these examples, the aggregate numbers would support conflicting images, the diversity of American society further undermines the stereotypes. Within the total figures on resource consumption, there is a wide range of American behavior, from the gas guzzling, portly commuter in his Escalade to the environmentally concerned ascetic in his Chevy Volt. They are all Americans.

Innovative High Technology, High Skills, and Energetic

Innovation and high technology have been staples of imagery of the United States for a long time: "Every European knew that America meant wealth, that wealth meant business, that business meant capitalism and the capitalist, and that—basically—the source of all good things, at least in the twentieth century was technology. These identifications have survived every pressure the modern era has brought to bear."[27]

It is difficult to measure a nation's innovation and technology in comparison to those of others, but the *Economist* tries. In its latest Innovation Index, for the year 2009, combining human resource skills, market incentives structures, and interactions between the business and scientific sectors, the United States leads the world. The American rating is well above those of the other major Western industrial economies. For example, it is more than 20 percent above the ratings for France and the United Kingdom.[28] The United States ranks seventh in research and development expenditures as a percent of GDP, after Israel, Sweden, Finland, Japan, South Korea, and Switzerland. In view of the size of the American GDP, American total research and development expenditures are vastly above any other nation—more than twice those of runner-up Japan.[29] These statistics tell of a society that is not complacent in its economic and industrial leadership. "America is nearly universally admired for its technological achievements"[30] and for inventions and applications, from the cotton gin to the geosynchronous satellite, from the electric light to the laser. America earns its reputation for innovation and modernity.

Cultural Backwater, Cultural Leader

Intellectual capital is also gauged in ways that do not directly deal with the economy but figure largely in the images of America, especially in Europe with its special claim as the originator and keeper of Western high culture. Fanny Trollope reported in 1832: "The only reading men I met with were those who made letters their profession; and of these, there were some who would hold a higher rank in the great Republic (not of America, but of letters), did they write for persons less given to the study of magazines and newspapers; and they might hold a higher rank still, did they write for the few and not for the many."[31]

This reputation stuck. To this day, the United States is rarely thought of as an intellectual society, even though it is known everywhere for its universities. Do the statistics support its lowbrow reputation? In the aggregate, they do not. In money spent on books in 2002, Americans led the world by far—more than three times the expenditures of the Germans; more than six times the expenditures of the British; and almost eleven times the expenditures of the French. When recalculated on a per capita basis, the Americans fell to fourth as a book-buying public, at about two-thirds of the average Japanese expenditure, but still more than double the average French expenditure.[32] Money spent on music purchases in 2009 tells a similar story—by far the highest total purchases and the tenth highest per capita purchases.

Much of what Americans read and listen to is highly commercial, without a fair claim to lasting high cultural importance. This is not entirely negative. There is no debate that the United States leads in the creation, propagation, and consumption of pop culture. The movie industry claims that it is the only American industry with a positive trade balance with every other country with which it does business.[33] Foreign ticket sales represented nearly 68 percent of the roughly $32 billion global market for Hollywood films in 2010.[34] Few of these films would dispel the image of the United States as a place of little cultural distinction. The impressions people get from the Hollywood "dream machine" are glamorous and creative. American celebrities are revered abroad, however shallow and absurd their professional output and personal lives may be. In part, it is the success of the mass culture emanating from the United States that drives foreign elites to feel threatened in their positions of cultural leadership and to sniff about the absence of high culture in American life.

How can we measure intellectual life? The picture is blurred by looking at total figures. America may be known for its legion of romance novelists, but there have been a dozen American Nobel Prize winners in literature. Only France's fifteen winners exceeds that count. In every other Nobel Prize category—physics, chemistry, physiology/medicine, and economics—the United States leads the tally, usually with more than double the prizes awarded to the nation in second place. These are not the results to be expected of a benighted society, as the United States is thought to be by many a smug European. The truth is complicated. While Americans as a group remain the butt of intellectual condescension abroad, in almost every one of the specific intellectual and scientific disciplines, from the arts and humanities to the hard sciences, Americans are considered leaders in the field by its other participants.

Even in such difficult to compare pursuits as painting and serious music, American reality defies conventional wisdom abroad. Following World War II, the United States, and particularly New York City, became the center of the painting world. Most avant garde movements, including abstract expressionism and pop art, found their originators and leading practitioners in the United States. Artists such as Jackson Pollock, Mark Rothko, Franz Kline, Helen Frankenthaler, Ellsworth Kelly, Willem de Kooning, Jasper Johns, Frank Stella, Robert Rauschenberg, Alexander Calder, Andy Warhol, Roy Lichtenstein, Robert Indiana, Cindy Sherman, Jean-Michel Basquiat, and Jeff Koons join a host of other familiar names in the firmament of American modern artists. European names such as Anselm Kiefer, Jean Dubuffet, Lucian Freud, Barbara Hepworth, Francis Bacon, Henry Moore, Alberto Giacometti, David Smith, and Damien Hirst are important in the movement too, but they represent a smaller group. The center of gravity for contemporary painting is in the United States.

The same is true for photography. Invented in France in 1839, developed in England and France in the mid-nineteenth century, and practiced with special artistry in pre–World War II France, modern art photography has become an American stronghold. Before World War II, the United States saw the work of pioneer modernists like Alfred Stieglitz, Edward Steichen, Edward Weston, and Ansel Adams. The Depression-era Works Progress Administration (WPA) nurtured a generation with a grittier eye for reality, including Walker Evans and Dorothea Lange. But the American photography community came of age after the war and achieved near-monopoly status for several decades. Imogen Cunningham, Irving Penn, Richard Avedon, André Kertész, Robert Frank, Diane Arbus, Sally Mann, and Robert Mapplethorpe are just a few of the familiar names on the American side; Henri Cartier-Bresson, Robert Doisneau, and Josef Sudek were all great European artists of the post-war period but represent a much smaller constellation. Much acclaimed new work is being done today on both sides of the Atlantic, as well as in Japan. However, the important position of the United States is clear.

Modern architecture is another field where eminent persons have come from a variety of nations, but the Americans have played a special role. The modern movement began simultaneously in the American Midwest and in central Europe during the last years of the nineteenth century. It thrived in pre–World War II Germany under the leadership of the Bauhaus school, as it did in Chicago under the influence of Louis Sullivan and Frank Lloyd Wright. However, after the war, helped by emigration of a large number of eminent Europeans, the United States became the center of the movement. The great Le Corbusier remained in France, but seminal figures such as Mies van der Rohe, Eero Saarinen, and Walter Gropius moved to America and did much of their best work as Americans. America became the center of the field. Later work by Louis Kahn, Philip Johnson, I.M. Pei, Richard Meier, and Frank Gehry helped entrench a long period of American leadership. Architectural stardom today is increasingly distributed across the world, but no one would consider the United States to be less than a center of excellence at the top ranks of the profession.

Serious music is a sophisticated art form with a strong American presence. Dominated before the war by Europeans, the mid-twentieth century emigration planted new leadership in the United States. Many of the émigré composers, such as Arnold Schoenberg, Igor Stravinsky, and Erich Korngold moved to Hollywood. Some composed for films. The movies remain the most prolific patron of serious music the world has ever known. The volume of original orchestral output in Los Angeles in any year outstrips that of Vienna in its nineteenth century heyday—even if the quality of Beethoven cannot be matched. Following the mid-century arrivals, there has been a line of notable American-born composers, including Leonard Bernstein, John Cage, and John Adams (among many others), whose eminence is at least the equal of the contemporary Europeans, including Benjamin Britten, György Ligeti, and Olivier Messiaen. Similarly, the second half of the twentieth century saw American preeminence in the performance of classical music by great soloists, including Gregor Piatigorsky, Jascha Heifetz, Arthur Rubinstein, Isaac Stern, Vladimir Horowitz, and hundreds of others, and by the great American orchestras present in each of the major cities of the country.

In all these fields of European high culture, the United States is at least a match for any other region of the globe. The persistence of images of America as a population of crude and ignorant people lacking in culture testifies to the indelibility of some images (especially those that support the self-esteem of the person maintaining the image) in the face of a contrary reality.

Some people might argue that the cultural leadership described above came about because of émigrés, not native-born Americans, so such achievements should not affect the picture of the United States. First, it is not entirely true. From Alexander Calder to Leonard Bernstein, the American cultural ascendancy relied on many who were in the United States from birth. Second, it is irrelevant in the context of America. The essential idea of the United States and a large proportion of the images of the United States are based on its being a gathering of émigrés and their descendants. All the facts and figures in this chapter that describe the United States include the problems faced by the illiterate, penniless, and desperate legal and illegal immigrants who add to the socioeconomic challenges in American cities. Similarly, those objective facts ought to include the accomplishments of Albert Einstein, Enrico Fermi, and so many others after they came to the American shore. If European cultures are to take credit for the accomplishments in America of these refugees, what blame are those cultures to take for forcing them to flee to America? No, in this analysis, and in all images of America, Americans should include all the people of the country, both native born and immigrants.

The American cultural lead is perpetuated by the emergence of the English language as the lingua franca of the globe. In a 2003 survey of twenty-one national populations, the Pew Research Center reported,

> Solid majorities in every country surveyed believe "children need to learn English to succeed in the world today." Nine-in-ten Indians (93 percent) and Chinese (92 percent) agree that learning English is essential, and this view is strongly held. Fully 87 percent in India and two-thirds of Chinese (66 percent) *completely* agree that children should learn English. Generally, even those people who say they dislike American culture, or say they are concerned about the future of their own culture, believe it is necessary for children to learn English.[35]

In France, which is renowned for its linguistic chauvinism, Education Minister Luc Chatel declared in 2011 that French children should be taught English in nursery school from the age of three. According to Chatel, "Today in France, not mastering English is a handicap."[36]

The English Speaking Union now estimates that about half the world's population now has some facility in English as a first, second, or foreign language. It is the language of all aircraft, 80 percent of Internet traffic, most business transactions, most scientific papers, and most diplomatic palaver. The days when a student needed to study German to go to medical school or French to go into the Foreign Service are over. Learning at least rudimentary English is a prerequisite for economic advancement in most of the third world. This reflects the American position in the world and helps preserve it. It provides an enormous advantage to the United States in presenting its culture and its points of view to the rest of the globe. At the same time, it is a constant reminder to others of the marginalization of their own languages and cultures.

Dominant in Sports, Jingoistic

Other objective indicators of the American position in the world are available in sports competition. Here wins and losses are tabulated and compulsively watched around the world. The ultimate standard of sports preeminence is the Olympic Games. The Games played a proxy role throughout the Cold War, allowing Eastern bloc nations, particularly the Soviet Union, East Germany, and Romania, to claim a leadership role on the world stage that their economies would not support. Despite the "sports factories" of these competitors, the records of Olympic medal counts show that the United States dominates aggregate gold, silver, and bronze medals won throughout the history of the Games. The American totals in each class of medal exceed the second-place Soviet Union by about 30 percent. In a sense, this competition was more of a proxy for the real-life contest between the nations than the Soviet Union knew at the time. Now, in the absence of the Communist competitors, the American medal count attracts resentment. Who wants to play in a competition that often seems like an American coronation, particularly when it is accompanied by constant shouts of "USA! USA! USA!" from the American contingent in the audience? It is fortunate for the Olympic Movement that China has picked up the gauntlet and has developed a new sports factory so that in 2008, with home court advantage in Beijing, it challenged the United States on overall medal count and exceeded the United States in gold medals. At

Vancouver in the 2010 Winter Games, the United States beat the Europeans at their own games, capturing a record total of 37 medals, but host Canada salved the world's wound with a top gold medal haul. Surely one of the strong appeals of men's World Cup soccer to the rest of the world is the absence of the United States as a serious competitor.

Militarily Dominant and Arrogant

When competition goes from the symbolic to the real, from sports to armed forces, the American position, objectively measured, is one of unchallenged preeminence in terms of expenditures, technology, reach, firepower, and every other quantifiable aspect except manpower. In 2009 American military spending exceeded that of the next nation (China) by a factor of almost seven and constituted 43.4 percent of the world's military spending.[37] This is to say that the United States military budget almost equals that of most of the rest of the world combined. Because of its huge economy, the United States was able to do this while spending only 4.3 percent of its GDP on the military.

Spending totals tell only part of the story. They understate the relative American position. As shown in the Iraq War, the American military possesses technological advantages that others cannot buy. Its satellite and ground electronic imagery and guidance equipment enables it to do precision targeting and keep its troops out of harm's way during battle. Historically, a small technical advantage, in the order of rifles versus muskets, was enough to assure victory. The American technical advantages are enormous and are so much so that no other country shows signs of making an effort to replicate the American position. For example, the United States Navy's thirty-nine Aegis-class guided missile destroyers are said to have the ability to track, prioritize, and target up to two hundred enemy aircraft at one time. What enemy has two hundred aircraft? China is investing in its military, but a 2003 Council on Foreign Relations study of the Chinese military estimated that China could not catch up with the United States military in the ensuing twenty years.[38] Since the United States military has this gigantic in-place technological lead and shows no signs of halting developments,[39] there is no reason to think China can catch up even after twenty years. This is historically unprecedented.

Still, the high-tech military of the United States cannot deal with all threats. As its virtual invincibility in every form of conventional combat is well understood throughout the world, the adversaries of the United States are compelled to attack in increasingly unconventional ways. Just as the United States could not defend against kamikazes in 1945, it does not have an adequate military answer to suicide attacks today. It is a paradox that modern weaponry with all its lethal power depends for its effectiveness in subduing an enemy on the humanity and rationality of its potential targets. Further, this power does not confer the ability to win the loyalty or trust of foreigners that may be necessary to crush an insurgency and control the outcome in a conflict. The post-war insurgency in Iraq and the long war in Afghanistan made that abundantly clear. Nevertheless, even without an ability to provide perfect security or assure victory in all conflicts, the American military provides an image of overwhelming power that is felt across the globe.

It is hard to describe the facts of the American economic, cultural, and military positions without seeming to slip into a tone of triumphalism. There is a justification for American pride in its accomplishments—and accomplishments they are. Its strengths in so many measures of economic, political, and cultural success (even allowing for its manifest cultural weaknesses) are not just the product of its blessed geography and natural resources. They are also the result of an especially industrious and creative population living within a superbly conceived and stable social structure, and the result of political choices made over the years that have been more often wise than unwise. The American position in the world is an achievement, not a given. Describing it to others, however delicately, invites a charge of arrogance and smugness. No one enjoys the self-description of the mighty. The historic American proclivity to declare itself "God's own country" and to proclaim, "We're number one!" at every opportunity is obnoxious and annoying. It gives rise to some of the most prominent negative imagery of the United States at the present time.

6

CONVEYING AND
DISTORTING IMAGES

With so many clear connections between historical and current images and American history and statistics, it is undeniable that there is normally some connection between imagery and reality. American history and current events do provide fodder for a collection of images. There are pictures of real places in America that are seen by tourists, in newspapers, and in films that get stored in people's minds. Most things of which people have heard actually did happen.

However, while America's past and current behavior (the reality of America), plays a significant role in filling people's mental bookshelves of images, it is not the exclusive source. People also have images in their heads that never happened and never existed—the product of fiction and of mistaken impressions; of propaganda, rumor, and other false reporting; and of error, exaggeration, and pure imagination. Some images are a mix of the real and the invented. Humans suffer from illusions and delusions. Nothing is set in stone. The brain is soft tissue, a complex system of changing chemicals and electronic impulses. It still hides its deepest mysteries from our understanding.

Culture affects our ideas. Humans are subject to ancient superstitions and long-standing grudges. People can fill their imagery with fantastic notions that have no root in reality. A broadly held Arab view that the United States was complicit in the Crusades of the twelfth and thirteenth centuries is a reflection of overactive imaginations goaded by demagogic suggestions to the populace. In Europe and elsewhere, the thought that the American government perpetrated the September 11 attacks is a concoction out of whole cloth but is no less believed because of its basis in fiction.[1] These and other invented images are ideas too. They occupy a place in the mind alongside the images derived from reality.

Further, people are selective in what they hear and see. Some of what people learn is remembered, and much is forgotten, adding to the incompleteness and the resulting distortion of imagery. Reports of reality usually travel an indirect route to the eyes and ears of people abroad. A look at the reportage and editorials in the pages of world newspapers reveals the spin in journalistic accounts of the stories they cover—to say nothing of the distortion implicit in the decisions not to cover other things that could create different images. Lawrence Wright, who wrote for the *Saudi Gazette* in Jeddah during the time of the 2003 Iraq War, described Arab press coverage of the war, including the *Gazette*'s, as follows:

On March 23rd, the front page of the *Gazette* showed an Iraqi child with his head blown off. The Arabic press and many of the satellite channels framed the bombing of Baghdad as "America's war on children." The lens of Al Jazeera focused on Iraqis kneeling in front of the coalition troops with their hands behind their heads: it was a war designed to humiliate the Arabs once again. . . . "The whole world is undoubtedly seeing the American cowboys as having come for only one aim: killing, destruction, and bloodshed," Khaled's newspaper proclaimed in an editorial that morning. One of the relentless themes of the Saudi media was that the twin objects of American power were oil and murder.[2]

If this is all a person reads in the press or hears on the television, what is he to think? The Saudi population is not reading a cross section of international newspapers and other media to get a balanced view of events. The 85 percent of the population who are literate are getting some of their news from the controlled print media, of which the *Gazette* is an example.[3] The other sources of news that reach everyone in Saudi Arabia who cares to follow international events (which is far from everyone) comes from doctrinaire government and private regional radio and television broadcasts, and from politicized sermons in mosques. The United

Nations' Arab Human Development Report of 2003 describes the Arab press as "*Authoritarian . . . Unidimensional . . . Official . . . Sacred*," and adds that "legalized restrictions on freedom of the press and freedom of expression in Arab countries curtail the independence and vitality of the mass media."[4] While the electronic press in Arab countries is growing rapidly in numbers of outlets, it is not escaping the restrictions placed on it.

The goal of press control is not always to promote negative views of the United States. Wright recounts that following the initial anti-American broadsides, "The next morning, at the *Gazette* office, Ramesh came into the local reporters' room with a mischievous look on his face. 'Well, we're all pro-American now,' he said. . . . All the editors-in-chief in the kingdom had been ordered to drop their anti-American line."[5] A loosening of press control in Arab countries may increase anti-Americanism in the Arab media reflecting popular attitudes.

Some information outlets are not merely influenced or indirectly controlled by the government—they are propaganda organs of the government. The images of the United States in Hitler's *Der Stuermer* or the USSR's *Pravda* and *Izvestia* were often either complete inventions or exaggerations of problems that were sufficiently twisted to be tantamount to falsehoods. Soviet citizens used to say, "There is no Pravda in *Izvestia* and there is no Izvestia in *Pravda*," which translates to, "There is no Truth in News and there is no News in Truth."[6] Today's *Xinhua News Agency* and *China Daily* continue in this tradition of state organs, in which the pictures of the United States vary with government policy rather than with the facts. Current benign coverage in China of most stories about the United States could easily return to the traditional Chinese talk about the "running dogs of capitalism" if relations reach an obstacle. Of course, the United States has its media outlets, such as Radio Sawa in the Middle East and the Voice of America, among others, which offer a set of pictures of their nation.

Not all media distortion comes from government involvement. The other influences that insert bias into press accounts include publishers', editors', and reporters' personal biases and incompetence; pressures by advertisers and sponsors; budgetary and space limitations that curtail coverage; reporters' pandering to the biases of their sources; and public demand for sensational news stories that fit what it wants to hear. Whether it is Fox News or Al Jazeera, the audience tends to tune to stations with which they agree. Prejudices feed on themselves as the media offers confirmatory images to viewers and readers who pay to see them. Some stories are distorted or omitted entirely by intimidation of reporters and publishers. The Algerian civil war of the mid-1990s went almost entirely unreported because more than a hundred journalists were killed by combatants as the reporters tried to get the story.[7] CNN admits that it colors its news from the Middle East to avoid having its local bureaus shuttered and its reporters attacked by the governments there.[8] Some stories are omitted due to lack of resources to station reporters in remote places. Chief among these was the completely ignored Second Congo War that began in 1998 and was said to have ended in 2003 but was still going on in 2010. The death toll by 2010 reached seven million people according to the figures of the International Rescue Committee.[9] We cannot form accurate images of that horror without ever having heard about it.

Increasing use of the Internet does solve some problems because the World Wide Web jumps over most governmental hurdles and goes directly to people. However, much material on the web is not only unedited, it is unverified by any process and not subject to even the loosest professional standards of reliability. It can be a deep pool of valuable accurate data, and it can be a swamp of inflammatory, scurrilous lies. At first, its main role was as sole repository of particularly sensational and forbidden material, such as pornography, the photographs from Abu Ghraib prison in Iraq, the beheading of Daniel Pearl, and other terrorist messaging. It played a much greater role in jumping over walls of censorship to perpetuate Arab uprisings in 2011 with YouTube recordings of otherwise unreported demonstrations and confrontations. However, it remains a source of unedited and unverifiable information, vulnerable to disinformation.

Books, news, and propaganda are not the exclusive channels for images. Beyond these sources there are visits to the United States; encounters with Americans; tales told by word of mouth—a teacher, an imam, a friend, or relative; and, importantly, images of America conveyed in entertainment. Fictional literature, movies, songs, and all the other creations of fertile imaginations carry images that might or might not be grounded in reality. Fiction usually makes no pretense of objectivity or veracity. As in the case of news reporting, entertainment, even documentary entertainment, is subject to the biases of the writer and editor and the constraints of space and funds. But the fictional nature of most entertainment licenses it to concoct complete fantasies that are put on the image shelf as images of America. Further, the reach of entertainment is deeper and broader than the reach of the news. It has a way of sticking in the mind.

There is the opening scene of the 2008 Disney-Pixar animated film *Wall-E* in which the refuse-collection robot, Wall-E, in the distant future, is overlooking the destroyed remains of a great American city. All is desolation and destruction, except for one small plant. The city was destroyed by its grotesque consumer culture. In a similar philosophical vein was Fritz Lang's German silent film of 1927, *Metropolis*, which showed views of the modern city as a monstrous interconnected series of New York–style skyscrapers with trains, planes, and helicopters traveling among them. It was rooted in H.G. Wells's futuristic vision, and to the audience it suggested America. Similarly, King Kong gets a hold of the Empire State Building in the 1933 movie and in Peter Jackson's 2005 remake. Views of American cities preponderate in filmed inventions of cities doomed to catastrophe. In history, most great cities have had catastrophic demolitions—such as the various burnings and sacks of Rome, the Great Fire of London in 1666, and the fire bombings of Rotterdam, Tokyo, Hamburg, and Dresden in World War II. Except for the Chicago fire of 1871 and the San Francisco earthquake of 1906, American cities have been spared those events. Yet there is something in the image of American cities that makes them prime targets for destruction fantasies. Recall *Independence Day* and *Batman*. Perhaps it is their phenomenal growth and the self-satisfaction implied in their success. In this light there are the remarks of Georges Duhamel in 1931: "In brilliant New York I have seen as many beggars as I saw in Moscow. . . . Of what account are the avenues that look like deep streams of wealth flowing between illuminated banks! Of what account are the mountainous buildings that evening crowns with flame!"[10]

America is not always a nightmare in the world of fiction. It is often a dream. America as a dream in foreign minds did not begin with the movies. It existed in the nineteenth century. But films and television have given it a powerful push and a visual representation. Hollywood makes escapist fare, from Mickey Mouse's *Steamboat Willy* and Busby Berkeley's 1930s musicals to the international television sensation *Baywatch*. Tom Hanks's fantasy portrayal of simpleton Forrest Gump in the 1994 film of the same name had a good run in American theaters, but for more than ten years it was the hottest feature film on DVD in Saudi Arabia.[11] Saudis enjoyed watching Gump on a tableau of the American South putting his life in the hands of fate and quoting his mother, "Life was like a box of chocolates. You never know what you're gonna get." The United States was a dream world.

Inherent in the entertainment medium are views of things and people that are larger than life, more beautiful, more exciting, more talented. The rest of Americans do not look like movie stars, do not have the lives of the rich and famous, and are not as exciting as rock stars or as talented as NBA basketball players. But those people, distorted and enhanced by their agents and handlers and by the tabloids, inhabit the minds of people seeing the entertainment output of the United States.

The surge in popularity of reality shows since 2000 might testify to the public's thirst for entertainment that is more connected to the real world and less distorted. However, experience with this style of programming indicates that the industry cannot avoid the temptation to distort, whether by selective casting and stage setting or by scripting the dialogue. The fact is that entertainment has no ambitions to be true. It is selling a product that attracts customer interest based on people's fantasies. Therefore, its contribution to people's store of imagery is a vast supply of pretend places and things. For children all over, the street scene of urban America is *Sesame Street*. When they are older, the images from Martin Scorsese's *Mean Streets* join it in the imagination.

Even realistic portrayals of decidedly imperfect lives can look dream-like to film viewers abroad. The 2009 film *Crazy Heart* features Jeff Bridges as dissolute (but touching) failed country music singer. In the foreground it is gritty and very truthful story of real lives. But it is set against a background of perfect weather and gentle people going about their business on roads without potholes in the magnificent scenery of the American Southwest. In fact, it is almost always sunny in American movies. The locale is heaven to the denizen of a foreign tenement. There is trouble in heaven, but it is still heaven.

Whether positive or negative, Arab or European, Asian or Latin American, print, television, books, movies, music, or the Internet, the images of the United States conveyed in the media inevitably distort reality. The person on the receiving end is looking at America through a foggy and rippled lens. In view of all these impediments to perfect communication, whenever the images in people's minds have a connection to American reality, it is a fortuity.

These images conveyed in the media join the vast collection of images from other sources on the mental bookshelf. They are the building blocks in the mind from which views are expressed. The striking nature of this survey of images of America is the amount of contradiction among the images. That allows a person to supply vivid imagery to the expression of his opinions regardless of what side of the argument he finds himself on. The imagery does not determine the opinion; it enables the opinion. The opinion is determined by the person's predisposition that guides the person in selecting among his images to support his views. Predispositions are the second part of our inquiry.

PART II
Selecting Images

7

PREDISPOSITIONS

In order to express opinions about America, people must sort through their mental bookshelves and choose among the vast supply of images for the raw material to construct the expression. The search covers the images that are clear and accurate, as well as the fuzzy, half-remembered distortions and inventions. Background, beliefs, personality, and personal experience guide the search. They shape how people recall and make use of the images. They combine under the guidance of a predisposition or bias. People do not rummage through their imagery blindly; they are looking for things that conform to and support their inclinations. This selection process calls forth views of America that amount to a portion of a picture taken from what is already a portion of a picture. People generalize from these particulars, creating a stereotype of a stereotype. The process of selection as much as the creation of the original images determines the ideas about America that are voiced.

Predispositions can be highly volatile or firmly fixed. They can be emotionally charged feelings or casual tendencies. People with happy recent experiences with the United States may search their minds for favorable images, while those feeling negatively may be looking for the unflattering pictures in their minds. While each person has a different set of images in his brain, on a subject as vast as America, everyone has some of both types available to be read. (Osama bin Laden's favorite television show as a child was *Bonanza* with its attractive views of the American West.[1]) By selecting among images in the mind, a person is equipped to articulate and support an opinion of America. The images become the content of the expression of the predisposition. It should be no surprise that when public opinion surveys are taken on a national basis, favorable or unfavorable predispositions toward the United States vary predictably with positive and negative images in that country at the time of the survey.[2] In other words, when they do not like you, they will say you are ugly. International polling reported that on a worldwide basis during each calendar quarter from the beginning of 2005 to the end of 2007 as the United States was seen unfavorably during the Bush administration, there was a gradual decline in positive perceptions of American scenery.[3] To the same effect, the 2009 Pew Global Attitudes Survey found that after the 2008 election of President Obama, favorable opinions of the United States in the Muslim world had increased only marginally, if at all, but "the most notable increase occurred in Indonesia, where people are well aware of Obama's family ties to the country and where favorable ratings of the U.S. nearly doubled this year."[4] This increase in favorable predispositions toward the United States among Indonesians from 34 percent to 62 percent was matched by the imagery. A total of 47 percent of Indonesians described the United States as a "partner," up from the prior year's 23 percent. The other Muslim states that were polled and whose favorable predisposition had not much improved did not adopt that image. Where the predisposition to the United States is favorable, its image is as a partner, and where the predisposition is unfavorable, its image is not as a partner. Similarly, in August 2011, in the aftermath of American military support for the anti-Gaddafi Libyan uprising, a grateful rebel soldier in Benghazi, Omar el Keish, waved the Stars and Stripes and said of his Arab countrymen, "Libyans love America . . . They love the flag because it stands for freedom and democracy."[5] So, as soon as the normally anti-American Arab street in Libya switched its predisposition toward the United States, imagery of freedom and democracy was at the ready in their minds to support the new view. The image plays a supporting role to the predisposition.

The unpredictability of events in the world and in each person's life frustrate any attempt to fully anticipate an individual's momentary predisposition toward America. The fleeting nature of some predispositions is reflected in the high level of volatility of results in international polls on whether people have a favorable image of the United States. When the family of Iraqi scientist Mohammed Munim al-Izmerly learned that he had died in American custody of apparent abuse by interrogators, his daughter Rana said, "I will hate Americans and British people for the rest of my life."[6] The reaction is understandable and not without justification. It leads her to call forth her mental library of bad images of the United States and Britain. But would she have voiced similar views before learning of his arrest or of his death? When her fury abates, will she paint such a broad brush over all Americans and British people? Perhaps not. Hers is a predisposition based on an event—an important and life-changing event with a long-lasting effect—but an event nevertheless.

Not all events are damning. Many friendly foreign attitudes toward America come from positive events or circumstances in a person's life—a tenderly remembered visit to the United States; a beloved relative who lives there; encounters with friendly and generous American tourists, business people, or soldiers; a liberation from occupation or dictatorship by American forces or policies; or any other gratifying personal experience with Americans or its government. Despite the low favorability ratings the United States perennially receives in Greece (presumably rooted in American support for a past military dictatorship), it seems rare to meet a taxi driver in Athens who does not say he has a beloved brother in Pittsburgh. Many Europeans of the older generations will still speak with sincere gratitude and affection for the Americans they got to know and for what the Americans did during World War II and its aftermath. In early December 2009, American journalist Abigail Hauslohner was on a rural bus in remote Yemen. This is Osama bin Laden's homeland and the nation from which the "underpants bomber" Umar Farouk Abdulmutallab was soon to be dispatched for a flight to Detroit. Friendly passengers on the bus invited her to attend a wedding at a nearby town with the unfortunate (but coincidental) name of Al Qaeda. The next morning, after an evening overflowing with joy and hospitality, the women of the town saw her off and wished her a happy journey, and "the female wedding guests showered me with hugs and kisses. 'Don't forget me,' a 5-year-old named Mona said. One of the groom's brothers offered another suggestion: 'Be careful. There are bad people out there.'"[7] The universe of such happy intersections with America gives rise to the generally favorable opinions of the United States that have pertained through history and are still expressed in high percentages by people in many parts of the world. In May 2003 after the start of the bitterly divisive Iraq War, the Pew Research Center poll still showed substantial majorities in countries as diverse as Great

Britain, Kuwait, Canada, Nigeria, Australia, and Italy expressing favorable opinions of the United States.[8]

Most predispositions do not arise from any particular event, and many are anti-American. They are shared in the instincts and emotions of large numbers of people who tend to harbor negative predispositions toward the United States due to long-held biases based on psychology, political theories, and cultural norms that evoke deep and continuing resentment. Resentment has no content—it is a generalized feeling of dislike. Only after incorporating an item or two from the supply of negative imagery available in the resentful person's mind does antipathy become the expression of an anti-American viewpoint. Such long-lasting resentments include xenophobia, nationalism, envy, romanticism, and the anti-modernist norms of traditional societies. When these biases guide a person, images drawn from reality as well as images that are completely invented provide the building blocks for angry attacks on the United States. When the opinion is expressed through a recollection of a litany of negative images that have an undeniable connection to American history, conditions, or policies, anti-American stereotypes take on a persuasive veneer of reality.

Considering human nature, it is surprising that any foreigners like the United States. The amazing thing about the recently recorded declines in favorability found by worldwide public opinion polls is the heights from which the measures fell and to which they returned in 2009, 2010, and 2011. People do not generally like foreigners. Fear of strangers is probably an evolutionary development that protected people who for eons lived in a dangerous, unpredictable world. The approach of a stranger was unlikely to be good news. Consistent with this, foreigners' attitudes toward the United States even at their worst were generally no less favorable than the attitudes they had toward most other foreign nations. A poll of European attitudes in late 2002 showed that the level of warm feelings toward the United States was almost identical to those held by the various European publics toward each other.[9] Polling in March 2004 showed that while 37 percent of the French had a favorable view of the United States, only 33 percent of Americans had a favorable view of France.[10] It is always hard to be popular as a foreigner.

A spirit of nationalism institutionalizes the natural suspicion of foreigners. It is patriotism's ugly twin. In the minds of many people, loving your own country automatically leads to a dislike of other nations. Such dislikes of outsiders are glue for holding a group together. They are familiar companions to racial pride, tribal loyalty, team spirit, school spirit, and any number of other clubby relationships in which a group makes comparisons with outsiders. Group psychologists researching social identity theory have explored this phenomenon and vouch for its reality. Studying groups of Germans and British subjects, they conclude, "According to our findings, a positive national identification is associated with out-group devaluation as soon as the basis for in-group evaluation changes to comparisons with other national groups."[11] Any layman who has heard sports arena chants of "We're number one!" does not need to read the studies to know this truth. Christopher Hitchens remembers his English boyhood in the 1950s: "So I was brought up, at home and at school, with an ambivalent view of 'our American cousins.' Like many poor relations, we consoled ourselves Englishly with the thought that we made up in good taste and refinement for what we increasingly lacked in money and influence. Americanism in all its forms seemed to be trashy and wasteful and crude, even brutal."[12]

For a member of society, it is difficult not to be swept up in these views of outsiders. Conformity is among the strongest social pressures. The pressure to toe the line grows significantly when the in-group focuses on a foreign group. Researchers have tried to measure this aspect of social identity theory: a group of individuals together in a restaurant were evenly split on their views of vegetarianism and meat eating until a new group sat down alongside them and were strident advocates of one of the two alternatives. As soon as the first group learned of the new group's preference the first group coalesced around a new adherence to the opposite of the new group's view. A sense of belonging is enhanced by the presence of an out-group, and that sense of belonging strengthens the force of cultural norms. That is, the awareness of the out-group polarizes opinion in the in-group and increases the usual pressure to conform.[13] These findings amount to a prediction of what clearly exists: a tendency for people to conform to widespread attitudes of anti-foreign contempt, whatever their personal proclivities might otherwise be. People unite in their anti-Americanism. It can unite an otherwise divided nation. In both Canada and Belgium, anti-American prejudice is among the few things some people agree upon. It can unite neighboring nations. The European Project, meant to create a sense of being a European as a citizen of the European Union, encourages pride in distinctly European culture and traits as contrasted to what are claimed to be American qualities: violence, ignorance, and obesity. It is a tie that binds. According to the French analyst Jean-François Revel, "If you remove anti-Americanism, nothing remains of French political thought today, either on the Left or on the Right."[14] The process of conforming to an anti-American norm can be a permanent fixture of national identity, or it can be a transitory "mob psychology" feeling found in temporary passion as part of a demonstration or riot. Either way, such a norm sends people to their mental bookshelf in search of negative imagery about the United States.

Sometimes predispositions for or against the United States affect parts of foreign societies rather than the whole. Legendary House Speaker Tip O'Neill said that all politics is local. In partisan competition among political factions and in the distinctions among social strata in many nations, one or another party or group is often associated with being in favor of the United States or against the United States. For those who identify as a member of an anti-American political party, such as the Communists in Italy or the Islamists in Algeria, an anti-American mind-set is ordained as a qualification of membership, regardless of any personal experience or particular thoughts on the subject of the United States. Even where the political distinctions are not so obvious, as in the contests between the Social Democrats and the Christian Democrats in Germany, the two parties distinguish themselves to some degree by contrasting their respective sympathies toward America and American policies. Attitudes about America can distinguish classes, as in India, where upper-class Indians are attracted by American (and English) values and policies, and the populous lower classes tend to be deeply suspicious of the former imperial power and its successor. In Europe the intellectual elite harbor a special disdain for the United States. It is a ticket of admission to the class. In these political and class differences within nations, views about all things American become a litmus test for intragroup loyalty.

All these tendencies of humans to dislike outsiders would apply to any foreign nation that comes to the attention of the in-group. It is normal. But the reaction America receives is far from normal. The natural human tendency to derogate the foreigner, to consider him inferior, intensifies when the country that is disdained is so obviously not inferior. The dominance of America in so many ways, and its close involvement with the lives and thoughts of people everywhere, creates a unique set of resentments. The American lead, perceived worldwide, affects minds and generates dislike.

French philosopher Jean Baudrillard provocatively interpreted the world's response to the events of September 11, 2001, as "vast jubilation at seeing the destruction of this world superpower, or rather, at seeing it, in a sense, self-destruct, a beautiful suicide. Because this superpower, by its unbearable potency, has roused all the world's innate violence, and thus (without knowing it) the terrorist imagination that dwells in all of us."[15] What is unbearable about potency? Why should it rouse the world's violence? Baudrillard removes responsibility for the acts of September 11 from its perpetrators and from the policies and actions of the United States and attributes it to the dominant American position in the world, rather than any way in which that dominance is exercised. In this explanation, it is not even American "dominance" that triggers the violent reaction, because dominance implies some dominating behavior. He says it is what America is, not what America does. Potency is the capacity to dominate whether it is exercised or not; it is potential dominance. For example, the United States does not now dominate China militarily, but China knows that it has the capacity to do so. To Baudrillard, it is this capacity that rankles. Even without the United States deploying its forces, all the other nations of the world are constrained by the enormous American capability. The United States is resented for being so powerful and for being the leader or the symbol of leadership of the West, in a world where the differences between the developed and underdeveloped worlds are so vast. In the words of the young Russian literary critic Dimitri Olshansky, "America has taken power over the world. It's a wonderful country, but it seized power. It's ruling the world. America's attempts to rebuild all the world in the image of liberalism and capitalism are fraught with the same dangers as the Nazis taking over the world."[16]

At the heart of this resentment is the depth and breadth of the American lead. For the nationals of other countries, it is bad enough to be in 2nd place, to say nothing of 192nd place. There is a sense of humiliation, especially in historically great powers and in historically great cultures, to be in a subordinate position. People naturally search for explanations, particularly explanations outside their own responsibility, for their reduced status. "Surely those who overtook us did so illegitimately; if not illegitimately, then immorally; if not immorally, then at a cost in culture or humanity that we justly chose not to pay." When Russia's great socialist playwright Maxim Gorky confronted the overwhelming success of New York in a 1906 visit, he explained it as a Faustian bargain:

> I love energy. I adore it. But not when men expend this creative force of theirs for their own destruction. There is too much labor and effort, and no life in all this chaos, in all this bustle for the sake of a piece of bread. Everywhere we see around us the work of the mind which has made of human life a sort of hell, a sense- less treadmill of labor, but nowhere do we feel the beauty of free creation, the disinterested work of the spirit which beautifies life with imperishable flowers of life-giving cheer.[17]

This self-justification of the humbled creates an image of the power- ful as having achieved their preeminence by cheating, brutalizing, steal- ing, or other means beneath the accuser. This is a comfort, and it is a recurrent theme, though it invariably ignores the accusers' own national history of cheating, brutality, theft, etc., that somehow did not leave their nation in the same position of primacy. Was Czarist Russia really the model of "life-giving cheer" to the revolutionary Gorky?

American power inflicts another psychological wound. To many abroad, a sense of disenfranchisement comes from knowing that the Unit- ed States is constantly making decisions that affect their lives and that they have no say in them. America, by its leadership position, is legislating for the world whenever it makes a decision or takes an action. If it pushes the value of the dollar up or down, it affects others; if it closes foreign military bases, it affects others; if it changes the rules on securities issu- ances in the New York market, it affects others. America may do so with the knowledge that foreigners are affected, and this may irk foreign sensi- bilities; and America may do so without any realization that foreigners are affected, which may annoy them even more. Is it worse to be treated as a dependent or as a cipher?

The opening act of the American Revolution was the Boston Tea Party in 1773, which declared the American refusal to accept the imposi- tion of taxes over which the colonists had no vote. For the first 125 years of American history, the franchise was steadily extended. Now, nothing is more fundamental in the American ethos than the concept that peo- ple get to participate in the decisions that concern them. Americans are not alone in this idea. Throughout the world of democratic nations, and many in which democracy is denied, people value the right to vote. In 2010 about 62 percent of eligible Iraqis turned out to vote in the face of terrorist explosions.[18] Of course, foreigners do not get to vote in American elections. Yet people everywhere know that the results of American elections matter for them in a way that no foreign elections matter for Americans. In most places they can demonstrate against United States policies, but they cannot vote on those policies. No one is proposing to change this situation—no country will extend its franchise to foreigners—but this reality has a bitter effect on the 95 percent of the world population that is left out of American decision making and is thereby impotent in dealing with some important aspects of their lives. In the 2004 presidential election, the London newspaper the *Guardian* ran a web-based campaign, "Operation Clark County," to encourage its British readers to write to voters in Clark County, Ohio, to urge them to vote for Senator John Kerry. The newspaper saw that county and state as potentially pivotal in its hope to see President Bush unseated. It provided Ohio voter names and addresses and offered a reward of a trip to Ohio.[19] The intense interest in American elections by people everywhere was again visible in the satisfaction taken in the election of President Barack Obama. Their preference for him was overwhelming. "It allows us all to dream a little," said Oswaldo Calvo, a Venezuelan political activist in Caracas.[20] By contrast, Americans take no symmetrical interest in any election happening abroad. Foreigners resent their exclusion from American decision making, even if they would make the same decision.

Child-like dependency on American decisions reinforces another feature of the American leadership position: America as the Establishment. Anyone anywhere in the world who is unhappy, who is disgruntled, who is unfulfilled in life, may look for someone to blame. Consider this recent report on German attitudes:

> "It's because they are poorer in the east than in the west, and there's a kind of anger at America for this," said Christoph Dieckmann, a former dissident Protestant minister from eastern Germany who now works as a reporter for the weekly Die Zeit. "They blame America for their poor economic state." . . .

To a great extent, eastern [German] disappointment with the results of national reunification has contributed to what some commentators called a generalized resentment, a feeling that the Ossis, as the East Germans are called in the western part of the country, are not so much antiwar or anti-American as they are, simply, anti.[21]

In today's world, anyone who is "simply anti" is likely to look with disapproval at the leading player in the global establishment, the United States. There is an irony in this, in that the United States is an agent of political, cultural, and economic change in most of the world. It is often antiestablishment. In many areas (though not in all) it does not play the status quo role normal to dominant powers of the past. In being the most powerful state, it comes under fire both from those espousing change and those resisting it. Many criticisms of America and its activities are criticisms of the American policy involved, but many are just the primal screams of the disaffected against the strong. The attacks on September 11, 2001, were not random—they were assaults on the greatest world-renowned symbols of the existing order: the World Trade Center, the locus of financial power, and the Pentagon, the headquarters of military power. They had also targeted the U.S. Capitol, the home of political power. Among other things, the attacks were the ultimate antiestablishment cri de coeur. In a gentler way, the antiglobalization demonstrations that stalked World Trade Organization meetings beginning in 1999 were the same sort of rage against the machine.

American primacy interacts with other more complicated negative attitudes. America plays the role of a leading protagonist in dramas in people's minds arising from aversions to its liberal philosophy, its commitment to modernity and change, and its tantalizing demonstration of a life that is fuller, freer, and wealthier, but out of reach. In these conflicts the United States matters for what it symbolizes. As Italian commentator Cesare Pavese said in 1947, "After several years of study, we comprehend that America was not another land, another historical beginning, but merely a gigantic theatre where, with more frankness than was possible anywhere else, the drama of everybody was being enacted."[22] We will consider each of these dramatic conflicts in turn.

8

ROMANTICISM VERSUS DEMOCRATIC LIBERALISM

At the moment of the collapse of communism in the Soviet Union and Eastern Europe, American political philosopher Francis Fukuyama wrote a provocative book entitled *The End of History and the Last Man*. Despite its title, he did not suggest that the calendar had stopped turning or that human conflict had come to an end. His thesis was that the fall of communism marked the end of the long struggle among competing ideologies, and that liberal democracy was the victorious system—the only one left standing.[1] This analysis had ongoing appeal to advocates of liberal democracy. In 2002 Michael Mandelbaum wrote,

> Peace, democracy, and free markets are the ideas that conquered the world. They are not, of course, universally practiced, and not all sovereign states accept each of them. But for the first time since they were introduced—at the outset of the period that began with the French and Industrial Revolutions and is known as the modern era—they have no serious, fully articulated rivals as principles for organizing the world's military relations, politics, and economics. They have become the world's orthodoxy.[2]

It is true that today (despite al Qaeda's threats) there is no armed, centrally directed force credibly threatening to impose feudalism, fascism, communism, or some other "ism" on the world's liberal democracies, and that autocratic leaders in many nations in which liberal democracy is still only a dream routinely proclaim their devotion to it. Nevertheless, contrary to Fukuyama's and Mandelbaum's conclusion, there is a competing vision for the organization of society, and it has a hold on the minds of billions of people. It is a collection of romantic ideas that are the opposing twins of all the concepts that constitute the syndrome we call liberal democracy or liberalism. They have existed since before the founding of the United States, and ever since, they have colored images of America abroad. Much of what passes for reaction to current events or circumstances is no more than a regurgitation of a romantic critique uttered repeatedly since the early 1800s. Romanticism is liberalism's antithesis, the yang to America's yin. It has and will always shadow liberalism's ideals.

The elements of liberal democracy are an interrelated collection of ideas born in ancient Athens and expounded by French and English Enlightenment philosophers in the seventeenth and eighteenth centuries. America's founders knew well the writings of Descartes, Voltaire, Montaigne, Montesquieu, Rousseau, Hobbes, Locke, and other thinkers of the day. Among their ideas were the concepts of the free individual as the basic component of society, the social contract by which the individuals come together to form a society for the common good, progress, rationality, individual liberty tempered by the terms of the social contract, equality of opportunity, equality before the law, personal responsibility, and the perfectibility of man on earth. These are the principles behind the liberal system of peace, democracy, and free markets. These principles were automatically accepted in the American communities on the edge of the wilderness, where self-reliance and freedom from government control were natural endowments. In their local governance structures, colonial leadership wrote constitutions embodying these ideals. As their conflicts with English rule and its increasing efforts to impose control over their distant subjects grew, the rebellious Americans turned to these ideas in formulating their statements of principles. These concepts run through the ringing manifesto Thomas Jefferson wrote in the Declaration of Independence: "We hold these Truths to be self-evident, that all Men are created equal, that they are endowed by their Creator with certain unalienable Rights, that among these are Life, Liberty, and the Pursuit of Happiness—That to secure these Rights, Governments are instituted among Men, deriving their just Powers from the Consent of the Governed."

The American rebels concisely declared the first practical application of the theories of the European political philosophers whom they admired. They announced equality among men, and the social contract. They implied a democracy in the consent of the governed. They enunciated the rights of man, given by God and therefore unalienable. They said that these rules apply to "all Men" and that they are of universal application. They said that men's liberty is guaranteed and that men must be free to pursue happiness. By that phrase they implied that happiness is not something awarded by fate or birth, but is achieved in this life through its energetic pursuit. All of this was said to be self-evident. These assertions might have seemed surprising to many at the time, since these "self-evident" and "unalienable" truths and rights then were a governmental model employed nowhere in the world. Today, after over two centuries of American liberal democracy and after the falls of fascism and communism, they apply only to a minority of the world's population. Nevertheless, they form the founding principles of the United States and attract the unanimous allegiance of its citizenry, regardless of political party.

By 1787 the former colonials had won their war with England and drafted a constitution that embodied the world's first effort to apply to a nation's government the full panoply of the principles of liberal democracy. With the Constitution's ringing opening of "We the People . . . " the Americans left no doubt that this would be a democracy. The Constitution itself, having been ratified state by state following the extraordinary public debate reflected in the Federalist Papers, came as close as anyone could to an actual social contract in the sense of Hobbes and Locke. At times Jefferson even proposed renewing the Constitution with every generation to keep alive the claim of it being a true contract among the citizens.

The Constitution's checks and balances declare its faith in the common man while responding to the doubts of those who predicted the descent of democracy into mob rule. Its structure represents its authors, who believed in reason and personal responsibility. It is a pragmatic solution to human imperfections. In its compromises and its provision for amendment, the Constitution eschews utopianism.

The Bill of Rights, added to the Constitution after its adoption in 1789, guarantees free speech, tolerance, and pluralism in its First Amendment. This assurance of freedom of conscience and rejection of a state religion restated the centrality of individual rationality in the affairs of men.

The Fifth Amendment protected private property from unfair governmental taking, confirming free markets as the economic system of the country.

These events in America astonished and electrified Europeans. Philosophical debates about the nature of man and government had been the exclusive province of the most sophisticated European thinkers. It never occurred to them that the people they saw as backwoodsmen and refugees would be the first to put such principles into practice. In fact, for the Americans it was not a radical step, because their very remoteness had allowed them to naturally develop political and social relations among themselves that approximated the Lockean ideal. Except for the Southern plantation society, whose fall would come violently in the Civil War, American society was not analogous to the feudal, aristocratic societies of the old world. To move to a republic based on liberal democratic principles, all the Americans needed to do was remove the roles of Parliament and King George III and create the mechanisms of the new government. The Americans, in their farming and commercial world, already had the world's lowest taxes and the greatest liberty for individuals (white, male individuals, at least) to "pursue happiness" on this earth. In the revolution, they formalized and preserved the democratic liberalism into which they were born.

Before the American Revolution and the Constitution, the typical eighteenth-century European Enlightenment thinker was a member of the intellectual elite who could not contemplate America except with the deepest condescension. The Enlightenment thinkers of Europe were immersed in study of the works of philosophy of ancient Greece and Rome. They appreciated the neoclassic architecture of Georgian London. They enjoyed the paintings of seventeenth- and eighteenth-century artists who avoided religious and royal themes in favor of illustrating domestic scenes and common (though often wealthy) people. They appreciated the ordered, intellectual, classical music of Handel, Haydn, and Mozart. The liberal democrat in royalist, pre-revolutionary Europe would look from the window of his elegant study toward the Atlantic and be repelled by the thought of a people living on the edge of a wilderness.

The most frequently cited images of America and its inhabitants by European writers of the Enlightenment era are those by the French naturalists Georges-Louis Leclerc, the Comte de Buffon; and abbé Cornelius de Pauw. Buffon, who is credited with originating the study of anthropology, wrote the monumental multi-volume *Natural History*, first published in

Hertford House London (1788) (home to the Wallace Collection),
an example of the neoclassic architecture of Georgian London.
© Mark Walley and licensed for reuse under Creative Commons.

The Enlightenment movement toward painting domestic scenes is
typified by Johannes Johan Vermeer's *The Milkmaid* (ca. 1658–61).
© Wikimedia Commons.

1749. In it he claimed that the climate and natural conditions in America caused all things living there to be less in strength, size, and other qualities than those in Europe. He said that "in this New World, there is some combination of elements and physical causes, something that opposes the amplification of animated Nature." Animals "shrink and diminish under a niggardly sky and an unprolific land. . . . All the animals that have been transported from Europe to America . . . have become smaller . . . and those which were not transported [and] which are common to both Continents . . . are also considerably less than those of Europe." He called the American Indian "a kind of weak automaton incapable of improving or seconding [Nature's] intentions. . . . Though each [Indian] nation has peculiar customs and manners, though some are more savage, cruel, and dastardly than others, yet they are all equally stupid, ignorant and destitute of arts and industry." Indian men, he said, have "been refused the most precious spark of Nature's fire. They have no love of women. . . . In the savage the organs of generation are small and feeble. He has . . . no ardor for the female. . . . Nature, by denying him the faculty of love, has abused and contracted him more than any other animal."[3]

In 1770 the Dutch-born French cleric Cornelius de Pauw wrote his exhaustive *Recherches philosophiques sur les Americains*. He laid the blame on the humidity of the American climate for his observation (never having been there) that all life forms, even those of European emigrants, degenerate or become monstrous when living in America.

> It is known that dogs taken from our countries lose their voice and cease to bark in the majority of regions of the New continent. . . . The animals of European and Asian origin that had been transplanted to America immediately after its discovery have become stunted: their size diminished and they lost a part of their instinct or of their capacity. . . . The climate of the New World contains a secret vice that up until now opposes the augmentation of the human species. . . . The women of Europe become infertile in America far sooner than in their native countries.

The Native American fared even worse than under Buffon's eye: "Nature has peopled America with children, out of whom it is impossible to make men. . . . Even today, after three hundred years [since Columbus], not one of them can think. Their fundamental characteristic is stupid insensibility. Their laziness prevents them from learning anything. No passion can stir their soul. They have neither intelligence nor perfectibility."[4]

These views reflected the common European Enlightenment image of nature and man in the New World before the American Revolution made it the proving ground for the rationalist experiment. European Enlightenment thinkers had always expected the revolution to erupt first in France, where feudalism was overripe for destruction and where society needed radical revamping. In the France of 1789, the large, completely disenfranchised urban bourgeoisie made up of artisans and merchants had grown up over many generations. With each passing year, it bore a greater burden for the support of the unproductive noble and clerical estates. Inspired by the American example and beginning with King Louis XVI's calling together of the Estates-General, the French Revolution exploded. In its beginning, with the Declaration of the Rights of Man, it exemplified all the ideals of the Enlightenment that drove the American patriots. It began with an enormous admiration for all things American.[5] The great difference was that the French environment was not one in which the population had grown up in a version of the new system. To establish democratic liberalism in France required the extirpation of the ancien régime. Heads rolled at the guillotine. The Reign of Terror and the feared mob rule ensued. The convulsions ended in Napoleon's declaration of an empire, with himself as emperor, and the intoxicating and ultimately devastating Napoleonic Wars ending in defeat in 1815.

In the midst of all this, the economic and social power of the bourgeoisie grew. The middle class did end up empowered. Many in the former aristocracy and the former peasantry participated in the new commercial economy. Others were left out and became embittered. The philosophers, writers, artists, and other eighteenth-century champions of the Enlightenment were deeply disillusioned by the violence and destruction of the process as well as by the new parvenu leadership of French society.

The aristocrats never liked ideas that called for their demise. The intellectuals who had spearheaded the Enlightenment were so disgusted by the events of the revolution that they turned on it as well as on the ideas behind the revolution. In the wake of the French Revolution, the writers, artists, poets, and other creative Europeans broke with rationalism and democratic liberalism and created its opposite: romanticism. The monarchists, landless former peasants, and others outside the new order climbed on board. This confrontation between romanticism and the Enlightenment has defined a deep divide in Western society ever since.

The birth of romanticism can be timed with rough precision to the first decade of the nineteenth century. It can be heard in the evolution of Ludwig van Beethoven's music. In 1803 Beethoven began composing his Third Symphony, now known as the *Eroica*. Up to that time, he had been a great admirer of the French Revolution and of Napoleon Bonaparte, exulting in their overthrow of royalty and in their dedication to liberalism. Beethoven's first two symphonies were perfect examples of rational classicism. They were reminiscent of, even inspired by, Mozart and Haydn. Their form was restrained, orderly, and modest. With his third symphonic venture, he strove to do something grander, something on an epic scale. He announced his intention to dedicate the piece to Napoleon. However, in 1804, Napoleon crowned himself emperor of France. With this hypocritical return to autocracy, added to the illiberal brutality of all that had preceded it in Paris, Beethoven lost faith in the revolution and scratched out Napoleon's name in the partially finished piece. After this revanchist conversion to an illiberal worldview, Beethoven premiered the composition on April 7, 1805; it bore a dedication to his royal patron, Prince Franz Joseph Maximilian von Lobkowitz.

Changing a dedication did not itself complete the change of heart for the composer. That followed apace. Beethoven's work on the *Eroica* Symphony was almost finished by the time he lost faith in the Enlightenment. The new composition was bigger than its previous symphonies and had a radical opening blast of two loud chords. It was stunningly beautiful. But it was still an orderly, classical piece. Musical sonata form was observed. It did not take sweeping new musical directions.

In the next few years, in his new mood, Beethoven finished work on the incomplete, classically composed Fourth Symphony and turned to both the Fifth and Sixth Symphonies, works reflecting his new view of the world. He premiered the Fifth and the Sixth on the same day, December 22, 1808. In keeping with his newfound fondness for pre-Enlightenment ways, the astonishing Fifth Symphony, with its striking four-note introductory motif, was dedicated to two noblemen. It was an original, breathtaking departure, but in some ways it was too special. Alone, it could not set the world on a whole new approach. It was and remains inimitable. Others could follow this lead only in their dreams.

It was the Sixth Symphony, the *Pastoral*, that changed the musical world. Beethoven had begun sketches for it as early as 1802, perhaps nudged by Haydn's naturalistic oratorio, *The Seasons*, and then he set it aside. He labored on it in earnest after being stimulated by his frustration with Napoleon and the Revolution. It opens with a peaceful, sweet passage in the happy key of F major, intending, as Beethoven himself indicated, to imitate "the cheerful impressions excited by arriving in the country." The entire work was designed to evoke the joys of a bucolic life, in contrast to the turbulent, ugly environment of modern liberalizing, industrializing Europe. It announced to the world that beauty and meaning are in the rural ways, the old ways. It was constructed with an unconventional five movements rather than the usual four, and it avoided order and rationality. It embraced sentiment as Beethoven's work never had before. The symphony ends with a passage marked by a beautiful musical figure evoking a shepherd's horn call. With that call, Beethoven opened a century of romantic music, art, and literature created to celebrate everything the bourgeoisie ignored or opposed. Serious music composers followed his lead unwaveringly, amplifying on this theme, until at least the time of Gustav Mahler in the beginning of the twentieth century.

Simultaneously, other artists were reacting similarly. Among the other disillusioned former liberal democrats was the English poet William Wordsworth, who had written about the start of the French Revolution, "Bliss was it in that dawn to be alive . . . When Reason seemed the most to assert her rights."[6] By 1807, he published "Ode":

> Then sing, ye birds, sing, sing a joyous song!
> And let the young Lambs bound
> As to the tabor's sound!
> We in thought will join your throng,
> Ye that pipe and ye that play,
> Ye that through your hearts today
> Feel the gladness of the May!

Clearly, romanticism was in full flower in English poetry. Its image of the world was the very opposite of the conventional life as brought forth in Europe by the French Revolution. With only momentary interruptions, the art world has been a steadfast alternative or opposition voice to all things mainstream Western society has meant and done since the horn call of the *Pastoral* Symphony.

The artistic split from post-revolutionary European society widened with the Industrial Revolution of the early nineteenth century. As factories grew and spoiled the countryside, they created wealth and power among people who had no sophistication, merit, or rank under the old order. This created another opportunity for an alliance of the defrocked (and now impoverished) feudal elite with the artists and thinkers, few of whom had a place in the new industrial and commercial world.

William Blake, an early champion of the French Revolution, wrote these famous lines in 1804 in his poem "Jerusalem":

> And did those feet in ancient time
> Walk upon England's mountains green?
> And was the holy Lamb of God
> On England's pleasant pastures seen?
> And did the Countenance Divine
> Shine forth upon our clouded hills?
> And was Jerusalem builded here
> Among these dark Satanic mills?

From this disillusionment arose a complete worldview that countered and continues to counter the conception of the pursuit of happiness through progress and individualism. The opposition of these two views has defined opposing social forces within Europe from 1804 until today.

Nineteenth-century artists did not spend much time thinking about America, but when they did, their images were very different from those of the Enlightenment critics of the supposed degeneracy of the natural world there. European artists and American artists trained in Europe and inspired by European thought began to celebrate the American landscape and the American Indian as inspiring contrasts to the progressive, liberal, striving lives of the white citizenry.

Consider these views of the American Indian after the commencement of the romantic movement. Thomas Jefferson, the leading champion of the Enlightenment and of liberal democracy, in 1818 continued to describe Native Americans in a manner that would have been comfortable to the European Enlightenment writers, Buffon and Pauw:

> What, but education, has advanced us beyond the condition of our indigenous neighbors? And what chains them to their present state of barbarism and wretchedness, but a bigoted veneration for the supposed superlative wisdom of their fathers, and the preposterous idea that they are to look backward for better things, and not forward, longing, as it should seem, to return to the days of eating acorns and roots, rather than indulge in the degeneracies of civilization?[7]

Shortly thereafter, in 1823, James Fenimore Cooper, the American novelist later decried at home for his aristocratic and Frankish views, published the first in his series of novels called the *Leatherstocking Tales*. Among them, there is this contrasting description of the American Indian from *The Last of the Mohicans*:

> At a little distance in advance stood Uncas, his whole person thrown powerfully into view. The travelers anxiously regarded the upright, flexible figure of the young Mohican, graceful and unrestrained in the attitudes and movements of nature. Though his person was more than usually screened by a green and fringed hunting-shirt, like that of the white man, there was no concealment to his dark, glancing, fearless eye, alike terrible and calm; the bold outline of his high, haughty features, pure in their native red; or to the dignified elevation of his receding forehead, together with all the finest proportions of a noble head, bared to the generous scalping tuft. . . . The ingenuous Alice gazed at his free air and proud carriage, as she would have looked upon some precious relic of the Grecian chisel, to which life had been imparted by the intervention of a miracle; while Heyward, though accustomed to see the perfection of form which abounds among the uncorrupted natives, openly expressed his admiration at such an unblemished specimen of the noblest proportions of man.[8]

In 1854 another world-renowned American writer who obtained his romantic credentials in Europe,[9] Henry Wadsworth Longfellow, penned *The Song of Hiawatha*. Among the better-than-human images of the Indian Hiawatha contained throughout this epic poem are these two stanzas describing the moment when the white missionary arrives "by the shore of Gitche Gumee" to begin the assault on the Indian way of life:

> And the noble Hiawatha,
> With his hands aloft extended,
> Held aloft in sign of welcome,
> Waited, full of exultation,
> Till the birch canoe with paddles,
> Stranded on the sandy margin,
> Till the Black-Robe chief, the Pale-face,
> With the cross upon his bosom,
> Landed on the sandy margin.
> Then the joyous Hiawatha
> Cried aloud and spake in this wise:
> 'Beautiful is the sun, O strangers,
> When you come so far to see us!
> All our town in peace awaits you,
> All our doors stand open for you;
> You shall enter all our wigwams,
> For the heart's right hand we give you.[10]

These were the romantic views of the Indian that became the standard interpretation among artists and romantic thinkers throughout the world. Not only did this interpretation beautifully describe the dignity of a dying people, it also served as an emblematic opposing narrative to the view of the ascending middle-class culture exemplified in Jefferson's comments. It served as an implicit protest.

It does so even today. Imagine Uncas's or Hiawatha's surprise to find in today's Germany clubs of Indian hobbyists who do as Alex Biber of Oberriffingen does:

> Alex Biber's day job is designing semiconductor technology. Away from work, he becomes Beaver, a Cheyenne warrior.
> Biber the engineer drives on the autobahn and wears blue jeans.
> Beaver the brave wears hand-tanned buckskin and rides a horse,

commanding the steed in an ancient language once used by Plains Indians. Biber, his wife and two daughters live in a 91-year-old farmhouse, but the family vacations in tepee villages in humid Central European forests.[11]

The romantic interpretation of the Indian was never the view of the general public in the United States in the nineteenth century. In 1831 and 1832, the American painter George Catlin went west and sympathetically sketched and painted the Indians of the Great Plains. He returned to Washington, D.C., and offered to give the works to the government for its new national museum. Congress flatly refused them. He then took them to Europe, where the admiring view of the Indian held by the romantic elites assured him greater success. Today, many of these pictures

American painter George Catlin's *Au-nim-muck-kwa-um, Tempest Bird* (1845) was among more than one thousand images of Native Americans he painted or sketched. Rejected at home but embraced by European audiences, the work ultimately found its way to American museums. *Image courtesy of Smithsonian American Art Museum, Washington, DC/Art Resource, NY.*

are prized possessions of the Smithsonian Institution. In the nineteenth century, an idealization of the Indians was contrary to the spirit of a middle-class nation intoxicated with Manifest Destiny. The ultimate expression of the dominant American attitude on the subject of the Indians was General Philip H. Sheridan's 1870 comment that "the only good Indian is a dead Indian." The march westward of the American public, aided by government policy and military support, continued until white Americans occupied the entire continent.

The Indians, in the futility of their resistance, became the ideal focus of the romantic critique. The story of the American Indians is one of sad, inevitable defeat. Still, it is not obvious that the story should have such a central place in the sympathies of European and American romantic thinkers. Why did they not show the same sympathy for the native peoples of Russia and central Asia who were also brutally murdered and displaced during Russia's two-hundred-year conquest of their continent? The difference is that the Indian demise was at the hands of the hated bourgeoisie. Indian culture and behavior came close to the romantic ideals and stood in contrast to the dominant American society that was built on the Enlightenment principles that the romantics considered abhorrent. The Indians believed in fate. They lived in a tribal community organized on the model of a family. They revered their history, ancestors, bloodlines, and tribal groups. Within the tribe they respected hierarchy, and members of the tribe accepted their place within an unchanging structure. They exalted in the particular differences between their group and outsiders and did not assert universal principles of how mankind outside their group should behave. These were the people of Wounded Knee and Little Big Horn. They placed high value on personal dignity, will, and heroic, even doomed, acts of defiance. They shared all property communally. As Jefferson claimed, they showed little interest in rationality, education, or progress in the Western sense. With some isolated exceptions (such as the Cherokee nation), they did not adopt inventions such as the wheel and the written word, even after their utility was repeatedly demonstrated. They accepted a world in decline.

The Indian ways formed an almost perfect contrast to the Enlightenment model of universal principles, individuality, reason, progress, private property, and a society based on the consent of its individual members.

In their victimization, Indians became a sympathetic rallying point for all those standing apart from the liberal zeitgeist.

What the composers, artists, and poets quickly sensed in the wake of the French Revolution gradually developed into an accepted litany of romantic ideals as part of a stated, coherent social critique by a series of European writers beginning at mid-century. Karl Marx and Friedrich Engels began their 1848 *Manifesto of the Communist Party* with a resounding romantic attack upon the newly ascendant bourgeoisie along with an undisguised nostalgia for feudalism:

> The bourgeoisie, wherever it has got the upper hand, has put an end to all feudal, patriarchal, idyllic relations. It has pitilessly torn asunder the motley feudal ties that bound man to his "natural superiors," and has left no other nexus between man and man than naked self-interest, than callous "cash payment." It has drowned out the most heavenly ecstasies of religious fervour, of chivalrous enthusiasm, of philistine sentimentalism, in the icy water of egotistical calculation. It has resolved personal worth into exchange value, and in place of the numberless indefeasible chartered freedoms, has set up that single, unconscionable freedom—Free Trade. In one word, for exploitation, veiled by religious and political illusions, it has substituted naked, shameless, direct, brutal exploitation.[12]

Five years later, Arthur de Gobineau published his *Essay on the Inequality of Human Races*. With it, he sailed the romantic critique into new waters. Gobineau is best remembered, where he is remembered at all, for his combining of earlier strands of thought on racial types into a race theory in which culture is determined by race, and natural human leadership is represented in the aristocracies of various societies, particularly those in western Europe, who are the closest descendants of the original, creative, superior "race," the Aryans.[13]

According to Gobineau, civilization is doomed by constant miscegenation, destroying strength, creativity, and intelligence. He believed that the Enlightenment idea of the equality of man encourages this "mongrelization" and thereby accelerates the pace of destruction by poisoning the gene pool of the former aristocracy. His own family history predisposed him to this analysis, his parents having been prosperous minor nobility who fought on the monarchist side in the French Revolution and became impoverished in the new France. He despised the French Revolution for having brought low the natural leadership, of which he saw himself as a member. He despised the mass of the French people who now held the power and wealth that he saw as his birthright.

Most importantly, he began the romantic analysis of bloodline as the seat of vitality, intelligence, and meaning in life. He looked to a past better than his day or the future, as the best bloodlines are continually diluted. He saw America as a temporary haven for "the last possible form of culture,"[14] despite its Enlightenment principles, because of its isolated Anglo-Saxon bloodlines. Even there he foresaw an inevitable decline under the influence of immigration. He brought to the artists', composers', and poets' instinctive reaction to the liberal world of commerce and manufacturing a whole set of sociopolitical theories that led to the same places: exaltation of nature, group identity and particularism, historical inevitability, fate, hierarchy, irrationality, will, heroism, and pessimism. It was mythology dressed up as science—a science used to attack the whole rational structure of science. He created a romantic constellation around the polestar of the élan vital of racial purity.

Gobineau's belief in fate was vindicated when, in 1876, the German opera composer Richard Wagner rescued him from obscurity. Gobineau became a part of the circle of intellectuals influencing Wagner who developed a distinctively German brand of romantic racial thinking in opposition to Europe's prospering liberal industrial and commercial culture. Two men in the group, Ludwig Schemann and Houston Stewart Chamberlain, picked up Gobineau's baton and wrote extensive popular works adapting Aryan racial theories to an attack on the soulless modern life around them. Schemann, borrowing from both Gobineau and a nationalist German writer, Paul Anton Boetticher (who wrote under the pseudonym Paul de Lagarde), narrowed the idea of the Aryan to the Norse and Teutonic peoples whom he said were the bloodstock of the current German *volk*. They alone could rise to resist the materialism of the modern world and reinstate a lost sense of culture and meaning to life that was being destroyed by the grasping multitude.

Wagner's English-born son-in-law, Houston Stewart Chamberlain, took the romantic Aryan theory further in his 1899 book, *The Foundations of the Nineteenth Century*, in which he endowed the Aryans with a monopoly on youth, strength, vigor, and creativity. In his writings (as in Wagner's thoughts and compositions) the pure Aryan, with his superior culture, history, and blood, is under constant assault by the Jews, a people who work to corrupt Aryans with their culture of individuality, private property, commerce, science, and rationality. In his worldview, the Jews lack spirituality, nobility, or a soul. To be "Jewish" did not require Jewish birth or faith. It was enough that you took on what he saw as the dispositions of the Jews. Even Ignatius of Loyola, founder of the Jesuits, qualified.

Chamberlain's writings achieved wide circulation in Germany. From Chamberlain there was a direct line to the mind of his reader and admirer Adolf Hitler.

Wagner's operas provide a visual and musical statement of the same romantic point of view. They dwell on themes of inspired will, spirit, and fate in ancient settings. In his great cycle of four operas, the *Der Ring des Nibelungen*, there is the hero, Siegfried, with the blood of the gods in his veins, executing amazing acts of will and courage before his and the gods' inevitable doom. There is magic. Nothing is rational; nothing is ordinary. There is mystery and there is spectacle, in an otherworldly way. The settings all portray images of a lost epoch of pure German culture in primeval times. The music is lush and overwhelming. There is no place for the material world of the everyday. The operas of the *Ring* are the full flowering of romanticism—a literary and musical genre that stretches from Mary Shelley's *Frankenstein* to J. K. Rowling's *Harry Potter*, from Modest Mussorgsky's *Night on Bald Mountain* to Cirque du Soleil's *O*.

Out of Wagner's orbit also came the most influential thinker of the romantic anti-liberal critique, German philosopher Friedrich Nietzsche. On hearing the overture to the opera *Die Meistersinger von Nürnberg*, Nietzsche was overcome.[15] Nietzsche was a student of Jacob Burckhardt, the Swiss anticapitalist philosopher, and Arthur Schopenhauer, the German philosophical guru of transcendence over a life of striving. He became one of Wagner's acolytes in Bayreuth during a formative period of his intellectual life, from 1872 to 1876. Nietzsche was drawn to the exaltation of personal traits of will, power, and vitality in Wagner's scenarios. His focus was on human qualities he associated with aristocracies. He did not emphasize racial theories or religious bigotry but saw in his Aryan admirable qualities of strength and even brutality that favored him over the well-mannered, civilized middle class of the Victorian age. He despised the weakness of the herd afflicted with the slave morality of a petty moral existence without spirit. Theirs was a life of meaninglessness and inauthenticity. He saw all of Western culture as sick, mediocre, and headed toward its own destruction for want of a vital force. For this society, God was dead.

In his 1882 novel, *Also sprach Zarathustra*, Nietzsche incorporated these themes. Borrowing from the ancient Zoroastrian religion, he introduced the *Ubermensch*, the Superman, the prophet and hero who rises above the mediocrity of materialist civil society, its manners, its dissipation, and its inevitable doom, and lives as a free spirit.

In historian Arthur Herman's words:

> Nietzsche's philosophy proceeded from the same vitalist assumptions as Gobineau's. Every civilization, they both stated, relied on a reservoir of organic life force for its existence, or will to power. But Nietzsche's most decisive influence would not be on racial thinkers but on cultural critics and artists. Nietzsche would inspire them to think of themselves as a counterforce to a decadent social order. The modern artist did not pretend to be the savior of modern society . . . since there was nothing worth saving. Instead, Nietzsche encouraged the notion that attacking the Western cultural and moral tradition was in itself an expression of health and renewal. . . . The antiestablishment critic, the artist, and the "immoralist"—from Picasso and Bertolt Brecht to the Sex Pistols and Madonna—form a new vitalist aristocracy in the modern cultural void.[16]

The tag team of romantic philosophers leading up to Nietzsche, the inspiration given by Nietzsche's writings, and the artists' own senses of estrangement from the bustling industrial and commercial growth of European society in the nineteenth century gave rise to an antiestablishment romantic mood in every art form. Architecture abandoned the rationality of neoclassicism for a series of styles recalling the Middle Ages, from Gothic to Romanesque. The Scottish essayist Thomas Carlyle campaigned against analytic reasoning and wrote books on the lives of "heroes" such as Oliver Cromwell and Frederick II of Prussia. The English artist, critic, and philosopher John Ruskin introduced the naturalistic painting of

The Gothic revival in nineteenth-century Europe. The Palace of Westminster (Houses of Parliament), London (1839–52), Sir Charles Barry and Augustus Welby Northmore Pugin, architects. *Engraved title from original drawing. From Charles Mac-Farlene and the Rev. Thomas Thomson's* The Comprehensive History of England Vol I, *published in 1867, showing the "new" Houses of Parliament viewed from Hungerford.*

William Holman Hunt, *Our English Coasts* (1852). Hunt was a member of the Pre-Raphaelite Brotherhood, which rejected the restraints and orderliness of classicism and reached for a naturalistic aesthetic. *Image courtesy of Tate Gallery, London/Art Resource, NY.*

The ruins of the Roman city of Volubilis (ca. 250 BCE), near Meknes, Morrocco. The romantic movement's turn against classicism led to a fascination with the decline of lost civilizations and their ruins. *Photo courtesy of the author.*

the Pre-Raphaelites, ultimately leading to the birth of the environmental movement. A fashion for civilizational decline arose among the artistic and restless of Europe who went in search of long-ignored remains of lost civilizations in the Middle East and around the Mediterranean from Persia to Morocco. In this they followed the lead of English romantic poet Percy Bysshe Shelley, whose "Ozymandias" spoke of lost grandeur in the sands of the Sahara:

I met a traveller from an ancient land
Who said:—Two vast and trunkless legs of stone
Stand in the desert. Near them on the sand,
Half sunk, a shatter'd visage lies, whose frown
And wrinkled lip and sneer of cold command
Tell that its sculptor well those passions read
Which yet survive, stamp'd on these lifeless things,
The hand that mock'd them and the heart that fed.
And on the pedestal these words appear:
"My name is Ozymandias, king of kings:
Look on my works, ye mighty, and despair!"
Nothing beside remains: round the decay
Of that colossal wreck, boundless and bare,
The lone and level sands stretch far away.

The romantic mood in the art and literary worlds among the aristocrats and thinkers of Europe was consistent and vibrant, but it did not capture the true spirit of the age of the nineteenth century. It remained antiestablishment. The romantics, despite their prominent voices, were on the margins of their societies. Peace generally prevailed in Europe, individual rights slowly grew, democracy made inroads, and economic productivity rose rapidly. The bourgeoisie prospered and gained ever greater power. The romantics dominated the written word and the arts, but the rationalists and capitalists held the upper hands of commerce and industry and increasingly ruled society, if not all the ministries.

The nineteenth-century advance of liberalism did suffer setbacks. The revolutions of 1848 created upheavals in Europe and fed some of the resentment of the intellectuals toward the new model of society. In the United States, the Civil War rent the nation but ultimately served to end its own provincial feudal vestige—the glaring inconsistency of slavery in the professed "land of liberty"—and cement the future of the country as an industrial nation. In France and Germany, the Franco-Prussian War of 1870 raised the curtain on a united autocratic Germany and introduced the short-lived Paris Commune of the romantic underclass. In the politics of Europe, monarchy still held sway in most places. Even in France, democracy was on-again, off-again.

The imagery the European romantics promoted of a soulless, mediocre, grasping, materialist civilization lacking in authenticity or culture was their attack on their own countrymen in the ongoing battle for societal leadership. It continues today in the class-ridden domestic politics of European countries. It was not invented to be directed across the sea to America. However, when the romantics looked at America, they saw a society that perfectly fit their critique of the bourgeoisie. The kind of rootlessness that magnified Americans' alleged inauthenticity and lack of culture seemed to confirm the romantic critique. After all, the United States was entirely bourgeois and proud of it.

Unlike many romantic European critics of America, Norwegian novelist Knut Hamsun actually visited the United States. He made two trips in the 1880s, during which he wrote articles for the Norwegian public on his experiences. His views were pure Nietzscheian romanticism:

> We . . . get a sense of the danger that arises from the mixing of different kinds of people in a free, uncontrolled, capricious environment. The danger is all the greater in America, where shiploads of immigrants—diseased and degenerate human raw material—stream in every day from all over the world.[17]
>
> The Americans have *not* grown up and emerged safely from their country's history of freedom. For they are constantly being uprooted and broken up and mixed with the flood of European raw material and criminal elements.[18]
>
> No, I do not think that liberty consists of *liberties* or that wellbeing is the only measure of success in life. . . . The Americans are a restless ambitious people. It is as if gigantic wheels were driving their whole existence with roaring speed. Once they hit upon an idea for getting ahead, they pursue it compulsively, working as hard as a slave, with boundless hope and great leaps of faith. People in other countries may be said to be engaged in a struggle for existence; here it must be called a struggle for *well-being*—for a kind of carnivorous, satiating existence, with the ability to afford intense sensual pleasures along with fat horses and rich food. The typical American has no real artistic sense or substantial literary, religious, political, or social interests.[19]

Hamsun later won the 1920 Nobel Prize for Literature. During World War II, he supported the Nazi puppet government of Norway led by Vidkun Quisling.

English writer Fanny Trollope, another nineteenth-century visitor, listed among her many complaints,

> I heard an Englishman, who had been long resident in America, declare that in following, in meeting, or in overtaking, in the street, on the road, or in the field, at the theatre, the coffee-house, or at home, he had never overheard Americans conversing without the word DOLLAR being pronounced between them. Such unity of purpose, such sympathy of feeling, can, I believe, be found nowhere else, except, perhaps, in an ants' nest[20]. . . . In taste and learning they are woefully deficient[21]. . . . I do not like them. I do not like their principles, I do not like their manners, I do not like their opinions.[22]

As British historian Simon Schama observed:

> Other characteristics of American life alienated the Romantics: the distaste for tragedy (a moral corrective to illusions of invincibility); the strong preference for practicality; the severance from history; and, above all, what German poet Nikolaus Lenau called *Bodenlosigkeit*, a willed rootlessness, embodied in the flimsy frame construction of American houses. Europeans watched, pop-eyed, while whole houses were moved down the street. This confirmed their view that Americans had no real loyalty to the local, and explained why they preferred utilitarian "yards" to flower gardens. No delphiniums, no civility.[23]

In 1888, James Bryce, British liberal lawyer and a sympathetic chronicler of the American scene, observed this contempt among romantic Europeans:

> I have never met a European of the middle or upper classes who did not express astonishment when told that America was a more agreeable place than Europe to live in. "For working men," he

would answer, "yes; but for men of education or property, how can a new rough country, where nothing but business is talked and the refinements of life are only just beginning to appear, how can such a country be compared with England, or France, or Italy?"[24]

The romantic critics' disdain for America is well reflected in Maxim Gorky's report of his visit to New York in 1906, commencing with a description that could have come from William Blake's anti-industrial pen:

> "Skyscrapers" [*sic*] are outlined against the fog. Rectangular, with no desire to be beautiful, these dull, heavy piles rise up into the sky, stern, cheerless, and morose. In the windows of these prisons there are no flowers, and no children are anywhere seen. Straight, uniform, dead lines without grace of outline or harmony, only an air of cold and haughty presumption imparted to them by their prodigiousness, their monstrous height. But in this height no freedom dwells. . . . In great houses dwell small people. . . . [25]
> I am involuntarily drawn to make a parallel between Europe and America. On that [the European] side of the ocean there is much beauty, much liberty of the spirit, and a bold, vehement activity of the mind. There art always shines like the sky at night with the living sparkle of the imperishable stars. On this side there is no beauty. The rude vigor of political and social youth is fettered by the rusty chains of the old Puritan morality bound to the decayed fragments of dead prejudices.[26]

These were the unanimous views of the literary romantics but, as in Europe's own society, not the prevailing views of the vast majority of people, not the spirit of the age. In the United States, more than anywhere, democratic liberalism was succeeding. Ordinary Europeans were voting their views by immigrating in swelling numbers. Ordinary Americans were expressing their views by displaying an overweening patriotic pride that tweaked the sensibilities of foreign visitors. Rudyard Kipling tells of events as the tourists gathered on the 4th of July, 1889, in Yellowstone National Park:

> They called it "patriotic exercises;" elected a clergyman of their own faith as president, and, sitting on the landing of the first

floor, began to make speeches and read the Declaration of Independence. The clergyman rose up and told them they were the greatest, freest, sublimest, most chivalrous, and richest people on the face of the earth, and they all said Amen. Another clergyman asserted in the words of the Declaration that all men were created equal, and equally entitled to Life, Liberty, and the pursuit of Happiness. . . . At duly appointed intervals the congregation sang "My country, 'tis of thee" to the tune of "God save the Queen" (here they did not stand up), and the "Star-Spangled Banner" (here they did). . . . What amazed me was the calm with which these folks gathered together and commenced to belaud their noble selves, their country, and their "institootions" and everything else that was theirs.[27]

American and European observers who did not share the romantic mind-set wrote favorably of America and its land of free markets and democracy. James Bryce captured the sensibility of the European romantic pessimists who railed against American society:

In Europe, whose thinkers have seldom been in a less cheerful mood than they are today, there are many who seem to have lost the old faith in progress; many who feel when they recall the experiences of the long pilgrimage of mankind, that the mountains which stand so beautiful in the blue of the distance, touched here by flashed of sunlight and there by shadows of the clouds, will when one comes to traverse them be no Delectable Mountains, but scarred by storms and seamed by torrents, with wastes of stone above, and marshes stagnating in the valleys. Yet there are others whose review of that pilgrimage convinces them that though the ascent of man may be slow it is also sure. . . . This less somber type of thought is more common in the United States than in Europe, for the people not only feel in their veins the pulse of youthful strength, but remember the magnitude of the evils they have vanquished, and see that they have already achieved may things which the Old World has longed for in vain.[28]

Two years before Gorky paid his dyspeptic visit to New York, distinguished German social scientist Max Weber lectured at the Universal Exhibition in 1904 in St. Louis. He had just begun his great work on the "Prot-estant Ethic" and his essay *The Protestant Sects and the Spirit of Capitalism.* He held a sympathetic view of America as an emerging world power that would soon overtake Germany. Echoing Tocqueville, he wrote that the American political system worked because "in the past and up to the very present, it has been a characteristic precisely of the specifically American democracy that it did not constitute a formless sand heap of individuals, but rather a buzzing complex of strictly exclusive, yet voluntary, associations."[29]

The mainstream in Europe and America recognized the success of the American system. By 1900 this remote, fragile outpost of a century earlier had become a worldwide empire with the largest economy in the world. Immigration swelled. Ten million came between 1865 and 1890. Fifteen million came between 1890 and 1914.[30] Electric lights, telephones, auto-mobiles, and the rest of the output of the world of science and reason were improving people's lives rapidly. The Gilded Age was a time of peace and unprecedented wealth for the majority.

The liberal experiment in America and Europe was so successful that it even made inroads into some artistic attitudes. Impressionist painting, based on scientific principles of vision exemplified by the work of Georges Seurat, challenged romantic painting of nature. New architectural ideas were beginning to match form to function and employ the technolo-gies Gorky so despised in his contempt of skyscrapers. By 1912 in Italy, a movement of "Futurism" in painting and sculpture would lionize science, machinery, and speed. Futurism's theoretician F.T. Marinetti declared its Manifesto in 1909, welcoming the machine, with all its speed and destruc-tive power, in words that would leave Wordsworth and Blake speechless: "We will sing of the great crowds agitated by work, pleasure and revolt . . . the gluttonous railway stations devouring smoking serpents; factories suspended from the clouds by the thread of their smoke; bridges with the leap of gymnasts. . . adventurous steamers sniffing the horizon; great-breasted locomotives, puffing on the rails like enormous steel horses with long tubes for bridle, and the gliding flight of aeroplanes whose propel-ler sounds like the flapping of a flag and the applause of enthusiastic crowds."[31]

However, even at its lowest ebb, romanticism was not dead. In 1894, after two years of education in Germany, the African-American scholar W. E. B. Du Bois returned with a new racial view of history and the future

Bourgeois life returns to painting in *Bathers at Asnières* (1884), by Georges Seurat. Seurat created a scientific approach to optics and color theory in his pointillist application of color. © *National Gallery, London/Art Resource, NY.*

The Flatiron Building, Daniel Burnham, architect (1902). This early Manhattan skyscraper pays homage to the Greek column and the classicism of the modern commercial and industrial world in its twenty-one stories built on a steel frame. *Photo © Paolo Ventura, paveita@gmail.com, and licensed for reuse under Creative Commons.*

Sculptor Umberto Boccioni's *Unique Forms of Continuity in Space* (1913), exemplifies pre–World War I's Italian futurism movement with its expression of strength, motion, and fluidity in bronze. Digital image © *The Museum of Modern Art/Licensed by SCALA/Art Resource, NY.*

that led him to publish *Souls of Black Folk* in 1903. With this, he started a Black Nationalist movement in the United States that depended on romantic notions of bloodline, spirit, and destiny. In 1896 German composer Richard Strauss, following Nietzsche, set *Also sprach Zarathustra* to music. The art nouveau movement in Paris decorated each stop of the bourgeois Metro with sinuous floral motifs that simultaneously enhanced and implicitly rebuked the machine-age underground transit system. In 1913 Russian composer Igor Stravinsky introduced his new ballet, *The Rite of Spring*, in Paris, evoking primitive, pre-rational music and dance. At the same time, in Munich, Oswald Spengler was at work on his seminal extension of Nietzsche, *The Decline of the West.* This influential book, first published as war raged in 1918, contended that modern liberal civilization was in its final throes, destined to die as earlier civilizations had, from its growing distance from spirit, nature, and culture.[32]

World War I will always be the Great War to Europeans. Liberals interpreted it, consistent with Woodrow Wilson's view, as the final bloody confrontation between liberal democracy and the remnants of monarchy and romanticism. They said that liberalism emerged triumphant with the Allied victory. In contrast, Lenin declared it to be the inevitable catastrophic collision among the liberal mercantile powers resulting from the greed of the capitalists which had set all the modern societies against each other in the hope of securing uncontested control over colonies and markets. Lenin's interpretation of events leading to the war may or may not have been wrong, but he was right that the events following the war did not open an age of supremacy for democratic liberalism. Despite the end of the autocratic rules of the czar, the kaiser, the sultan, and the Austro-Hungarian emperor, romanticism gained renewed impetus. The war shattered and impoverished all the principal European combatants and demolished the bourgeoisie's nineteenth-century confidence in progress. The war and the disillusionment that followed, coupled with economic distress (first inflation, especially in Germany, and then the Depression), infected arts, letters, popular culture, and much else. It made the middle class search for answers among the romantic ideas of those who had previously been marginalized.

In Russia, even before the war's end, Lenin's Communist victory imposed dictatorship and defied most of the principles of the liberal catechism. Lenin echoed Marx's scorn for the bourgeoisie and his appeal to culture:

> We are blamed for the destruction caused by our revolution. . . .
> Who are the accusers? The hangers-on of the bourgeoisie, of that
> very bourgeoisie who, during the four years of the imperialist war,
> have destroyed almost the whole of European culture and have re
> duced Europe to barbarism, brutality and starvation. These bour
> geoisie now demand we should not make a revolution on these
> ruins, amidst this wreckage of culture. . . . How humane and righ
> teous the bourgeoisie are![33]

Lenin's state socialism decried individuality and the idea of a state created by social contract. His autocratic rule was in the romantic tradition of that which is ordained by inevitable historical processes—a product of fate. His view of society was the ancient romantic tribal view of society as a family, in which the leader plays the role of the father, and the members of society owe him loyalty and obedience. He acts for the good of the whole, as he sees it, without regard to injury that may afflict individual members in the process of protecting the family. In his polemic of 1906, Gorky said, "[In America,] to no one seems to occur the simple thought that a nation is a family."[34] In Russia, this thought became the rule.

Communism did share liberalism's view that there are universal principles (though illiberal ones) applicable to all societies, and Communism also departed from romanticism's faith in bloodlines. It shared liberalism's belief in progress, though through a process of historical inevitability toward a dictatorship of the proletariat. It also claimed to respect science, rationality, and pragmatism.

However, it opposed liberalism in its most crucial aspects. It saw the market economy of capitalism as the central evil and therefore decried private property, personal responsibility, faith in the common man, and democracy. Soviet socialist realist art exalted "heroes of socialism" and acts of will. It saw warfare as a principal means to expand its reach. It had no place for tolerance, freedoms of speech or assembly, or other "bourgeois liberties." It had no place for religion, whether separate or joined with the state. It was a utopian ideal, which set up a powerful state as a largely romantic antagonist to democratic liberalism.

On a second front, in 1922 Benito Mussolini's Fascism rose in Italy to embody in a state the second ascendant romantic alternative. Along with its cousins, soon to be born—Adolf Hitler's German National Socialists, Francisco Franco's Spanish Royalists, and their later imitators, allies, and sycophants all over Europe from Vichy France to Greece to Norway to Hungary to Romania—liberalism's inverse images became law all over Europe in reaction to World War I and the subsequent economic and political upheavals.

In fascism, state intervention in the name of industrial policy is substituted for free markets; group identity, race, bloodlines, and nationalistic cultural claims are substituted for tolerance, pluralism, individual rights, and universality; paternalism, hierarchy, and historical class lines are sub-

The much larger than life soldier that forms the Zaisan Soviet War Memorial (ca. 1950) in Ulaanbaatar, Mongolia—which honors Soviet soldiers killed during World War II—is characteristic of social realism with its romantic adoration of the hero. *Photo courtesy of the author.*

stituted for equality of opportunity and social mobility; will, heroism, and utopianism are substituted for reason, pragmatism, and compromise; faith, fate, revelation, and historical inevitability are substituted for personal responsibility; autocracy and the family model of society are substituted for democracy and a systems of checks and balances on the power of government over individuals; agnosticism or a religion joined to government are substituted for the separation of church and state; and a belief in a larger society in decline is substituted for a belief in human progress.

During the rise of communism and fascism in the 1920s, 1930s, and 1940s, romanticism flourished. For artists Europe's romantic revival made it the place to be. Aside from its abundance of homegrown culture critics, from Kafka to Weil, Europe drew America's finest artistic voices into a 1920s Parisian exile from stultifying middle-class America. Ernest Hemingway was its most emblematic purveyor of romantic paeans to irrational spirit and will in his writings about bullfighting and war. F. Scott Fitzgerald depicted the crass, soulless materialism of America's rich in *The Great Gatsby*. Gertrude Stein, in her poetry and in her art collecting, challenged middlebrow pretensions with her devotion to the avant garde. In declaring of her hometown, Oakland, California, "There is no there there," she encapsulated the romantic view of the void of conventional American life.

Even at home, these post-war attacks on the American liberal world of the striving ordinary man proliferated, including Theodore Dreiser's novel *An American Tragedy*, about an ambitious young man pursuing his Horatio Alger dream in a murderous way, and Sinclair Lewis's novel *Babbitt*, skewering Midwestern American small-town life. The image of mainstream Americans contained in the work of these and other post-war writers, living here and abroad, was of sterile, pointless, money-obsessed lives. Nietzsche's romantic attributes of vitality and authenticity are absent. Americans are portrayed as the walking dead.

Disapproving romantic portrayals of America and Americans by native European artists intensified as America's economic and cultural importance grew among the war-weakened Europeans. America became a symbol, standing for all that was declining in civilization. In 1931 Georges Duhamel went to visit what English poet Rudyard Kipling called "the grotesque ferocity of Chicago"[35] and emerged, convinced he had found in America the avatar of a hellish future:

> In that ridiculous moral atmosphere in which swarms not a great nation, but a confusion of races, how can one possibly find that sublime serenity which art must have if it is to quicken and flower?[36] . . . . America? I am not talking of America. By means of this America I am questioning the future; I am trying to determine the path that, willy-nilly, we must follow.[37]

In these passages Duhamel set out the romantic complaint about a metaphorical America as a subhuman swarm of racially mixed insects engaged in materialistic activity bereft of the spirit required for art. Artists blamed America for all that was wrong with Europe. The antiliberal European fear of all things modern became congruent with a fear of Americanization, whether or not the United States had anything to do with it. In this forerunner of the charge of cultural imperialism, America became a metaphor for the European liberalism that the romantics despised. In playing out the bitter domestic European battle between romanticism and liberalism, it became and has remained an effective slur to tag all of modernity and the liberal project as Americanism.

Germany's leading twentieth-century philosopher, Martin Heidegger, gave deep intellectual legitimacy to similar themes in the 1920s, 1930s, and 1940s. Faithful to Nietzsche, Heidegger condemned the technocratic modern world of wage slavery and consumerism that extinguishes human spirit and eliminates the role of nature in people's lives. Attacking both America itself and the disposition known as Americanism, he wrote, "The primacy of sheer quantity is itself a quality, i.e., an essential characteristic, which is that of boundlessness. This is the principle we call Americanism."[38] "The surrender of the German essence to Americanism has already gone so far as on occasion to produce the disastrous effect that Germany actually feels herself ashamed that her people were once considered to be 'the people of poetry and thought.'"[39] In his 1935 lectures, as an active supporter of Hitler's regime, he stated that the domination of America by a "cross-section of the indifferent mass . . . has become an active onslaught that destroys all rank and every world-creating impulse of the spirit and calls it a lie. This is the onslaught of what we call the demonic (in the sense of destructive evil)."[40]

As the 1920s and 1930s wore on, romanticism's influence spread from its traditional preserve in the minds of sophisticated writers and artists, aristocrats, and the underclass to capture the imagination of beleaguered members of the bourgeoisie, many of whom were suffering in the Depression-era failure of the capitalist system. It is their support that put and kept fascism in power. Writings attacking the liberal canon spread from the pens of the intelligentsia to Nazi pseudophilosopher Alfred Rosenberg and his patron, Hitler, and to the popular press. They reached an enormous audience.

Hitler spoke of culture, bloodlines, fate, will, and the decline of civilization:

> The ultimate cause of such a decline was their forgetting that all culture depends on men and not conversely; hence that to preserve a certain culture the man who creates it must be preserved. This preservation is bound up with the rigid law of necessity and the right to victory of the best and stronger in this world. . . . Blood mixture and the resultant drop in the racial level is the sole cause of the dying out of old cultures; for men do not perish as a result of lost wars, but by the loss of that force of resistance which is contained only in pure blood.[41]

Hitler's racial theories, incorporating Gobineau's Aryan mythology and his own anti-Semitic fixation, were synthesized in Rosenberg's *The Myth of the Twentieth Century*—required reading in the schools of the Third Reich. Rosenberg pointed out the contrast between Nazism's romantic notions and America's democratic liberalism in the context of predicting America's demise unless it abandoned its liberal tenets:

> The American declaration of freedom was the model for the *Droits de l'homme* of the Paris revolution. Admittedly, in order to further capitalism, the battle cry of "Rights of Man" was heard, and the liberation of the blacks was accomplished in the southern states.
>
> Today every single American curses this black liberation. The American liberal is bound and determined to force his ideas on America, for as a State, the antiquated Liberalism thumps the dub [sic] of 'Freedom' on all citizens even if it must be beaten in with rubber truncheons. . . . If the insane principle of the equality and equal rights of all races and religions is one day finally given up, there is yet hope.[42]

The Nazi image machine adopted the entire canon of romanticism. The German propaganda film *Triumph of the Will* began with Hitler, godlike, descending slowly through the clouds over Gothic spires to regimented crowds of men in uniform. There are repeated scenes of torchlight parades, recalling medieval times. Vital young men are shown in vigorous exercise in the woods. Hitler is depicted before the adoring mobs, with his steely-eyed gaze emblematic of the will of the *ubermensch*. Had Richard Wagner been alive, surely he would have been called upon to direct this film in place of Leni Riefenstahl and to compose a hymn.

The romanticism of Germany in the 1930s was capped by the Berlin Olympic Games of 1936. Founded in 1896 by a French aristocrat, Pierre Frédy, Baron de Coubertin, the modern Olympics were and remain the romantic ideal in action. Beginning and ending with parades, emphasizing the singing of anthems, nationalistic pride, and feats of personal heroism, the Games take on the spirit of Wagnerian spectacle. In 1936 the Berlin Games added their own primitive touch that has stayed with the Games ever since—the torch relay from Olympia, Greece, to the site of the Games.

Even Leon Trotsky, a Soviet romantic in his own right, writing in the late 1930s from his refuge in Mexico, was appalled by the primitivism of Nazism, which he blamed on the failures of capitalism:

> Today, not only in peasant homes but also in the city sky-scrapers, there lives alongside the twentieth century the tenth or thirteenth. A hundred million people use electricity and still believe in the magic power of signs and exorcism. . . . What inexhaustible reserves they possess of darkness, ignorance and savagery! Despair has raised them to their feet; fascism has given them the banner. Everything that should have been eliminated from the national organism in the . . . course of the unhindered development of society comes out today gushing from the throat: capitalist society is puking up the undigested barbarism. Such is the physiology of National Socialism.[43]

In the ensuing carnage of World War II, the liberal democracies and the Soviet Communists together emerged victorious. Right-wing romanticism was discredited, but the philosophical elements of romanticism embraced by the Left remained the counter to democratic liberalism.

Heidegger's aversion to technology and his call to surrender to "Being" and spirit descended directly to the post-war school of Existentialism pioneered by Jean-Paul Sartre, the French novelist and philosopher of the Left. In one of his earliest works, *Nausea*, Sartre painted this picture of bourgeois French society:

I watch the grey shimmerings of Bouville at my feet. . . . These little black men I can just make out in the Rue Boulibet—in an hour I shall be one of them.

I feel so far away from them, on the top of this hill. It seems as though I belong to another species. They come out of their offices after their day of work, they look at the houses and the squares with satisfaction, they think it is *their* city, a good, solid, bourgeois city. They aren't afraid, they feel at home. All they have ever seen is trained water running from taps, light which fills bulbs when you turn on the switch, half-breed, bastard trees held up with crutches. They have proof, a hundred times a day, that everything happens mechanically, that the world obeys fixed, unchangeable laws. . . . They are peaceful, a little morose, they think about Tomorrow, that is to say, simply, a new today; cities have only one day at their disposal and every morning it comes back exactly the same. They scarcely doll it up a bit on Sundays. Idiots. It is repugnant to me to think that I am going to see their thick, self-satisfied faces. They make laws, they write popular novels, they get married, they are fools enough to have children. And all this time, great, vague nature has slipped into their city, it has infiltrated everywhere, in their house, in their office, in themselves. It doesn't move, it stays quietly and they are full of it inside, they breathe it, and they don't see it, they imagine it to be outside, twenty miles from the city. I *see* it, I *see* this nature.[44]

Through the rest of the twentieth century, a line of European writers and theorists followed Sartre, conducting a drumfire of attack on the United States and its culture, both as reality and as a symbol. They included, among many others, Albert Camus, Frantz Fanon, Michel Foucault, Jacques Derrida, and Jean Baudrillard. Their themes came in various doctrinal guises, from communism to New Left theory to deconstructivism to post-modernism to multiculturalism. The essence was always romanticism as introduced in the era of Beethoven's *Pastoral* Symphony and iterated through the nineteenth century up to Nietzsche's call for acts of will and authenticity. All of them see modern urban liberal life as a void. In Camus's 1942 novel, *The Stranger,* pointless homicide is an antidote to the emptiness of contemporary life; six decades later in the French post-modernist novelist Michel Houellebecq's 2002 book, *Platform*, pointless sex is the antidote to the emptiness of contemporary life. All of them endorsed the Soviet propaganda attacks on the West, accusing it of plutocratic and crass commercial exploitation of the masses in a heartless and soulless capitalist system. All of them promote particularism and group rights over universalism and individuality. All of them claim a faith in nature against rationalism and decline against progress. All of them would have seconded Baudrillard's comments in his 1986 travelogue, *America*, in which he echoed the established romantic line that America "exorcises the question of origins, she does not cultivate the origins or the mythical authenticity, she has neither a past nor a founding truth. . . . [45] America has the power of in-culture. . . . The future power lies with peoples without origins, without authenticity, and who will know how to exploit that situation to the limit. . . . All myths of modernity are American."[46] Bernard-Henri Lévy sees this prevalent anti-Americanism of the Left as "the progressivism of the imbecile," which for the Left in Europe has become "a fixed ideological star."[47]

▪

Not all anti-American attitudes are driven by romanticism, but those that are have survived two hundred years. As early-nineteenth century German philosopher Georg Wilhelm Friedrich Hegel postulated, there are ideas (theses) that contest with their opposites (antitheses). If the contest is resolved so that a new thesis is developed, a new antithesis will arise to challenge it. Democratic liberalism and romanticism appear to play these roles. The very existence of a liberal idea in the minds of some people seems to assure the presence of the opposing idea in the minds of others. No central organizing force is needed to bring this forth. There will always be the alternative narrative. There is a mind-set throughout the world (including in the United States) that believes in fate; scorns reason; cherishes group identity and bloodlines; finds comfort in hierarchy, status, and class; sees government in a larger tribal sense with obligations running from the governed to those who govern; sees a world in decline; and expects salvation only in the afterlife. There are those who reject the liberal notions of personal responsibility and have no attraction to the ideas of pluralism and tolerance. There are those who find no meaning in a conventional life.

For most people liberalism and romanticism are not hermetically sealed categories but are just tendencies. Often a person will accept some of the ideas associated with the Enlightenment while holding to others that are of the romantic tradition. A confirmed liberal can contemplate nature on occasion, and a true romantic can handle a business transaction. Still, the tendencies are there, and they enable the prediction of attitudes and the understanding of images.

Some adopt romantic ideas out of abiding belief, some as a marker of intellectual pretension or class lines, and some as a badge of sophistication. Especially in Europe, it is easy to recognize in the views of the former aristocracy and of the intellectuals and artists the old-fashioned snobbery that sets them apart from their own middle class, as well as permanent arrivistes such as the Americans. "The bourgeois, often philistine, unheroic, antiutopian nature of liberal civilization can make it difficult to defend. Where the free market dominates, as in the United States, intellectuals feel marginal and unappreciated, and are inclined to be drawn to politics with grander pretensions."[48] Regardless of their origin, these politics are broadly held points of view, and they have been with us for a long time. Much of what purports to be expressions of rage or disdain arising from the latest Hollywood film or American foreign policy pronouncement is the old romantic wine in a new bottle.

The Europeans, whose society is so close to America's and who created the Enlightenment, appear to be decrying America and American culture as they generate frightful images of America. For example, leftist French writer Frantz Fanon wrote in his 1961 work *The Wretched of the Earth*, "Two centuries ago, a former European colony took it into its head to catch up with Europe. It has become so successful that the United States of America has become a monster where the flaws, sickness, and inhumanity of Europe have reached frightening proportions."[49] But Fanon and others are actually engaging in a long-running battle within their own countries across class lines. For those in this internecine battle, the United States plays a role only as a symbol. When France's General Commission of Terminology and Neology attacks the ever-expanding use of American expressions in the French language, they may say they are attacking an invading American onslaught. In fact, the United States makes no effort to export its language to France. Rather, they are attacking their own bourgeoisie for their attraction to Americanisms. The French general public prefers calling a surfer "*un surfer*," despite the insistence of the Académie française that he be "*une aquaplanchiste*."[50] When José Bové and his band of dairy farmers, successors to the French feudal peasantry, burned down a McDonald's restaurant, they said they were defending against an American invasion. In fact, the McDonald's restaurants are there because the French middle class patronizes them. There are over 850 McDonald's in France. Similarly, Disneyland Paris, a frequent target of disdain by French sophisticates, was the most visited tourist attraction in Europe in the summer of 2008.[51] Surely this was not based on the small volume of visiting American tourists. When we see uniformly romantic imagery of the United States in the press and in literature in Europe, it reflects the dominance of this way of thinking among those who rule the press and academia in those societies. Almost all of them, Left or Right, underclass or elite, consider the European middle class vapid, vacuous, and superficial, and consider all things vapid, vacuous, and superficial to be American. The disdain for the United States is directed as much or more at the Americanized and commercially dominant middle classes in Europe as it is against the United States.

Similarly, leadership by the old elites, who are among the foreign ministry cadres of Europe as well as among international relations journalists and foreign policy scholars, helps account for their (and their students') expressions of open and widespread admiration of violent and solitary romantic figures like Che Guevara, Yasser Arafat, Mao Tsetung, and various third-world liberation and terror movements. Such movements oppose the United States and thereby also oppose all that Europe is and has. The European elite, but not the European business establishment or general public, can be counted on to admire every illiberal movement and personage who stands in the way of American foreign policy. Romanticism will always drive the views of a small but influential segment of European society as long as its opposite drives the views of the dominant culture.

Frequently what appears to be a purely political opposition to American society or foreign policy is more of a culturally based expression of opposition to the strength of the United States as the standard bearer of the Enlightenment, and a sympathy for such romantic figures as desperate guerillas who fight lonely battles against all odds; suicidal terrorists who accept their fate in heroic, futile grand gestures; and cruel tyrants who preside over impoverished countries as stern fathers do over their families. European elites clucked about the disgrace of American slavery in the nineteenth century but supported the feudal South in the American

Civil War. Apparently blind to brutality and tyranny, European intellectual elites sympathized with communist opponents of American policy in China, Cuba, and to a large extent, all of America's opponents in the Cold War. From T. E. Lawrence's exotic Bedouins to today's Palestinians, European intellectual elites have a passion for the contemporary version of the American Indian: the romantic, fundamentalist Arab peoples of the Middle East who are in obdurate opposition to the Enlightenment culture of the Americans and to the archetypal liberal democrats, the Israelis. To European romantic elites there is both justification and nobility in the savagery of terrorist attacks on ordinary people in Western societies so long as they are perpetrated by today's version of the noble savage. European-style thinkers and writers in Europe and elsewhere (including romantic thinkers in the United States) greet such attacks with the approval they also give to the success of the Sioux at Little Big Horn.

An example of this genre is the work of James Cameron, a Canadian writer/director, in his script for the 2009 film *Avatar*. He states that his story of an attack on a happy nation of natives of a distant planet by mercenaries of the Pentagon has an underlying political message in opposition to despoiling the environment.[52] But it is much more than that. It is a broad tour through romantic political notions. The rude and crude Americans are portrayed as President George W. Bush had been, disdaining negotiations in favor of frontal military assaults. They lay waste to a community of poetic, beautiful, primitive tribesmen who live a spiritual existence as a single large family, honoring their ancestors in an unspoiled primeval forest. They are colored blue, the color of Lord Krishna in Hindu mythology. Krishna is said to have spent his life protecting humanity and destroying evil. Leaving no doubt of the film's position on recent political debates, the Americans say they are attacking preemptively through tactics of shock and awe. They bring death and destruction in order to obtain subsurface minerals America needs to maintain its industrial output. The tremendous tall tree the victims worship collapses in a slow fall reminiscent of the World Trade Center. The initial defeat and expulsion of the natives has the look of the Choctaws during the Trail of Tears. The entire battle recalls the final defeat of the Indians by a violent assault on them at Wounded Knee, but the film turns around for a Hollywood happy ending in the surprise defeat of the Americans; cue General Custer and Little

Big Horn. The Palestinians did not miss the point: they promptly began demonstrating against the Israelis on the West Bank in the blue costumes of the Na'vi tribe of *Avatar*.[53]

Romanticism among the West's intellectuals also reveals itself in the embrace of particularist ideologies like multiculturalism and antiglobalization. In their resistance to the assimilation and homogenization inherent in the universalism of democratic liberalism, they are expressing the old romantic ideals of love of culture and tribal identity.

While its roots are in Europe, romanticism knows no borders. Even American artists and intellectuals are overwhelmingly so disposed. The infatuation of Hollywood with director Michael Moore and his anticapitalist message was undiluted by their own (and Moore's) personal wealth. American academics and authors such as Professor Jared M. Diamond, with his book *Collapse: How Societies Choose to Fail or Succeed*, easily embrace narratives of decline and ruin that fit so well into a romantic vision.[54]

The liberal universalist thought that the people of the world who do not now live in democracies are all impatiently awaiting their liberation by America collides with the devotion of the intellectual elite to romanticism. When the United States undertakes its mission to bring its liberal modern world to the outposts of romanticism, the traditional critics voice their rage. In advance of, and even in the wake of, the successful American military purge of the neofascist Iraqi autocrat Saddam Hussein, the European romantics rose in full throat. English playwright Harold Pinter wrote,

> There is . . . a profound revulsion and disgust with the manifestations of US power and global capitalism which is growing throughout the world and becoming a formidable force in its own right. I believe a central inspiration for this force has been the actions and indeed the philosophical stance of the Zapatistas in Mexico. The Zapatistas say. . . . "Do not try to define us. We define ourselves. We will not be what you want us to be. We will not accept the destiny you have chosen for us. We will not accept your terms. We will not abide by your rules. The only way you can eliminate us is to destroy us and you cannot destroy us. We are free."
>
> These remarks seem to me even more valid now than when I made them on September 10 [2001]. The "rogue state" has—

without thought, without pause for reflection, without a moment of doubt let alone shame—confirmed that it is a fully-fledged, award-winning, gold-plated monster. It has effectively declared war on the world. It knows only one language—bombs and death. "And still they smiled and still the horror grew."[55]

European intellectuals rewarded Pinter with the Nobel Prize for literature in 2005. His acceptance speech was a rambling anti-American rant on the theme that "the crimes of the United States have been systematic, constant, vicious, remorseless."[56]

The vanguard of the widespread foreign and domestic opposition to the Bush administration's evangelism of liberal democracy by force of arms against Iraq was a large cross-section of the West's poets, writers, and intellectuals—the traditional keepers of the romantic flame. In the spirit of such kindred souls as Noam Chomsky, Susan Sontag, and Susan Sarandon, Greek composer and intellectual Mikis Theodorakis addressed a rally against the invasion of Iraq, which had just overthrown Saddam Hussein, and declared that Americans are "detestable, ruthless cowards and murderers of the people of the world. From now on, I will consider as my enemy those who interact with these barbarians for whatever reason."[57] The Obama administration's enlarged wars in both Afghanistan and Pakistan are also opposed by the same people.

In contrast, there are the views of the liberal democratic approach to life typified in comments by Czech writer Ivan Klima, whose Enlightenment credentials were confirmed in his leadership of the anti-Soviet Prague Spring protests of 1968. In the same publication as Harold Pinter's outraged attack, he expressed this image of America:

I regard attacks by fanatics on American citizens in New York or anywhere else in the world as being, above all, an attack on the civic freedoms that America embodies and thus an attack on my own freedom too. To view them in any other way ultimately means siding with the reactionary and totalitarian forces which spurn democracy, civil rights, racial and sexual equality and the freedom to live according to one's own convictions and to profess—or not— any belief.[58]

These comments on both sides are not just politically inspired images of America. They are expressions in the arena of politics of the competing syndromes of cultural and philosophical ideas identified as romanticism and liberal democracy. The presence of the Enlightenment view will inevitably call forth its opposite. At times, such as now, Enlightenment ideas will predominate in society; at times they will be under siege. Romanticism will ebb and it will flow in inverse proportion to the hold of democratic liberalism. For those stirred by a romantic attitude toward life, it is not a passing mood. It cannot be deflected by changes in policy or by persuasion and propaganda. So long as the United States remains the icon of democratic liberalism, these two competing predispositions will animate the search for the imagery used to attack or defend the American way of life and America itself.

9

TRADITIONAL SOCIETIES

Think of yourself as an Afghan Taliban insurgent in the summer of 2010. You were working after midnight at a pitch-black roadside location in an isolated, rugged part of the country to set up an improvised explosive device (IED). Something went wrong. It exploded too soon. You were not injured, but you knew you could not stay there after the sound of the explosion. So you ran as fast and far as you could. You put a good distance between you and the explosion and found a dozen of your comrades. You all made your way up a dark, hidden country road to escape. Things were going well. All was silence and darkness. Then, in an instant you and your associates were all destroyed by a precisely targeted Hellfire missile shot from the wing of a remotely piloted Predator drone and guided to its target through the eye of the missile by another remote pilot. The pilots, sitting in front of computer screens in a trailer on an air force base near Las Vegas, Nevada, had watched you from the moment the IED exploded. The images were transmitted to them from the infrared night cameras on the Predator drone and the Hellfire missile. As you lay mortally wounded, your final thoughts might have included anger and regret. Surely, your thoughts about your American enemy were not friendly. But you were impressed.

Surviving onlookers in primitive, rural hamlets in Pakistan and Afghanistan have witnessed these precision performances. Illiterate villagers who have never left their mountain valleys are introduced to America by these demonstrations of seemingly miraculous vengeance from the sky.

144

To an unlettered person, especially a religious person, things like this can only be the work of God or Satan. Surely the United States is not God. Like Satan, modernity and technology frighten and tantalize at the same time. From moments such as these and from countless other contacts between the modern world and traditional societies, the people on the traditional side of the divide have stored a library of mental imagery of the United States as an avatar of modernity and change and as a contrasting reality to their own lives. This collection of images is called upon regularly to explain, justify, or challenge their own station in the contemporary world. Predispositions in the minds of traditional people guide their selection of images that applaud and accept modernity or images that revile and reject it.

Through the ages, human existence in most parts of the world maintained itself in equilibrium of unchanging patterns. Interrupted by the occasional war or natural disaster, countless generations passed their biographies down to their heirs. Religious traditions and fatalism explained the natural world. Few changes occurred that could be called progress. Tradition, hierarchy, and constancy ruled people's lives. Depending on conditions such as climate and the presence of threatening neighbors, life was more or less brutal and brief. Humans were typically gathered in tribes or larger communities of closely related people. Leadership of the groups was on the model of the family, with a tribal elder serving as chief. Even larger groupings, with a person in the role of king, were modeled on the family writ large. Gender roles were clearly understood. Status and occupations were inherited.

There is a temptation for people everywhere to gaze wistfully back upon a simpler time and to return to those days, to abandon the benefits of medicine, science, communication, and all the rest of modernity, in exchange for the certainties and psychological comforts of an angst-free life of never-ending cycles of the seasons. For many there is no need to return to an earlier age. This pattern is still alive in all sorts of places, especially rural and semi-rural places in Asia, Africa, and Latin America. However, where it exists, it is increasingly under siege from encroaching modernity and outside influences entering the minds and lives of the people of traditional communities and destroying the ancient balance. Traditional people can enthusiastically seek out the Western world, succumb to its blandishments in a posture of fatalistic acceptance, or fight a rear-guard, ultimately losing, battle against the force of change. In most places, and even within some individuals, there is a combination of these three responses.

An imam in a Pakistani village may live a meager life, but he enjoys the status of temporal and religious leadership. The unvarying routine of prayer, teaching, and pastoral duties within his community can be a satisfying one. The effects of newly arrived satellite television on the youth of his town, evident in their new T-shirts and alien music, might be harbingers of the end of his position in society. It imperils his grasp on their minds and on their respect for him. How can he not despise such a change? He is likely to cling to the old ways, as does Ajmal Qadri, leader of the Pakistani Islamic political faction, Jamiat Ulema-e-Islam, who said in 2000, "I believe that a clash of civilizations is inevitable . . . and in this clash, the fittest will survive. We are much more cultured than America and the West. The West is bereft of the strength that comes from families. Plus, the West is run by Jews. Americans and the Jews have begun a new crusade, which is known as globalization."[1]

Dismay with change is not limited to the leadership of the old culture. All people steeped in the old system, even people treated badly by the old system, may react defensively to the arrival of change that marginalizes their culture.

> They have to admit that their ways were out of date, that everything they produced was worthless compared with what was produced by the West, that their attachment to traditional medicine was superstitious, their military glory just a memory, the great men they had been brought up to revere—the poets, scholars, soldiers, saints and travellers—disregarded by the rest of the world, their religion suspected of barbarism, their language now studied only by a handful of specialists, while they had to learn other people's languages if they wanted to survive and work and remain in contact with the rest of mankind. . . . Yes, at every turn they meet with disappointment, disillusion or humiliation. How can their personalities fail to be damaged? How can they not feel their identities are threatened?[2]

This collision between the West and traditional societies is unavoidable given the success of the West economically and the advance of modern communications. There is hardly a corner of the world into which news of the wonders of modern society, even of the "wonders" of a secular and libertine lifestyle, has not penetrated. Westernization does not have to be foisted upon them by a colonizing force of arms. The people of the village, both the wealthiest who may want to use their riches to move in larger spheres outside the traditional village and the most suppressed and repressed who may want to cast off the shackles of the old ways, are the motivating forces for adopting Western ways. The ruler of Dubai, who has built a twenty-first-century city in the sand, says, "We want to rekindle that spirit of daring in the Arab world. There aren't any other viable options, because we are in danger of being left behind in a relentlessly competitive world."[3] Nevertheless, whomever either invites in a new culture or has one imposed on him will experience a sense of dislocation that he must weigh against the advantages gained by the change.

> This reality [of modernization] is experienced differently by those born in the dominant civilization and those born outside it. The former can change, advance in life, adapt without ceasing to be themselves. One might even say that the more Westerners modernize themselves the more completely in harmony they feel with their culture. Only those among them who reject modernity find themselves out of touch. For the rest of the world's inhabitants, all those born in the failed cultures, openness to change and modernity presents itself differently. For the Chinese, Africans, Japanese, Indians and American Indians, as for Greeks, Russians, Iranians Arabs, Jews and Turks, modernisation has constantly meant the abandoning of part of themselves. Even though it has sometimes been embraced with enthusiasm, it has never been adopted without a certain bitterness, without a feeling of humiliation and defection. Without a piercing doubt about the dangers of assimilation. Without a profound identity crisis.[4]

A key to this identity crisis is the element of choice—both the choice of modernization versus tradition and the choices inherent in daily modern life. Traditional societies give people a prescribed path. There is no option of religion, profession, spouse, political leader, or even clothing or food. All is dictated by tradition. The Western supermarket can have a devastating, disorienting effect on the new arrival. Making more important life choices can leave a person adrift. The verities of life are gone. Simple things become complicated. People who expected to be thrilled by the personal freedom of the modern world often want to flee to the breast of a comforting tradition that made their choices for them. These mixed emotions raise paradoxes of longing for change combined with resentment toward the West, and especially its leading example and expositor, the United States. The English journalist Henry Fairlie observed this phenomenon in 1975, saying: "The energy of the American presence in the world is both welcomed and feared, both a cause of hope and a source of anxiety, because with its idea it keeps unsettling the established forms of the past. Not merely old but ancient customs are surrendering to a presence that is not imposed and yet seems irresistible, to an idea that appears to be more powerful than the slogans of any revolution."[5]

The traditional village leader or intellectual in the old culture who is under threat of irrelevancy clings to his precarious status and is a straightforward critic of the new. He is invested in seeing that modernization fails. The conflicted members of society, reaching for a freer, more comfortable, or more cosmopolitan life, want at least some of what the West has to offer, but may not want all of it, and they begin to sense a nostalgia for what they are losing in the process of modernization. Typical of this is the comment by a young Indian woman who had been working in India at a call center, talking to Americans on the phone:

> I've been making calls for the past 6 months now, probably 200 calls every day. So earlier my perspective about America was all too rosy since that's what you see on television and thorough the media—that it was the best country and the land of opportunity—and it is definitely. But I think the people there are very lonely and some of them are very depressed. Their family ties seem to be wavering off and I don't think it's all that nice. Every place has its own problems.[6]

The disorientation, dislocation, anomie, and nostalgia that people feel in confronting encroaching modernization are common to all traditional societies that are in flux, whether in Morocco, Kazakhstan, or Alaska. The strength of these feelings is intensified manyfold when the traditions that are threatened are the culture of a once great civilization now in decline, and when they constitute patterns prescribed by a still-vibrant religion. In the Arab world, the culture that is now confronting and resisting modernity was the world's leader for hundreds of years. The Arab culture of the last third of the first millennium was the cultural and scientific paragon—"the ornament of the world."[7] In the several centuries following Mohammed's death in 632, and particularly following the triumph of the Abbasid clan over the Umayyad Caliph in Damascus in 750, the Arabs were the cultural leaders of the world. The new Caliphate in Baghdad preserved the classical texts of ancient Greece and Rome and translated them into Arabic. Consistent with the need to precisely regulate the timing of religious observances, they advanced mathematics and astronomy, adapting the concept of zero from contacts in India and devising algebra. They invented the astrolabe. They created beautiful poetry.

The remnant of the Umayyad tribe traveled to Andalusia, in present-day Spain, and created a second hub of great Islamic civilization, organized on a pluralistic model with contributing roles for Christians and Jews. Science and poetry flourished there too. This culture, headquartered in Córdoba, conceived an architectural style with continuing influence all over the world today. It absorbed the Arab texts translated in Baghdad from the ancient languages and provided for their translation into Latin and the vulgate European languages of Spain and France, laying the foundation for the European Renaissance.

The beginning of the end of this golden age occurred in 1009 with a Taliban-like fundamentalist assault on Córdoba, resulting in the sack of the fabulous palace Madinat al-Zahra. The Almoravid clan of orthodox Berber tribesmen from Morocco had crossed the Strait of Gibraltar and come upon the diverse society of the Umayyad Caliph, proclaiming that any community in which the Islamic believers (the Umma) consorted on almost equal terms with the Christian and Jewish infidels (the Dhimma) was a desecration of the Islamic faith. They prescribed a learning program limited to Islamic religious texts. The prime minister of Malaysia, Mahathir bin Mohamad, addressing the Organisation of the Islamic Conference, now the Organisation of Islamic Cooperation, on October 16, 2003, described this change (though he ignored the effect of pluralism):

The early Muslims produced great mathematicians and scientists, scholars, physicians and astronomers etc., and they excelled in all the fields of knowledge of their times, besides studying and practicing their own religion of Islam. As a result the Muslims were able to develop and extract wealth from their lands and through their world trade, able to strengthen their defences, protect their people and give them the Islamic way of life, Addin, as prescribed by Islam. At the time the Europeans of the Middle Ages were still superstitious and backward, the enlightened Muslims had already built a great Muslim civilization, respected and powerful, more than able to compete with the rest of the world and able to protect the umma from foreign aggression. The Europeans had to kneel at the feet of Muslim scholars in order to access their own scholastic heritage.

But halfway through the building of the great Islamic civilization new interpreters of Islam came who taught that acquisition of knowledge by Muslims meant only the study of Islamic theology. The study of science, medicine, etc., was discouraged.

Intellectually the Muslims began to regress. With intellectual regression the great Muslim civilization began to falter and wither. But for the emergence of the Ottoman warriors, Muslim civilization would have disappeared with the fall of Granada in 1492.[8]

Looking only at intellectual leadership, for which Islam justly prided itself for hundreds of years (and ignoring the Islamic community's myriad other issues of poverty and despotism), the Arab world, and the Islamic world in general, have sunk to intolerable depths. In the millennium from the fall of Córdoba to today, not only the Arabs of Spain but the entire Arab world has translated fewer books into Arabic than Spain now translates into Spanish in an average year.[9] "This disparity was revealed in the first half of the 1980s when the average number of books translated per 1 million people in the Arab world during the 5-year period was 4.4 (less than one book for every million Arabs), while in Hungary it was 519, and in Spain 920."[10] In 2002 the UN found that "about 65 million adult Arabs are illiterate, two thirds of them women. Illiteracy rates are much higher than in much poorer countries."[11] The UN's *Arab Human Development Report 2009* found that under continuing autocratic rule in the region, little or nothing had changed for the better.[12] These are fruits of the long Arab decline beginning with the rise of fundamentalism in Spain.

The Muslim civilization did not enter its dark ages all at once in 1009. Some of its greatest military conquests were yet to come. But, with repeated Berber victories in Andalusia—first by the Almoravid clan and then by the even more fundamentalist Almohad clan—the centralized, cosmopolitan Andalusian society collapsed. In 1031 the Córdoban caliphate dissolved, and the Iberian peninsula split into an archipelago of city-states called Taifas—most of them Muslim but growing increasingly Christian over the centuries. Iberian society became ever more turbulent and contesting, with declining tolerance for minorities and fading cultural importance. Finally, the completion of the *Reconquista* by the Catholics in 1492 marked the end of the Spanish flowering of Muslim intellectual life and of any form of Muslim (or Jewish) life on the Iberian Peninsula. Within the following twenty years the remaining Muslims and Jews in Spain were commanded to convert to Christianity or be put to death.

While Andalusia and the Arab caliphs were declining, other centers of Islam had significant victories. Salah al-Din (Saladin), an Islamic Kurd, assumed leadership of Egypt in the late twelfth century, established the Ayyubid dynasty, and led Arabs to victory against the colonies of Christian Crusaders in Palestine and on the Syrian coast.[13] Non-Islamic Mongolian and Turkish tribesmen conquered the fading Abbasid Caliphate in Baghdad in 1258 and subsequently converted to Islam. These newly minted Muslims, with a corps of slave fighters (Mamluks) from the Caucasus and Central Asia, defeated the Ayyubids and what remained of the Christians in Palestine and established control of the area from Baghdad to the Nile.[14] In turn, in the fifteenth and sixteenth centuries, the Ottoman Turks streamed out of Anatolia, conquered the Eastern Christian capital of Constantinople in 1453, and then expanded to the Balkans and Central Europe while establishing non-Arab Islamic rule over almost the entire Arab world. Meanwhile, in the mid-fifteenth century, the Tatars of the Golden Horde took control of Russia and large parts of Eastern Europe and shortly thereafter converted to Islam. However, by the end of the century, the Christian Orthodox Russians reversed their defeats and freed themselves from "the Tatar Yoke."[15] During the sixteenth and seventeenth centuries, another locus of non-Arab Islamic power irrupted from Persia. The Persian Empire competed at times with the Ottomans, prospered in

Iran, and more importantly, gave birth to the Islamic expansion into the Indian subcontinent. The Indian Mughal Empire, ultimately headquartered in Delhi, was one of Islam's brightest stars. It shined most brilliantly in the mid-seventeenth century, with the Taj Mahal and the founding of Delhi. It disappeared into the British Raj in 1858.

While the Mughals began to regress in India, the Ottomans also passed their apogee in Central Europe. Having conquered Buda, and having controlled all of Hungary and the Balkans, the Turks attacked Vienna twice and came close to the city gates. The second effort, in the summer of 1683, ended in humiliation for the Turks and for Islam. Bernard Lewis quotes the contemporary Ottoman chronicler Silahdar as saying, "This was a calamitous defeat, so great that there has never been its like since the first appearance of the Ottoman state."[16] By 1698 the results of this debacle were memorialized in the Treaty of Carlowitz that began a process of territorial diminution of the Ottoman Empire, culminating in the empire's collapse after World War I.

Islam's shift from a thriving and expanding religion and culture to a civilization under siege on its entire perimeter had a debilitating psychological and cultural effect on Islamic societies throughout the world. Lewis describes it as follows:

> In modern times, Islamic tolerance has been somewhat diminished. After the second Turkish siege of Vienna in 1683, Islam was a retreating, not an advancing force in the world, and Muslims began to feel threatened by the rise and expansion of the great Christian empires of Eastern and Western Europe. The old easy-going tolerance, resting on the assumption not only of superior religion but also of superior power, was becoming difficult to maintain.[17]

The response chosen by the Islamic world, particularly by the Arab world that had been in decline for so much longer, was to turn in upon itself and reject contact with the ascendant Western civilization. The moment chosen to do this, the 1680s, could not have been worse for Islam. This was the time of the publication of Isaac Newton's *Principia Mathematica*, which laid the foundation for the rapid growth of science. This was the time of René Descartes's "cogito, ergo sum," which signaled a new era in philosophical inquiry. This was the very beginning of the Enlightenment in Europe, to be followed immediately by the Industrial Revolution. Islamic peoples, locked in a defensive crouch, missed them both. Islam, which had taken in all the knowledge of the pagan ancients, now had no interest in foreign languages. Islam saw its stunning architecture copied in the rising West but never itself borrowed from the buildings of the Gothic or Renaissance European styles. Westerners traveled through Islamic lands, but Muslims did not reciprocate. As in the case of the Native Americans, Arabs and Ottomans sought to adopt Western guns and other military innovations but otherwise had little or no interest in the inventions of the industrial West. Islamic Mullahs popularized a saying of Mohammed that people should "beware of new things, for every new thing is an innovation and every innovation a mistake."[18] In 1728 Ibrahim Muteferrika applied in Istanbul for a license to open the Islamic world's first printing press, writing, "It is vital for the Muslims, formerly in advance of the West in sciences, not to let themselves be eclipsed." By 1745 his press was shut down by edict of the mullahs.[19] Islamic countries became frozen in the amber of tradition.

Europe came knocking in a new and more threatening way in 1798 when Napoleon occupied Egypt. Before that most of Islam's contacts with the West, both when expanding and when contracting, were at the edges of Islamic rule. This was an invasion of the heartland. To the embarrassment of the Egyptians and the Ottomans, only the British could and did dislodge the French. The entire Islamic region, from Morocco to Indonesia, became a part of the world in which the West had unfettered freedom of action. The Europeans took colonies in Southeast Asia and North Africa, fought wars among each other in the Crimea, supported independence for Christian Greece and Serbia, and ultimately created artificially divided nations from among the Arab remnants of the former Ottoman Empire. They awarded themselves League of Nations mandates to govern the newly created states. Not until the decolonizing years following World War II did these peoples generally achieve self-determination—and sometimes even then against stiff European resistance, as in the Algerian war that lasted from 1954 to 1962.

Slamming the door on the outside world is a common response for a once-great civilization in decline. Islamic countries were not the only places to turn inward when threatened by the burgeoning Christian West. Japan had been a thriving empire with extensive contacts with the West,

154 ■ American Avatar

particularly the Portuguese and Dutch traders, through its designated international port, Nagasaki. In the early seventeenth century, the new Tokugawa shogun became alarmed at threats to his rule by the efforts of Europeans to spread Christianity in Japan. His reaction was to close Nagasaki and isolate the nation completely from outside influences. Japan, then, missed the progress of the West in the ensuing two hundred years. When in 1853 a small fleet of American warships sailed into Uraga Harbor at Edo (Tokyo), the shogun's regime was powerless to resist the insistence by a modern state that it open its borders. This humiliation triggered self-examination among Japanese elites that resulted in the overthrow of the shogun and the installation of a new imperial regime in 1868, followed by an aggressive effort to catch up. By the early twentieth century, Japan had absorbed all the latest notions of Western thinking, including fascism. Japan stands today as the epitome of a modern democratic, industrial, and commercial society.

Historically China had been a great and expanding nation. By the middle of the Qing Dynasty, it was on the defensive. In 1760 the Chinese emperor decreed that Westerners would no longer be allowed into the Middle Kingdom except at the port of Canton. China stayed locked up through the eighteenth century, when in 1793 the emperor turned back a consular delegation from the English king displaying new British mechanical inventions and proposing trade relations. His famous letter explained, "We have never valued ingenious articles, nor do we have the slightest need of your country's manufactures. Therefore, O King, as regards your request to send someone to remain at the capital, while it is not in harmony with the regulations of the Celestial Empire, we also feel very much it is of no advantage to your country." By 1840 Chinese isolation was met with the Opium Wars. Still defiant, China was invaded by Europeans again in 1860. Finally, helpless before the modern armies of the West, the emperor began receiving foreign delegations in 1873 and sent to London China's first foreign ambassador. Thereafter, China has swung between isolation and openness. The Cultural Revolution of the 1960s and 1970s was the most recent and most brutal rejection of outside influences. Only since the Tiananmen Square incidents of 1989 has China confidently opened to the world. In doing so China has embraced almost every scientific and cultural advance available—even market capitalism (though not democracy).

In the cases of both Japan and China, great ancient cultures reacted to threat by turning inward, as did Islam. Both of them suffered defeats and occupation by Western powers. However, when forced to open, both of them ended up adapting to Western modernity and welcoming change.

Samuel Huntington predicted in 1993 in his article "The Clash of Civilizations" that the West was about to go into a decline in power and influence in all measures, including wealth, intellectual achievement, military power, and cultural influence, and that all the traditionally competing cultures, including Chinese, Japanese, and Arab cultures, would reassert themselves and overtake the West.[20] Within just a few years, the error of that prediction became obvious. The Western, particularly American, economic and military boom of the 1990s reasserted Western dominance. The world's cultures do retain linguistic and other cultural differences. Some of these differences are celebrated and enshrined to find comfort in tradition in the face of advancing cultural homogenization—but homogenization is the dominant trend. People all over the world are moving to a version of contemporary Westernization. That does not mean they are all wealthy—in fact, most are poor—but it does mean people's lives are increasingly alike from Mexico City to Jakarta to Manila to Rio de Janeiro. The geography looks different, the people speak different languages, and the weather is different, but urban lives in crowded high-rises, commutes through traffic-clogged streets, and work in offices and factories are much the same from place to place. If there is to be a clash, it will not be between competing civilizations. It will be between the wealthy and successful Western societies, including Europe, America, Japan, South Korea and the other places where modernity functions well, and the poor societies of the Middle East, Asia, the Americas, and Africa, where modernity's success is not assured and where frustration at the inability to share in modernity's bounty is growing. In both cases, modernity on the Western model is the measure of success. Most of the principles of the Enlightenment, including rationality, progress, and individuality, are increasingly accepted by the average person everywhere. This is the fruit of globalization.

There is a large exception. Unlike the Chinese and Japanese, powerful elements in the Islamic world, especially its Arab core, continue to resist modernization. The Islamic civilization is different from the others, and the difference is rooted in the overlay of a comprehensive religion on the culture—a religion that, when strictly interpreted, embodies a philosophy antagonistic to the Enlightenment thinking of the modern world and antagonistic to nonbelievers. The Islamist reaction to the globalization of the Western value system is more than a resistance to domination by outsiders, a frustration at the failure to acquire a Western standard of living, and a fear of change; it is an adherence to a competing view of life and human existence. It is a strong attachment to attitudes that match most of the ideas that constitute the European antiliberal, romantic syndrome.

In Arabic, "Islam" means "submission." Islam takes a fatalistic and passive view of life. Events are all the will of God. The phrase "Inshallah" ("God willing") is sprinkled in Arab speech like punctuation. The Koran says, "No one dies unless God wills. The term of every life is fixed."[21]

Under Islamic doctrine, Mohammed received the Koran as a recitation of the word of God, commencing in 610 and ending with Mohammed's death in 632. Thereupon, the revelation ended, and the words of the Koran and their meanings became immutable. They do not evolve, and they do not progress. The Holy Law of Islam, the sharia consists of the rules governing the behavior and rights of members of Islamic society appearing in the Koran and are similarly inalterable. Another source of Islamic doctrine is the hadith, the record of sayings and deeds of Mohammed during his life that complements the other scriptural material and helps explain the sometimes mysterious or seemingly contradictory meanings of passages of the Koran. These too are not subject to amendment but do provide a basis for the complex and changeable analysis of the other traditional documents by the large cadre of judges (*qadi*) and legal experts (*ulama*) in the Islamic religious community. Their role has been to interpret the scriptures but not change them. Only God legislates and only God decides. The Koran says, "Whatever the subject of your disputes, the final word belongs to God."[22] This all stands in direct opposition to major precepts of Western liberalism: beliefs in progress, change, personal responsibility, and a community formed by social contract among individuals wherein the civil laws are made and altered by men.

Further, and of central importance to Islam, "Your God is one God. There is no god but Him."[23] Anyone who purports to legislate or rule alongside God challenges this central monotheistic tenet of Islam. By strict interpretation, secular governments constitute polytheism. In the Koran, God asks, "Do the unbelievers think that they can make My servants patrons besides Me? We have prepared Hell for the unbelievers to dwell in."[24] Muslims must not "render unto Caesar" anything, because only God rules. Mohammed, in his lifetime, conflated religious, military, and political leadership. In traditional Islam there is no room for the liberal ideas of secular government or separation of church and state. "Muslim religious thinkers of stature have looked at secularism, understood its threat to what they regard as the highest values of religion, and responded with a decisive rejection."[25]

Without liberal Western ideas, Islam is not easily compatible with democracy. King Fahd of Saudi Arabia has commented that the "democratic system prevalent in the world is not appropriate in this region. . . . The election system has no place in the Islamic creed" because Islam views the leader as a "shepherd" who is responsible for "his flock."[26] In the immediate aftermath of the Iraq war in 2003, two leading Shiite sheiks in Baghdad said, "We don't want a formal democracy that will give Iraqis the right to say what they want, but the government will do what it wants." "We are all against the coalition because they are infidels. . . . We are demanding an Islamic state."[27]

Under sharia, the Enlightenment idea of equality before the law applies to Muslim men only. As the Koran says, "Men have authority over women because God has made the one superior to the other, and because they spend their wealth to maintain them."[28] Where Islam rules, Christians and Jews are subordinate to Muslims. As in today's Saudi Arabia, they pay a special tax and must not practice their religions publicly or proselytize. Other infidels are guaranteed no rights at all.

Islam rejects the Enlightenment and Puritan concept that through hard work a person can achieve God's kingdom in this life on earth. "You shall receive your rewards only on the Day of Resurrection. Whoever is spared the Fire and is admitted to Paradise will surely triumph; for the life of this world is nothing but a fleeting vanity."[29] With this, Islam departs from the Western idea of personal striving for a better life.

The strict Islamic believer is likely to assume a stance of superiority by virtue of greater internal spirit and "soul" over the ant-like Western infidel who labors for wages and will never reach paradise. The believer lays claim to Gobineau's élan vital. He applauds the doomed courage of the martyrdom of the suicide bomber. He applauds grand gestures of futile sacrifice. He forswears pragmatism and compromise. Wagner's uber-romantic opera *Siegfried*, with its scenes of slaying dragons and vaulting through flames, could have been set in the world of Islam.

As a religion that incorporates the romantic critique of Western society and reigns in traditional societies where the other problems of adapting to change and modernity are also present, Islam is in unavoidable conflict with the West and thus with America. Scholar Paul Hollander has written,

> The most obvious and clear link between anti-Americanism and modernization is encountered in Islamic countries and other traditional societies where modernization clashes head on with entrenched traditional beliefs, institutions, and patterns of behavior, and where it challenges the very meaning of life, social relations, and religious verities. . . . In a recent case, the indignant male members of a Kurdish family in Sweden were "provoked" by the transgressing female of their family who had the temerity to have a job and a boyfriend and dress in Western ways. She was finally killed by her father.[30]

Where Islam and the Enlightenment do agree is universalism. Each believes it has the universal truth. With that, their collision is assured.

Of course, religious verities are not always clear. Any scripture, including the Koran, contains ambiguity and contradiction. The Egyptian theological oracle of the Islamist Muslim Brotherhood, Sayyid Qutb, wrote, "There is only one place on earth which can be called the house of Islam, and it is that place where an Islamic state is established and the Shari'ah is the authority and God's laws are observed. . . . The rest of the world is the house of war."[31] On the other hand, the Koran states, "Unbelievers, I do not worship what you worship, nor do you worship what I worship. I shall never worship what you worship, nor will you ever worship what I worship. You have your own religion, and I have mine."[32]

Further, among Islamic people not everyone is an orthodox believer. Commencing promptly after Mohammed's death, a dispute about succession led to the schism between Sunnis and Shiites. That split is characterized by differences in Koranic interpretation and bitter enmities that remain behind some of the major political disputes of today. Over the years, lesser discords and fissures and newly created branches, from Sufis to Wahhabis, have added variety to Islam. As in all major religions, there are people who practice in accordance with what they believe to be literal interpretation of scripture and those who give scripture an allegorical interpretation. Outsiders have characterized the difference generally as a difference between fundamentalist and moderate Islam. Also, as in any religion into which people are born, there are practicing believers and non-practicing believers—people who are not dissenters but for whom religious worship is not an important part of their lives. When the call to prayer sounds in Egypt, only a minority respond to it. In Saudi Arabia, participation is much higher. There is no way precisely to measure this disinterest, but it is obvious that Koranic injunctions on daily prayer and Islamic pronouncements on women's attire are followed with widely varying levels of observance around the world.

Also, to some degree all religions are anti-Enlightenment in that they seek to explain life in ways that depend on faith rather than reason. All religions assume that they offer the correct answers. They exist in the realm of revealed truth, not free inquiry. History is clear that there is a tension between strictly interpreted Christianity and the scientific method, as witnessed in events from Galileo's battles with the Inquisition to the American Christian fundamentalists' continuing struggles against Darwin.

For all these reasons, it would not seem compulsory that Islamic religious dictates based on Koranic references should account for broad popular attitudes about modernization, but they do. Even for nonbelievers Islamic doctrines are a pervasive influence on the mindset. They define the culture, and they define it to be romantic. Among the Arabs, even in the many countries where theocracy does not exist and even where there have been open efforts to modernize and introduce secular rule on a Western model, the Western model consistently chosen, from Gamal Abdel Nasser in Egypt to Saddam Hussein in Iraq, has been fascism, not democracy. Periodically, Arab tyrants have been overthrown, only to be replaced by other tyrants. As in Japan's first effort at Westernization, the romantic Arab mind-set prefers government in the manner of the one period in Europe since the Enlightenment when romanticism held sway. It prefers government by a Western system that deprives the people of the benefits and struggles of making choices. Arab society is permeated by romanticism in both its religious and its political sphere, whether or not it is governed by an official theocracy. Unlike Europe, where romanticism is the philosophy of the left and right extremes and of intellectual and artistic elites, in the Islamic world, it is shared by the general public.

Add to this romanticism the consternation felt throughout the Islamic population, and particularly by the Arab population, that it was once the "ornament of the world" but is now powerless and poor. Consistent with the mentality of anti-Enlightenment pride, fatalism, and irrationality, the defeats of the distant past and the near past cannot be accepted as the fault of the believers. To believers, all good things come from God; conversely, all bad things must be the work of the devil. This thinking requires scapegoats.

When Ayatollah Khomeini began to refer to the United States in 1979 as the "Great Satan" and to Israel as the "Little Satan," Westerners took these phrases as quaint epithets with no deeper meaning. To ears conditioned to Islamic sermons and seeking to explain years of defeats, these names hit home. Those two nations of infidels, those centers of the world's most non-romantic, bourgeois societies, stood accused of perpetrating all the ills that had befallen the Islamic region. Typical of this thinking are the comments of Samir Ragad, chairman of the *Egyptian Gazette*, expressing his frustration over Saddam Hussein's defeat by the Americans:

> Frankly, we believed that Baghdad would remain Iraq's impregnable citadel. We thought that Baghdad's walls would turn into swords to decapitate the invaders. Saddam Hussein had misled us into believing that the invaders would never take Baghdad. But the home of five million people collapsed in record time.
>
> Why did the Iraqis not blow up the bridges over the Tigris and Euphrates to prevent the invaders from reaching their planned targets? It is a disgrace that these huge Iraqi troops relaxed idly and woke up to the roar of gunfire on all sides. It is now clear that the traitors are many and those who gave in to the Satan temptation outnumber them.[33]

In a way, the Satan metaphor is particularly apt for how the United States is perceived in the Islamic world. Whatever baleful influence the United States has had in the region has been by temptation, by the sheer attractiveness of what the devout Sayyid Qutb called "this rubbish heap of the West."[34] Unlike the Europeans, the United States never held a Muslim colony. Until its wars against Saddam Hussein (except for the long-forgotten action against the Barbary pirates), the United States never did battle against an Islamic country. On the contrary, in recent years, the United States has sided with the mujahideen in Afghanistan against the Soviets, and with the Bosnian and Kosovar Muslims against the Serbs. The United States stayed neutral in the Christian-Muslim civil war in Lebanon, famously tilted in favor of Muslim Pakistan for years in its dispute with India over Kashmir, and was sympathetic at first (before terrorism became the issue) to Muslim Chechen ambitions for independence in Russia. As to economic relations, the American role in the Arab world has been as an open-handed aid donor to Egypt and Jordan, and as a free-spending oil prospector and oil purchaser at world-market prices. Yet the resentment of the United States in these countries far outstrips anything existing in such countries as Japan, Germany, or Vietnam, which the United States demolished in wars with horrific collateral losses of civilian lives. It exceeds the resentment in Mexico, from which the United States wrested vast valuable territory. It is much more than any resentment in the Philippines, which the United States held as a colony for decades after putting down an indigenous independence insurrection. In fact, it exceeds the resentment everywhere else in the world.[35] To quote a young Palestinian, "America has to pay for its foreign policy, which is against Muslims."[36] Even accounting for the American defense of Israel's security and for the post–September 11 war on terrorism, the strength of this attitude cannot be explained by American actions with respect to the Arab world.

The tempting success of the United States stands before the Islamic world, and especially the Arab world, as a silent (and sometimes not silent) reproach for their obvious failures. In that, it bears the burden of defeats inflicted on them by others going back before the founding of the American republic. "We feel deeply the humiliation, the marginalization of the whole Muslim world," said the chairman of Britain's Imams and Mosques Council.[37] With their romantic notions of courageous resistance against the inevitable, and long having taken solace in their relative weakness and poverty by the excuse that they are morally, spiritually, and culturally superior, the Arab people cannot react rationally or pragmatically to their own decline or defeat. The managing editor of the *Arab News* explained the shocked reactions of Arabs everywhere to Saddam Hussein's demise: "The pride the Arabs felt in the initial stages of the invasion, before those leg-

endary 'pockets of resistance' halting the advance of the world's only superpower were revealed as a myth, has been replaced by immense shame
and humiliation. The images of US soldiers taking a picnic in the heart of
Baghdad will haunt the Arab psyche for generations to come."[38]

Faisal Shahzad, the American immigrant from Pakistan who tried to
blow up Times Square in May 2010, wrote in his e-mails, "Everyone knows
how the Muslim country bows down to pressure from west [*sic*]. Everyone
knows the kind of humiliation we are faced with around the globe."[39]

As the United Nations' Arab Human Development Report observed,
"A significant part of Arab intellectual endeavour seems to seek refuge in
ideological headlines that either take the form of slogans to glorify and effect a nostalgic revival or that encourage self-pity, blame others for adver-
sity and do not do justice to Arab societies."[40] Their unelected leaders pan-
der to these feelings of humiliation and self-pity and entrench their power
by diverting public frustration to external enemies, particularly the powerful outsider, the United States. They sell the idea that the United States
is all-powerful and behind every policy of which the public would not ap-
prove. President Hosni Mubarak of Egypt, who ruled autocratically with
almost $2 billion of annual aid from the United States, filled his state-run
media with anti-American diatribes. Ironically, opponents of the regime
followed the same anti-American line, assuming the power of the United
States was responsible for propping up the dictator. The Americans were
blamed by both sides, the regime's supporters and the regime's detractors.

The United States is the target of the feelings of humiliation because it looms so large. Even when others join it in action, as in the war
in Afghanistan, it is seen as the only actor. Even when the United Nations imposes sanctions, they are described as "American sanctions." The
forces encroaching on traditional Islamic society may encompass all of
democratic liberalism, modernity and Westernization, Christianity, and
the white race, but all they see is the United States. It fills people's minds
and appears to them to control even the minutiae of their lives. America's
very existence dominates and emasculates. A young Jordanian hoping to
get a visa to move to the United States voices his despair: "America, Fadi
says, is just too powerfully present in the lives of his generation of Arabs.
America decides what young people will wear or what music they'll listen
to. America decides whether there will be war or peace. It's so hard for a

young man to feel proud of being an Arab, he says, when it is America that determines his chances for happiness and success."[41]

Still, there are other voices among the more than one billion people in Islamic nations. Increasingly, they are speaking out. The great Arab poet Adunis calls for a "revolution of subjectivity" to free people from tradition. He recognizes the damage that has occurred to traditional Arab culture but calls on Arabs to participate in Western culture as creators, not just as consumers.[42]

A Qatari engineer educated in the United States took the following pragmatic view of the United States and its role in the world at a conference in the Middle East:

> The United States is in tune with many of the requirements of the contemporary world, and if there is going to be any leading power at all, it is the best qualified to play that role. Any such state must be democratic, law-abiding and sometimes needs to utilize force to implement that law. Only the United States with its strong economy, technology, and military power has that capability and the will to sacrifice.[43]

A leading Egyptian political analyst, Osama al-Ghazali Harb, expressed the view that scapegoating is the wrong response to the shameful conditions of the Arab world:

> What we, as Arabs, should truly feel humiliated about are the prevailing political and social conditions in the Arab world—especially in Iraq—which allowed someone such as Saddam Hussein to . . . assume the presidency. We should feel humiliated that Saddam was able . . . to single-handedly initiate a number of catastrophic policies that transformed Iraq, relatively rich in natural, human and financial resources, into the poorest, most debt-ridden country in the Arab world, not to mention the hundreds of thousands killed and displaced. We should feel humiliated that some of our intellectuals, supposedly the representatives of our nations' consciences and the defenders of their liberty and dignity, not only dealt with Saddam, but also supported him. . . . The Arabs should have been the ones to bring down Saddam, in defense of their own dignity and their own true interests.[44]

Words such as these reverberated in the home-grown revolutions of the Arab Spring of 2011. Perhaps democracy will get a foothold in the Arab world and romanticism will fade, as it did years ago in Japan. Islam lives side by side with democratic liberalism in Western nations and with growing democracies in non-Arab Turkey, Bangladesh, India, Malaysia, and Indonesia. Recent public opinion surveys find "a considerable appetite in the Muslim world for democratic freedoms."[45] The uprisings confirmed this. With the advent of democratic political participation, and with a real advance into the Islamic world of the prosperity and freedom which modernity promises, the traditional sense that there is a satanic force—the United States—looming above everyone may fade. On the other hand, a failure to deliver on the hopes of Westernization and democracy to those who long for it would again throw the frustrated modernizers into the arms of the revanchist advocates of traditional Islam and autocracy, who otherwise would be a shrinking minority.

The challenge for America is not to change Islam or seek to convert the most religious people to a secular point of view. It is to provide the bulk of the populations of the developing world the sense that all that America represents might be possible for them or their children. In analyzing attitudes in the Arab world and the rest of traditional societies, it is important to grasp that there are people whose aversion to modernity is solidly grounded in its threat to their livelihoods, their positions, and their deeply held beliefs. They will not change. They will harbor immutable anti-American predispositions so long as America is seen as the motive force behind Westernization. However, in view of the inevitability of modernization in some form and the inability to recreate lost cultures in any event, they are a shrinking minority.

The growing and much more challenging anti-American predisposition is among those who long for modernity and are frustrated, and may be more frustrated in the future, by the failure to attain modernity's benefits or by modernity's failure to match their image of it. These people accept and admire America, or at least the America in their minds. They want their world to change. An America that falls short of their expectations generates a bias based on disappointment—the grievance of a spurned suitor.

10

DISAPPOINTMENT: ENVY AND THE AMERICAN DREAM

As the 2011 Pew Global Attitudes Survey shows, most people have a pro-American bias. The vast middle-class majority in Europe who are not of the romantic mind-set identify with American liberal democracy and its common Western culture. The great majority of people in traditional societies, Islamic or otherwise, who hunger for change and modernity, want the world America inhabits to invite them in. These are sympathetic observers of United States who draw on a store of flattering imagery in their minds. But, when unfulfilled, their desires and expectations can lead to disappointments that have the reverse effect of creating bitter predispositions against the United States.[1]

These admirers come in two (often overlapping) varieties: those who want what they believe Americans have, and those who expect America to be a certain thing and to act in certain ways. As usual, the imagery on which they base their beliefs and expectations has both a basis in reality and a strong component of distortion and pure imagination. They are both forms of the American Dream as experienced abroad. Abkow Edow, a Bantu refugee from Somalia, recalled, "In Somalia, I dreamed of the United States, even though I didn't know anything about it."[2]

To many, America is a contemporary Eldorado, with streets paved in gold. It is a land of unlimited opportunity where every child can become president. The sun is always shining, and the people are always friendly and beautiful. Its conduct in foreign affairs is never self-interested but always considers their particular and personal needs. "America" is a metaphor for their perfect place. It is Shangri-La. Here are the makings of a love-hate relationship. Such a relationship starts with attraction and can sour with disappointment to envy and disillusionment. These are emotions with potentially devastating consequences.

Envy

While the United States actually is not Shangri-La, the chasm between the lives of Americans and other Westerners and those of the rest of the world is broad and deep. The average person among the globe's top 10 percent—an average American, Belgian, Swiss, Japanese, or other Westerner—is four hundred times as rich as the average person in the bottom 50 percent of the earth's population.[3] The West's youth glide through healthy lives. Malnutrition is almost unknown. Rather, the challenge is obesity. A majority of them get at least sixteen years of education. Universal literacy opens their eyes and minds to a wealth of ideas and opportunities. Increasingly, their schooling is interrupted by a gap year to explore and "find themselves." As adults, most Westerners choose their spouses, their occupations, and their locations. They have housing that is warm in the winter and cool in the summer. They have cars. For all the legitimate modern concern about industrial pollution, today's Westerners live in urban areas and interior spaces that are sparklingly clean compared to historic standards of public sanitation and the smoky, coal- or wood-heated homes and kitchens of yesteryear. Whatever health care system their nation offers, they can expect access to the latest medical care and pharmaceuticals. They have had a steady advance in life expectancy. Girls born in the West in 2007 can expect to live to eighty-two, and boys will survive to seventy-seven.[4] Throughout their long lives, they are free to come and go, to travel the world. Despite the unhappiness they may experience in their individual lives and the concerns about personal finances and the physical and psychological aches and pains that afflict all mortals, they are more likely to spend the bulk of their worries on the joys and sorrows that come from relationships and the search for meaning in life than any people, anywhere, at any other time in history.

Life is not fair. In the non-Western 80 percent of the world, every night one billion people go to bed hungry.[5] Boys born in Russia in 2007 can expect to live fifteen years less than those born in the wealthy nations of the West.[6] Children born in 2007 into the forty-two nations classified by the World Bank as "low income" have a life expectancy about twenty years less than those born in the West. In Sierra Leone children's life expectancies are more than thirty years shorter.[7] One in seven children in sub-Saharan Africa does not make it to age five.[8] If children do get to school age, there is no assurance that they will get to school. Approximately seventy-two million children in the developing world who were eligible for primary school were not enrolled in 2005.[9] Less than two-thirds of youngsters in low-income countries complete primary school.[10] The effect on literacy is obvious: in Nepal 57 percent of adults are literate; in Pakistan, 54 percent; and in Senegal, 42 percent.[11] One billion people entered the twenty-first century unable to read or sign their names.[12] As diseases such as malaria and AIDS afflict the poorest nations, children are orphaned. In 2005, 15.2 million children (mostly in Africa) lost one or both parents to AIDS.[13] Over 2.4 billion people around the world lack access to a toilet and other basic sanitary facilities, including 638 million in India.[14] Globally, about 1.5 million children die each year due to a lack of water, sanitation, and hygiene.[15]

For those who run the gauntlet of childhood and survive, the prospects are grim. In South Africa in 2008, only 36.5 percent of the population was in the work force, and 22.9 percent of that small work force was unemployed.[16] In 2008, 31 percent of South Africa's population was under fifteen years old.[17] How can its economy absorb the onslaught of these people as they mature? The same question applies to Uganda, Guatemala, and over forty-four other countries with under-fifteen populations that exceeded 40 percent of the total population in 2010.[18] The answer is that they cannot. For the poor majority growing up in today's world, there is no gap year to travel the globe. Travel takes money they do not have and visas they cannot get. They have no chance and no need to "find themselves." They know where they are.

From the other side of the divide, all the "stuff" and all the opportunities of the West are tantalizing. Juan de Recacoechea's *American Visa*, Bolivia's most celebrated novel, highlights this longing for America. It recounts the twists and turns of a small town Bolivian schoolteacher as he desperately pursues his vain hope to obtain a visa to visit his grown son in Miami. It sets its quest of false starts, adventures, and calamities against the broadly held Bolivian aspiration for entry to the gringos' magical El Norte. To Bolivian readers, the fictional character Mario Alvarez is all too familiar. In his longing for his American dream, he does not destroy America, but he destroys himself.[19]

The idea of America as a subject of longing is not limited to the world's poor and oppressed. From its earliest days it has been a siren's song to those who had dreams of a different life for any reason. It is a hovering presence in their minds. Jenny Diski wrote: "As a child in fifties London, America was as distant a reality to me as ancient Egypt, yet present in my life. . . . Distant is not quite the word. America was like the moon: its remoteness was irrelevant, what mattered was the light it bathed me in, its universal but private reach."[20] When this longing can be satisfied, as it has been for many millions in American history, it brings the special satisfaction of a dream realized. When it remains out of reach, the effect can be volatile. As the British-Dutch writer Ian Buruma concluded,

> America . . . is a very different place to those who live in places where "America" is only a mirage, a kind of guilty wet dream in dry desert lands, a promise which can never be fulfilled. If you live under a tyranny, with no personal freedom and no hope of advancement, in a country that feels abandoned and perhaps even betrayed by the modern world, the pull of family, tribe and tradition may be all that is left. Then a very different utopia beckons the embittered pilgrim, one built on a mirage of purity, sacred community and self-sacrifice. In such a state of mind, it is not enough to avert your gaze from those seductive towers of Babylon. You might have to tear them down.[21]

An affable young Jordanian by the name of Fadi interviewed in 2003 is an example of this. He had a dream to move to the United States and become a famous computer programmer at Microsoft. It was an American dream. He failed to get a visa. If he had gotten a visa it is unlikely that he would have gotten a job with Microsoft. If he had gotten the job, he surely would not have become famous as a computer programmer. After all, how many famous computer programmers are there? Instead, bereft, bearded, and unemployed in Amman, he dawdled on the university campus watching the girls go by. He expressed his disapproval of the young women who were not covered in Islamic scarves, called hijabs. Still, when pressed, he admitted his actual preference for the bare-headed Western-looking women in alluring clothes and makeup, who paid no attention to him. He explained, "Of course I look . . . I'm a human being. . . . Maybe I prefer the Western-looking girls. But I wish they would wear the hijab." In his struggle with the conflict and frustration within him he talked about becoming a *shaheed*, a suicide bomber, blowing himself up and killing American troops.[22] This is envy—envy of a place where his dreams would come true; dreams of success and dreams of beautiful girls. To him, America and beautiful girls had become equivalent longings.

Fadi is not alone. He is more the norm. Another Jordanian, Muhammad Fawaz, a twenty-year-old student at Jordan University, was described in 2008 as an Islamic activist. His dream had been to earn a scholarship to study abroad, but he lacked the connections, the "wasta," to achieve that goal. The injustice of it drew him into the arms of the anti-American Muslim Brotherhood. In the Middle East, frustration among the young is a force that drives them to conservative Islam. "It is their rock 'n' roll, their long hair and love beads."[23]

As a floating desire, the America of the imagination can be a glorious idea in the ether, a symbol of hope, a goal, a thrilling fantasy, a temptation, and if not attained, a hovering cloud, a kind of taunt or mocking reproach. For both Fadi and Muhammad Fawaz, the realization that America was there and they were not was painful. The pain required some kind of solace, which was found in anger.

Americans are peculiarly oblivious to the reactions people elsewhere have to their advantages. They are even more mystified by reactions people have to imagined advantages, the role of their nation in the dreams of others, and differences between what the United States is in real life and what it is in other people's imaginations. Americans are generally unaware of envy in the minds of others. Envy is resentment directed toward another person or other people who have what the envious person wants and cannot achieve or possess.[24] It is the emotional reflection of thwarted ambition and frustrated desires. Envy arises from a kind of admiration and attraction, rather than revulsion and repulsion. If the desire seems within reach, as it does to a Mexican immigrant crossing the Rio Grande, his emotion is one of emulation and admiration. However, when the aspiration is blocked, when it cannot be fulfilled, it can transform into envy.

Envy of the West, and of the United States in particular, is not limited to American advantages in wealth, power, education, and personal comforts. People around the world long for many facets of American society that are even more unattainable to them: democratic institutions, opportunities for social mobility and personal fulfillment, religious freedom, civil rights, stable government, secure and peaceful communities, and a variety of other images that can elicit both sweet admiration and bitter envy.

Envy is a nearly universal emotion and often a powerful one. Each person may experience envy at different times, toward different people, and for different reasons, sometimes as a strong pull, sometimes as a passing tug. It feeds upon itself and reinforces other emotions. Resentment of others' good fortune may fuel self-pity and a gnawing sense of inadequacy. In turn, consciousness of being envious may stimulate feelings of shame and self-loathing. Blame for these painful emotions may be projected onto the original target of envy, spiraling resentment toward hatred, as if to say, "I hate him not only for having more than I can ever hope to have, but for making me feel so badly about it and about my reaction to it."

Though inspired by material and intangible desires, envy is directed toward a person or a group of people (a nation in this case). It is not a feeling directed toward the thing or the characteristic the envier wants. If a person craves another man's flashy car and sees no way to satisfy that craving, the resentment that results is directed toward the man, not the car. To satisfy envy he might do something spiteful to the man who owns the car, with no expectation that such an act will bring him the car. When a spurned boyfriend slashes the face of a beautiful ex-girlfriend, he does it out of frustration and spite with no hope or expectation that the act will win her affection.

One man seeing another having something he covets can be a fine motivator. A hope of achieving what others have can drive a lifetime of fruitful labor. In the United States, frequently children are told they might grow up to be president. Since there have been only forty-four presidents since the nation's founding, that statement should be considered false by all normal standards. Still, it is the central nugget in the gold mine of the American ideal of social mobility. By its general acceptance, the expectation of social mobility avoids the sense of frustration and encourages emulation as the dominant reaction by Americans to the social and economic advantages of others. The hope of advancement may be only a glimmer, but even a glimmer can substitute emulation for envy. Where emulation cannot possibly achieve the object of desire, where ambition is blocked, feeling of envy and spiteful behavior become the norm. Widespread feelings of envy in society is a formula for social discord. Societies have developed ways to deal with it.

In Europe, even though income gaps between the rich and the poor are no longer any greater than those in the United States, the perception remains that society is more stratified there. European leaders do not present themselves, as Bill Clinton did, as "a man from Hope." In Europe, no mixed-race son of a Kenyan who was raised by his grandparents could be elected as head of state or prime minister. Political appeals to the public based on class resentment have always succeeded in Europe but have generally failed in the United States. Yes, the United States has a progressive income tax, and every time a rate change is proposed, there are politicians saying the change will affect the rich in one way and the working man in another. However, these appeals get little traction compared to similar arguments in Europe, where political parties are numerous and well correlated to the various, seemingly permanent economic and social strata. In such communities of social stratification, the politics of envy have a significant place. As we get further away from the American situation, to societies far more sclerotic than in Europe, envy emerges as an even greater political and social influence.

Envy always entails comparison. In the past, envy and spite have been problems within societies or groups within societies, rather than in relations between different societies or nations. This reflects the need for the envious to be able to consider himself comparable to the person who is the object of his envy. In travels through rural and impoverished parts of India, the Western traveler in his car—with his watch, camera, sunglasses, expensive clothing, and other paraphernalia of wealth—does not feel the glare of resentment from the villagers. Instead he might (erroneously) believe that he has not been noticed at all. The villagers are not immune to envy. The villager with one water buffalo might be willing to kill his neighbor for having two water buffaloes. The immunity of the visitor from afar arises from the fact that, in the villager's mind, the life of the visitor is not comparable to his own. The villager might or might not covet the objects the visitor has but cannot put himself in the position of the foreigner in a manner sufficient to envy him. Similarly, the ordinary British working man or woman for various reasons may or may not think it would be better if the nation had no monarchy, but he or she is unlikely to envy the Queen's possessions or sumptuous life. She does not consider herself comparable to the monarch. Envy flourishes among people who can imagine trading places with others who are like them but are blocked from doing so by personal circumstances, the political system, or otherwise.

Societies have attacked the problem of envy among their members in various ways, including suppressing the development or mere appearances of differences among people, exaggerating the differences among people to avoid comparability, enhancing social mobility to avoid thwarting people's ambitions, and suppressing the expression of envy. Many societies adopt several of these techniques in combination.

In the primitive world of Papua New Guinea, there is the tradition of the sing-sing. In the remote highlands of New Guinea, people live a simple subsistence life of hunting and gathering supplemented by planting yams and tending to free-range pigs. The pigs are considered the unit of wealth and are used to pay debts and dowries. The people do not ask for much, and not much separates one life from another. They are generally naked or nearly so in the balmy high country climate. The men gather together in large "spirit houses" and the women and children live in identical thatched bungalows. Except for the tribal hierarchy of chief and shaman, a more level society is hard to imagine.

Every year or so, several adjoining villages (provided they are not at war) will come together for a sing-sing. This is an extended celebration in which the people feast on the pigs that are considered surplus. Those whose pigs have multiplied more than others contribute them to the community, and they are devoured in one great, leveling festival. Thus, in this close-knit village society, the potential disruption of envy is thought so intolerable to internal peace that differences among people's possessions are ritually destroyed.

This forced leveling is not much different from the tradition of repartition of communal farms (*mirs*) practiced for hundreds of years in Czarist Russia. Every few generations, the Russian feudal lords would call together their serfs who were working the lords' domains for a reallocation of land. The serfs would have been farming the land in strips that had been allotted to their grandparents or great grandparents on the basis of the size of their families at the time of the last repartition. Over the ensuing years, families that were large may have shrunk, and small families may have grown. In the repartition, the strips of land would be redistributed to take into account the changes in family size. This not only leveled the peasant society's wealth and avoided envy among them, but it also gave the land to those who had the most hands to do the work. It is thought that the receptivity of the Russian peasantry to Lenin and the Bolsheviks was due in large part to impatience among farmers for a repartition that had not occurred for over eighty years and was thought to be long overdue. In the delay, envy had been allowed to fester to an explosive degree among the peasants who had less land and needed more to support their families. As early as 1879, a socialist revolutionary movement calling itself Black Repartition insisted on Russian rural land reform and redistribution. After the revolution, commencing in 1929 with his assault on the Kulaks, Stalin gave them the ultimate repartition and leveling by entirely collectivizing agriculture in a bloody purge. It was more than most of them had in mind.

While the Russian nobility was periodically leveling the allocation of land to avoid envy by one serf against another, the radical differences between the nobility and the farmers in ways of life, dress, diet, language, and almost all other aspects of existence may have worked to avoid the comparability that would have created envy of the nobility in the minds of the serfs. This combination of avoiding differences within one segment of society and maintaining differences that were so enormous as to prevent comparison between two segments of society worked to keep the dangers of envy at bay through most of Czarist rule. However, by the early twentieth century, after generations without the customary repartition, almost 150 years (1762 to 1907) of a gradual process of freeing the serfs, more than 100 years of talk about Enlightenment politics among the intelligentsia, and the steady growth of a bourgeoisie in Russia who were not so distant from the farmers as to prevent comparison by the poorest Russians, the claims of equality among the poor and of noncomparability between the poor and the wealthier classes could not be supported. The politics of envy burst over Russia in the Russian Revolution.

Still, suppressing comparability among groups of people within society had worked to maintain stability in Russia for a long time. It worked elsewhere too. In India the caste system served in part to stifle the tendency of people with less to believe that they should be in the shoes of those with more. In that society, as in many others, traditions that regulated how people of particular stations in life should dress and behave made people of less well-endowed strata consider the advantages of others to be irrelevant to them rather than something unfairly denied to them.

In many societies with enormous differences among groups of people and among individuals, and where comparability may be unavoidable, the opposite approach is taken. Rather than exaggerate the gulfs between groups, the differences among people are carefully hidden to avoid exciting envy. Potentates of various kinds have ruled over Arab nations for over a thousand years. The leader—be he sultan, king, bey, or sheik—was not comparable to the rest of the population and could live in splendor without arousing dangerous envy from the population as a whole (though he had to watch out for the envy of his immediate and very comparable family members). The rest of the population of traders and herders were not different from each other in obvious ways. Within this general population, the expression of envy would be disruptive. It was avoided by suppressing the show of wealth by any person who might be envied. Rather than confiscating unusual wealth, as in a New Guinea sing-sing, the Arab tradition is to hide differences and avoid shows of wealth in public. All men in Saudi Arabia, including the royal family, wear similar white robes. High walls hide the fabulous houses and elaborate possessions of the wealthy. Head-to-toe black robes hide women, the men's most valued possessions, from the eyes of potentially envious neighbors. Behind the high walls, these robes often come off, and expensive Western dress is common. This distinction between public leveling and private grandeur highlights the fact that the sameness of public appearance is not only done for reasons of religious piety but to avoid the "evil eye" of envy.

Fear of envy's evil eye is a common trait throughout North Africa, the Middle East, and Central Asia. It is embodied in blue beads sewn into Turkish rugs, and throughout the region by spitting sounds whenever men mention some good thing that has happened to them. The same concept appears in other places such as Brazil, where *figas* (amulets in the shape of a fist) are worn around the neck to ward off bad luck. All these folk practices share a common theme: avoid the danger of unrestrained envy. Those cultures assume that if envy is provoked, it will be acted upon. Therefore, the display of advantages by the potential targets of envy is suppressed. Consumption is inconspicuous.

These ancient traditions for dealing with envy, such as confiscating extra wealth, hiding extra wealth, or exaggerating societal stratification and creating castes to avoid comparability, tend to stifle personal initiative. Economic stagnation can be a price paid for social peace through the avoidance of envy. If you cannot imagine hard work or even good fortune changing your lot in life, why try? If, as the Japanese say, "the nail that sticks out gets hammered," why persist with an innovative idea?

The Christian West has gone a different way. Instead of stifling the person who is envied and expecting the envious person to act on his impulses, it stifles the expression of envy by the envious. In Catholic doctrine, feeling and expressing envy is one of the seven deadly sins. In the United States, the expression of envy is virtually taboo. Americans rarely admit real envy. People will use the word colloquially to say they admire or covet something, but people do not admit to the resentment that is the true meaning of envy. In American society there are frequent discussions of emotional motivations for all sorts of actions. People discuss love, hate, greed, and plenty of other emotions, but not envy. The English language does not even have a word for "schadenfreude," a German term for the spiteful pleasure a person takes in the misfortune of someone else. It is not that Americans do not feel envy as others do; it is just that they repress and suppress its expression. People will admit that they murdered someone but not admit the motive was envy. In Channelview, Texas, in 1990, Wanda Holloway admitted that she hired a hit man (who turned out to be an undercover FBI agent) to kill Verna Heath, the mother of the teenage girl next door, because that girl was chosen for the cheerleading squad instead of Holloway's daughter. She admitted to the facts, revealing her lethal envy, though there is no record of her actually using the word. In the American context, this admission is startling enough to be well remembered nationally and to be the subject of a film.

Given the Western cultural inhibition on expressing envy, it is not surprising that American and (to a much lesser extent) European societies allow its members the freedom to accumulate and display to everyone all their achievements and acquisitions even though they might excite feelings of envy. The fortunate and the successful may flaunt their advantages. In Western society the person who succeeds is celebrated, not stifled. Yet there are degrees of such celebration. As a result of the risks inherent in their lower level of social mobility, Europeans are less tolerant than Americans of conspicuous consumption. Americans want to "keep up with the Joneses," even if it means buying a dream house with a jumbo mortgage and flashy clothes with an overdrawn credit card. European manners require greater circumspection in the display of wealth. European culture mixes a modest measure of suppression of the envied with strong suppression of the envious. In the United States, strong suppression of the expression of envy is combined with greater opportunity for social and economic advancement, so that people less often see their ambitions as being thwarted, and society is freer from of the dangers of envy.

These differences in American mores from those in Europe and, in turn, from those in the non-Western world relate to the creation of resentments toward America and the propagation of negative imagery. The solutions for coping with the societal disruptiveness of envy each work within their own systems, but they invite cross-cultural misunderstanding and contempt when viewed from abroad. Europeans have complained since the nineteenth century that Americans are braggarts. Fanny Trollope wrote about the open braggadocio of the comparatively wealthy New Englanders and how it collided with English notions of good taste:

> I know not a more striking evidence of the low tone of morality which is generated by this universal pursuit of money, than the manner in which the New England States are described by Americans. All agree in saying that they present a spectacle of industry and prosperity delightful to behold, and this is the district and the population most constantly quoted as the finest specimen of their admirable country. . . . I have heard them unblushingly relate stories of their cronies and friends, which, if believed among us, would banish the heroes from the fellowship of honest men for ever; and all this is uttered with a simplicity which sometimes led me to doubt if the speakers knew what honour and honesty meant. Yet the Americans declare that "they are the most moral people upon earth."[25]

Surely in the English milieu, such boasting would violate manners intended to guard against envy. In nineteenth-century America, the wealthy felt sufficiently secure from the danger of the evil eye that they could behave in a manner outside the English definition of "honour and honesty" without attracting condemnation in their own country. Behavior considered normal in the United States that dealt effectively with the social condition in the United States invited a scornful image when seen through foreign eyes by the application of the norms needed there to preserve social harmony.

In 1885 Knut Hamsun wrote home to Norway and introduced his indignant view of the United States, declaring, "On the other side of the ocean lies a country as big as twenty kingdoms and incomparably rich— America, the Millionaires' Republic."[26] In 1931, even as the Great Depression sapped American strength, trenchant French critic of America Georges Duhamel expressed it in the following way:

> How can the universe avoid being dazzled? Behold, people of Europe, behold the new empire! It has had two centuries of success, a constant rise; few wars, all of happy issue; it has kept its many problems at a safe distance; it feels the pride of being a numerous people, rich, feared, admired, a pride that begins to stir in the humblest passer-by, lost in the corridors of the ant-heap, a pride that is capable tomorrow of delivering a hundred million souls to the enterprises of their intoxicated leaders.[27]

Americans do not need to brag to excite envy abroad. All the components are there: a vast difference in power, wealth, and importance; a feeling among many abroad that the world system and other impediments block their access to similar achievements; and a growing sense of comparability between their lives and the lives of Americans. While each separate society in premodern days developed effective ways to handle the effects of envy within it, the newly developed "global village" has not yet adapted to being a single global society in which all feel free to compare themselves to others. A single society cannot be stable if it has an enormously wealthy, conspicuous consumer who is acculturated to being oblivious to the gimlet eyes of others and who is living in plain view of the poor for whom envy is an emotion they feel free to express and act upon.

It is not new that America is richer than the non-Western nations. The world has survived for millennia with vast differences between the richest and the poorest. What is new is the ability to compare. Distance no longer insulates America from the eyes and ears of the world's poor. Today, visitors to the remote Draa River valley of southern Morocco find the villages of adobe houses adorned with satellite dishes. By 2009 the Arab world had over two hundred satellite television channels.[28] Some of those channels show programs that open a window to American society that will unrelentingly chip away at the sense that the United States is too remote from their reality to be a fit object of envy.

The issue of comparability and familiarity breeding envy and hatred has always been a paradox. In seeking to ease resentments and increase cross-cultural understanding, the United States has fostered cultural exchange. It has long encouraged foreign university students to study in the United States. The Pew poll of 2002 that showed sharp increases in negative public opinion of the United States around the world did find the increases to be somewhat smaller among those who had studied here.[29] However, for a minority of those who got to know America by having visited as students, the familiarity they acquired gave them the comparability that triggered resentments that lead to full-blown pathological cases of envy. The hotly anti-American leader of Ghana, Kwame Nkrumah, studied at the University of Pennsylvania. The spiritual leader of the Muslim Brotherhood, Sayyid Qutb, studied at the University of Northern Colorado at Greeley. Perhaps these and others like them had unfortunate personal experiences when they visited, or, ironically, they may have liked it so much that they resented being excluded from being accepted fully as Americans. By being in the United States, they could make the comparisons that are essential elements of envy. Envy is a hatred born of admiration.

America cannot deal with envy in traditional ways. It will not voluntarily destroy its wealth in a worldwide sing-sing so as to avoid the differences that exist. Envoys from the developing world were disappointed in Copenhagen in 2009 when the United States declined to adopt global warming rules that were motivated in part by the desire to level differences among economies. The United States cannot stop the proliferation of new communications technologies that have enhanced comparability. The United States cannot hide its wealth by stifling and censoring communications programming. America's best opportunity to avoid envy is to continually work to lessen the distances between it and the potential enviers by helping bring to them the modernity and affluence they desire. Such leveling will avoid disappointing people whose admiration of what

Americans have can be satisfied by them attaining it, too. If their ambitions are realistic, their goals are achievable.

Disillusionment

The American lead has another, more metaphysical impact on foreign attitudes. Due to its cultural and economic success, America and the idea of America are pervasive and have entered into people's minds in a symbolic way. "In this age of American Empire, the image of the United States has taken on almost mythic dimensions, symbolizing, consciously or unconsciously, deeply held personal fantasies and fears."[30] The effect on people's attitudes can include admiration, hope, desire, and a host of longings and warm feelings. This phenomenon is not new. On his departure from the United States to return to Hungary in 1832, the writer Sándor Farkas Bölöni said, "Farewell once more, glorious country. Be thou the eternal protector and shelter of the rights of humanity! Be thou an eternal frightening landmark to tyrants! Be thou an eternal stimulating example to all oppressed!"[31] America continues to animate peoples' dreams around the world. In the 1990s a record eleven million people immigrated to the United States, and very few left. Another 5.6 million entered between 2000 and 2005.[32] The United States continues to accept the world's largest flow of refugees from political oppression. This is the ultimate compliment. But it has a hidden danger within.

In human affairs no expectations as high as some people hold for America can be fully realized. "America can be seen as simultaneously inspiring dreams of salvation while conjuring aching feelings of disappointment."[33] As Italian author Giovanna Dell'Orto puts it, "Outside its borders, the United States *is* the American dream."[34] Much of the negative imagery America arouses is the inevitable result of the positive imagery in the same minds—positive imagery that cannot always be matched by the reality of a too-human America. As Charles Dickens admitted in 1842, "I am a Lover of Freedom, disappointed—That's all. . . . This is not the Republic I came to see. This is not the Republic of my imagination."[35] Take for instance the world's opinions regarding the actions of the Soviet Union and those of the United States: Soviet brutality was ignored or excused, but American imperfections of a lesser scale were denounced. This double standard is the result of the high expectations that came with American leadership, both self-professed and objectively measured. So long as perfection eludes humanity, disappointment will be the unavoidable shadow of America's position as the repository of the dreams of people everywhere.

The United States has always promoted itself as a special place, one of higher standards of moral and material well being. Its zealous promotion of its ideals has had the desired effect. Now, after raising the world's expectations, it is hard to avoid people's demands that it meet them.

However, these expectations often go beyond the United States' own pretensions. America has become an avatar for dreams originating in the mind of the observer. There are expectations that the United States, in its fiduciary capacity as the world's leading power, must act only in the interests of others. But it is a sovereign nation that first must tend to its own security and prosperity. The United States may not always tell the truth, come to the aid of virtue, treat its own citizens in accord with the highest standards, or practice what it preaches. To hold the United States up against a nation that only exists in the imagination is to hold it up to an impossible standard. It must fail. The admirer must be disillusioned and, in many cases, embittered. As an Egyptian newspaper editor observed, "After September 11, I tried in my articles to persuade my readers to feel that what had happened in New York was bad, but the truth is that a lot of people here felt that the Americans deserved it. A great many were simply glad that Big Brother had been given a sock under the chin."[36]

Such bitterness that America is not the place of the Dream is expressed as a generalized resentment. Consider the following rant against America during the Cold War by British author Jan Morris:

> Something snapped in me, and I faced up to a conviction I had been trying to stifle for years: the reluctant and terrible conviction that the greatest threat to the peace of humanity is the United States.
>
> I can no longer stomach America's insidious meddlings across the face of the world . . . wherever I go I find myself more and more repelled by the apparently insatiable American urge to interfere in other people's business.
>
> Nowadays I hardly believe a word official America says. I didn't believe your spokesmen about the Korean airliner . . . about Grenada and certainly do not believe them about Soviet intentions. . . .

The Soviets are less likely to trigger a World War III than you are yourselves.

Of course you are both paranoiac—two ideologically stunted giants . . . whose preposterous dinosauran posturings menace the survival of everyone. But the Russians have cause to be paranoiac! They are a grand and tragic nation.

But you! The most powerful, the most *enviable*, the richest, the most fortunate nation of the world. You have no excuse for paranoia.[37]

For Jan Morris it was nothing in particular that the United States did or said. It was just America and its place in the world that made "something snap" in her. The "something" seems to be the European expectation that "America's extraordinary power should not be used in ordinary ways. . . . America has the chance to be a unique power in history, not the latest in a long series of empires ultimately betrayed by their own exuberance."[38] As a nation, it could not measure up to the standards she had set for it. She then searched her store of negative imagery to expound on perceptions as remarkable as "paranoiac" and "dinosauran." This disappointment that the America of the real world failed to behave in perfect harmony with the place in her imagination or the place she believed it was obligated to be can become explosive. It is the anti-American blowback from fantasized, disillusioned philo-American idealism. These are the thoughts of some of America's "friends."

Disillusionment has an emotional charge, as does envy. They are not cool, considered intellectual conclusions. As powerful feelings, they are volatile and dangerous. Note the frequency among contemporary anti-Western terrorists of people who are from middle-class families who left their homelands in search of entrée to the modern, American-style societies of their dreams. Think of the story of Mohammed Atta, the September 11 leader from Egypt by way of a technical college in Hamburg, Germany. He did not start out rejecting modern, Western society. He wanted to be part of it. He wanted to be an engineer. Who knows what frustration he encountered on his way toward that ambition? Such people who harbor ideas of America that turn out to be unattainable in real life and disconnected from anything the real America says or does can descend to a fury of disappointment.

No nation can be expected to behave in a way that diverts the emotions of every fevered mind. However, the United States should try to live up to its own billing. In so doing, it must maintain an awareness of what expectations its friends and admirers hold for it. The United States can work to mitigate the obstacles people elsewhere encounter that block the fulfillment of their dreams. But the United States cannot be expected to campaign to debunk people's excessive dreams of America as a wonderful place—a place of wonder. For all the dangers that go with it, it is better to be envied than pitied and better to be admired than scorned.

11

ENHANCING THE IMAGE OF AMERICA STRATEGICALLY

Americans sit uneasily on the world's perch. They obsess over what other people think of them. It was not always so. More than one hundred years ago, the astute English observer James Bryce commented that "[the Americans] are now not more sensitive to external opinion than the nations of Western Europe, and less so than the Russians. . . . A foreign critic who tries to flout or scourge them no longer disturbs their composure; his jeers are received with amusement or indifference."[1] Throughout the Cold War, the Soviet propaganda machine pumped out a steady flow of attacks on everything the United States did and stood for. Critics in Europe, Latin America, and Asia staged frequent "Yankee Go Home" demonstrations. The People's Republic of China incessantly referred to Americans as "running dogs of capitalism." Westerners sympathetic to the USSR, including the 10 to 15 percent of voters who regularly voted for the communist party in France, Italy, and other friendly countries, echoed every attack. English philosopher Bertrand Russell declaimed,

> The United States today is a force for suffering, reaction and counter-revolution the world over. Wherever people are hungry and exploited, wherever they are oppressed and humiliated, the agency of this evil exists with the support and approval of the United States. . . . [The United States intervened in Vietnam] . . . to protect the continued control over the wealth of the region by American capitalists. . . . People have come to see the men

who control the United States Government as brutal bullies, acting in their own economic interest and exterminating any people foolhardy enough to struggle against this naked exploitation and aggression.[2]

In those days, scathing criticism did not faze Americans. They dismissed the vitriol. Americans saw the comments of their adversaries as angry words, nothing more. Now, with no organized adversary (but plenty of disorganized adversaries), Americans engage in perplexed self-examination as a response to every negative image expressed abroad.

While polling shows that, over time, positive foreign perceptions of America are more common than negative ones,[3] and while this book has explored an abundance of both positive and negative images, the negative views are the ones more frequently and more loudly voiced in the streets and the media of the world. People who support America and its positions may feel that, as the leading world power, it does not need an active expression of their approval. Applause is not news and does not find its way into the newspapers. Also, in the case of America, with its democratic system and its responsiveness to criticism, those who object to its policies hope that America will listen and be swayed by their views. There is some flattery implicit in these attacks. As the United States prepared for the 2003 war against Saddam Hussein's Iraq, the world erupted in anger expressed against America. Hardly a critical word was uttered against the tyrant Hussein, except seemingly obligatory expressions about his being a nasty dictator who should be removed somehow (but not by any forceful manner which the United States proposed).[4] Was it that the United States and its policies were so much more despised than Hussein, or was it that, unlike Washington, Baghdad was impervious to criticism?

In many nations in which free expression and demonstrations are not permitted, venting against alleged American treachery is practically the only state-sanctioned form of angry public political speech. Finally, expressions of the negatives may predominate in foreign discourse because anti-American predispositions are concentrated in the minds of those abroad who form the media and cultural elite, who regularly articulate their views publicly, and who are inclined to romanticism.

Americans are wise to be more thin-skinned than in the past and to take the critics seriously. The world has changed. It was always true that the images of America and of Americans affected commerce, immigration, and tourism. Now more than ever, foreign views of the United States also affect its national security. Security, national and otherwise, is the ability to control outcomes. It is the ability to be sure that ventures end well and unfortunate events either do not occur or their consequences are avoided or minimized. The American capacity to control outcomes unilaterally was never complete, but today everyone realizes that the United States cannot achieve its ends or confront threats to its welfare alone. In the 1990s Secretary of State Madeleine Albright called the United States "the indispensable nation" in its role in the Bosnian conflict. She meant that the United States was a required participant in any major international engagement that would succeed. Until the United States joined the project, the European Union had met no success in dealing with the former Yugoslavia. The United States was the critical ingredient. She did not assert that it could have succeeded by acting alone.

The risks of going it alone were on display in the invasion of Iraq in 2003. Despite the administration's claim of a "coalition of the willing" of over thirty nations, the refusal to participate and active interference of major nations such as France, Russia, China, and Germany harmed the war effort and tagged the entire engagement with the opprobrium of unilateralism. Turkey denied the United States entry to Iraq through its land, and the United Nations refused to take the burdens of occupation off of the shoulders of the United States. The United States bore the entire financial cost of the war. Post-war pacification was delayed by years.

Some of the increasing reliance on coalitions to solve international issues reflects shifting relative power relations. The United States, for all its economic power and unique military capability, as described earlier, is not far ahead of some other nations when they act together. Both its economic and military leads will increasingly become subject to challenge by aggregations of countries. In China's case the growth is both economic and military. In the case of the European Union, there is economic growth arising from the admission of new members and consolidation. Both can compete with the United States more closely than in the past. Also, the capability to frustrate American purposes grows when problems find their way to international bodies such as the United Nations and NATO, where the formal influence of the United States is as one vote among many. The power of the United States to persuade other nations to follow its lead on their own or in the context of a multinational organization is steadily shrinking as the spread of democracy and universal open communications have made many more national leaders, including autocratic leaders, responsive to the opinions of their populations. The United States can no longer discount the passions of the "Arab street" or any other street. The careful effort to provide Osama bin Laden an Islamic burial at sea is a reflection of this realization. All of these changes mean that the importance of the image of America abroad to the United States' foreign policy and its national security continues to grow. Resentments prevent collaboration. The future of American power lies in its ability to be at the center of all the varied webs of international relationships. The United States' reputation among the leaders and the people of other nations determines how well it can assume this role.

Another change propelling the importance of the image of America to national security is a paradoxical result of the United States' large military machine—the rise of asymmetrical warfare by non-state actors. Today's enemies frustrate the United States with small arms, conventional explosives, and ideas. The United States has declared a worldwide war against terror. It is actively fighting insurgencies in a number of countries in Asia, the Middle East, and Africa. Negative images of the United States are heavy burdens in these fights. In the Vietnam War, the United States spoke of the need to win the hearts and minds of the Vietnamese. However, the American military had no idea how to do so, made few attempts to do so, and failed in that effort and in the war. In Iraq and Afghanistan, this objective moved to the center of military strategy in American counterinsurgency doctrine. In June 2010 a young Afghan university student declared, "The Americans are here for their own reasons, for their own benefit. If they really wanted to bring peace to Afghanistan, they could have done so already, whoever was in charge."[5] To win in Afghanistan, the United States has to turn this image around. Relying on the Pentagon to burnish the nation's reputation speaks volumes on the role that images play in national security.

Given the importance of the images of the nation, how can the United States enhance them to its advantage? The ability of government to influence imagery of the nation is limited. Images of America are not features of America or its government; they are creatures of the minds of people abroad. Many of the images have been developed over centuries and change only gradually. The United States and its people can take actions that add to the store of images, but they cannot erase what is already in people's memories. Still, with a well conceived, selective approach, much can be achieved. The survey of imagery and the analysis of predispositions contained in the prior chapters of this volume offer guidance.

The enormous and varied supply of historic and recent imagery of the United States in the world's minds has been and remains a most valuable asset. America is still the globe's finest national brand. This truth leads to a fundamental operational principle: do not sell to people what they have already bought. Instead, focus on the image problems that affect the United States, and deal with them. Even America's archenemies recognize that it developed a republican and democratic form of government and is a proponent of that philosophy. They acknowledge that it advocates personal freedom and human rights, free markets, progress, modernity, and scientific and technological advancement. Irreconcilable anti-Americans know the United States is a rich nation—and they hate it all the more for it. They know it prizes individuality, and they scorn that. They fly American airplanes, use American computers and software, occasionally drive American cars, often wear American brands of clothing, frequently eat at McDonald's, and regularly watch American films and television. Those are undisputed features of American imagery for friend and foe alike. Admiration for them does not improve behavior. Attempts to propagate these images are redundant and meaningless at best.

This was not always so. During the Cold War, totalitarian governments were quite successful in hiding the facts of life outside from their people. The Soviet Union managed to sell to its population the idea that they were living in a worker's paradise. Richard Nixon's Kitchen Debate and the American display of consumer wares that surrounded it in Moscow made sense as an effective stroke against the negative imagery of Russian propaganda. Now, with the end of hermetically sealed societies and the growth of the Internet and global communication, only North Korea seems to have some success hiding the facts from its people. Now, the image of American wealth needs no marketing abroad.

Some well-known aspects of American life that seem like virtues to Americans can unexpectedly backfire. In the immediate aftermath of September 11, the Bush administration retained advertising executive Charlotte Beers as its undersecretary of state for public diplomacy and public affairs. She generated an advertising campaign shown in the Arab world focusing on the happy, prosperous lives of Arab Americans to counter the idea that the United States is anti-Arab or anti-Muslim. The campaign was derided for its ineffectiveness and obtuse misunderstanding of the mindset of the Arab audience. Arabs in poor homelands know well the prosperity of their cousins who managed to do what they cannot: emigrate to the United States. As with the nineteenth-century German émigrés whom Friedrich Gerstäcker derided as criminals and scoundrels, those who leave are often not admired by those who are left behind. Prosperous Arab Americans have achieved a dream that is denied to those who cannot get visas or who for other reasons cannot follow in their footsteps. Showing the success of other Arabs heightened the sting of thwarted ambition in societies where envy is a natural, open response. Showing that those who managed to enter through the gauntlet of American impediments to immigration are doing well is not pleasing to those left behind; it is infuriating. The Bush administration needed to understand the image of acceptance and prosperity through the lens of the average foreign Arab person's predisposition toward the émigrés.

The analysis of predispositions must guide the effort to enhance the imagery of the United States. Since there are images enough in every mind to support positive or negative opinions, attention should focus on the ways of thinking that summon the imagery. Change them and you change the expressions of imagery. Persuasion will not change predispositions against the United States based on devotion to traditional culture and religion, holding a privileged position in an old way of life, and commitment to a romantic world view. On the other hand, predispositions based on admiration which might morph into resentment in the face of frustration, as with envy and disappointment, are important targets to affect opinions. These are the emotionally tinged love-hate relationships that are fluid and offer both danger and opportunity to the United States. To the extent that the American concern with its image is concentrated on national security and foreign policy, it should target its efforts on these predispositions and images that are volatile and important.

There are repeated themes voiced by people abroad who resent the United States in ways that convey disappointment in its policies or a kind of unrequited love that smacks of frustration and envy. If the United States can establish the following five positive images in the minds of foreign observers, it would deal with most of these critical concerns of foreign publics:

- The United States is steadfast and honors its commitments.
- The United States is an open society with an open mind.
- The United States accepts its obligation to act in the interests of others.
- The United States is compassionate to others and cares about their personal safety.
- The United States acts consistently with its philosophical principles of democracy and human rights.

These are the images that matter in executing foreign policies based on the need for collaboration with other nations. These are the areas in which the United States must overcome foreign skepticism. There are other images that matter in international commerce and culture, such as technological skill, quality, glamour, etc., but they need not be the focus of promotion by the government. Government should legislate and negotiate the environment in which the free flow of commercial goods, services, and cultural activities flourish, but it can rely on the private sector, with its enormous advertising budgets, to trumpet these marketing virtues abroad.[6] On the other hand, advancing crucial images that affect how the nation conducts its international affairs depends on the government. Sometimes these messages can best be sent by the practice of public diplomacy—communicating directly with foreign populations about American actions and intentions. At the same time, to be trusted, the United States must live by its own description.

Considering the first of these images, steadfastness and reliability are qualities best exemplified by action rather than words. A reputation for inconstancy that comes from a history of changing administrations and priorities worries potential partners. In the giant game of poker that is international relations, being caught bluffing a few times too many is disastrous. The concern that the United States had too often threatened and too seldom acted during the George H. W. Bush and Clinton administrations was among the motivating factors in George W. Bush's decision to carry out his threats to invade Iraq in the face of vocal international opposition.

In that case and many others, there are those who say they despise the United States both for the nature of its policies and for not clinging to them resolutely. Of course, ineffective and unwise policies should not stubbornly be pursued, and the voices of foreign and domestic critics may accurately point out flaws in policies. However, if a policy is the wise course for the United States, it is right not only to maintain it but also to explain it and defend it. Changing policies to appease foreign critics would be inappropriate and counterproductive. The people who oppose the United States because it supports a position or a group that they dislike are likely to see a change in American policy in response to such complaints as a sign of irresolution, vulnerability, and confusion. Any support the United States wins from such critics is likely to be momentary at best. Most often, such tactical reversals win no support at all. Abandoning one side of a dispute to please the followers of the other side invites the bitter enmity of the jilted party while making no friends among their enemies. Also, in insurgencies, as in Afghanistan, people who have to choose between the Americans and the local adversaries will choose the locals, however much they might fear and despise them, if they think the Americans will abandon them.

The second image, that the United States is an open society, is an article of faith among Americans, but not among people elsewhere. Once in the United States, people are free to move and free to prosper if they can. The nation's reputation for opportunity for those within its borders is secure and deserved. However, the exclusionary nature of its immigration laws and even its rules affecting tourist and business visitors are legendary and deeply resented abroad. Lately, the debates about undocumented aliens, whose illegal presence is a side effect of the exclusionary laws, have exacerbated the image of America as a closed society. The barred door turns all the good images of life in the United States into sources of resentment so that the image of closure has a multiplier effect in building ill will. "Yes, it is good, but only for the privileged few." Here too actions will trump words. An immigration reform that mixes a more generous, gracious, and efficient route for more people to make legal entry with more consistent enforcement of immigration laws (and fair treatment for the people now in the country illegally) will help. For temporary visitors, who are more numerous than immigrants, the nation must streamline its visa process and treat applicants with courtesy and efficiency that is presently lacking. Changes in these areas will not need to be sold to people; they will see them personally. As in the cases of Fadi, Muhammad Fawaz, and the Arab viewers of Charlotte Beers's commercials, avoiding the sting of rejection prevents admiration from curdling into resentment and vengeance.

Being a physically open society is a start. The United States must also be an emotionally and intellectually open society. America's old image of being inward looking and ignorant of the rest of the world has not dissipated. It has grown. This is inconsistent with world leadership. To genuinely be open to other ideas, its government must listen to others. If the United States ignores the views of others, it adds to their resentments. The Cairo newspaper *Al-Ahram* editorialized, "We must stand up and postulate the outrageous assumption that in order for us to know the American people, appreciate their ideals and value system, they will have to know the same about us, the Arabs."[7] A fourteen-year-old Jordanian girl commented, "We should be telling the Americans what is happening here. . . . They don't understand us. They think they know us. I have nothing against Americans. I just don't like the way they think."[8]

Karen Hughes, when she was undersecretary of state for public diplomacy and public affairs in the George W. Bush administration, covered the world on listening tours. Since then, the Obama administration has modestly increased the budget for public diplomacy in the State Department and instructed the embassies around the world to expand their exposure to people "outside the traditional elites" of the nations to which they are posted.[9] In his address in Cairo in 2009, President Obama, said, "There must be a sustained effort to listen to each other; to learn from each other; to respect one another; and to seek common ground."[10] These sentiments recognize the importance of this issue, but they have raised expectations and run the risk of disappointment, with its attendant dangers.

Listening to others will never be easy. Bureaucracies do not listen well to anyone. All nations, not just great powers, have their own priorities. Nations' foreign policies cannot be tailored to suit foreign opinion. However, in listening to others, the United States will learn (at least it will learn what they are thinking), and the act of listening itself is an emollient. In some ways, the relationship between the United States, in the glory of its power, and the many smaller nations of the world is metaphorically parental. To the junior partner in this relationship, there is nothing worse than being ignored. The only thing the Pakistanis have decried more than the involvement of the United States in their affairs is the period after the Afghan war of the 1980s in which they say the United States ignored them. The act of listening will be noticed and appreciated. The efficacy of this process can be seen in the practices of American soldiers in Iraq and Afghanistan, where consultations with village elders have become a major part of their engagement. It works.

Listening is only one step in being responsible for the well being of others. Overwhelming American power disenfranchises all non-Americans. People everywhere have become dependent on the United States to act on their behalf because it is often the only nation that can. Americans must accept the obligations that come with unfettered power over the lives of others—the obligations to act in their interest as well as in America's own interest and to take into account their views. This is not noblesse oblige in the traditional sense, arising from self-important social pretensions or from unfairly imposed colonial mastery. It is the necessary result of having power, even legitimately attained power, over other people's futures. Therefore, Americans must be concerned with criticism from abroad to a degree that is far greater than in all prior ages when they competed with the Soviets or with a group of other powers for world leadership.

The image that America acts only in its self-interest is one of the most deeply ingrained current critiques of the United States. It is partly driven by the need of any American government to justify major foreign initiatives domestically on the basis of the self-interest of American taxpayers. The domestic arguments receive full attention abroad. Typically, there is a multiplicity of motivations for any act by the government or anyone else, and the ones emphasized will be those thought to be most persuasive to the audience in question. The skeptic abroad will latch onto the self-interested logic sold to the American audience as the only reason to act, and consider high-minded rhetoric about his nation's best interests to be a cover story. In view of the mixed motives in all such actions, the critic is seldom entirely wrong. In World War I the Wilson administration had to justify war as a way to make the world "safe for [American] democracy," as opposed to the Fourteen Points of high-minded objectives that came later. When the American public heard the broader noble goals, they recoiled from them and the burden of international responsibility they would have imposed on the United States. Franklin Roosevelt could not justify engaging in World War II before there was an attack on American soil. In

Vietnam Lyndon Johnson needed to concoct an attack on an American destroyer as a provocation.

Nations normally act only in their own interests. The United States is unique in its pretension to broader principles and its determination to spread them by example or by intervention. People elsewhere, and not just people with an anti-American predisposition, will not take at face value American protestations of disinterested motivations. Thus, in Iraq the charge that the invasion was carried out to obtain Iraqi oil has been given worldwide currency despite the fact that the United States could have bought all the oil it wanted from Saddam Hussein if it abandoned its own boycott. When actions by the United States involve military force or occupation, the other inevitable charge is that the motivation is to assert imperial control. In its position of world power, the United States is closely scrutinized by people everywhere alert to any sign of neocolonialism. Denying these accusations in a public relations campaign only gives them credence. The only cure for these charges is to be true to the principles that the United States announced for its action and leave when the job is over. Over time, repeated faithfulness to announced purposes will reinforce the image of acting unselfishly and turn the critics who are subject to being turned.

Both listening to others and acting in the interest of others are special duties attending the position of world leadership. They come from the fiduciary relationship that pushes aside the usual expectations of sovereignty. Consistent therewith, there is a general expectation that the United States will show compassion for those who suffer poverty, injury, and disease. It must not ignore a tsunami in Indonesia and Thailand, an earthquake in Haiti, or an earthquake and flood in Pakistan or Japan. It cannot be indifferent to disease and genocide in Africa. These tragedies are opportunities, and in most cases the United States has been alert and useful in being first on the scene, often ahead of the local government. For a nation searching for ways to prove its goodwill, such calamities provide the demonstrations. With that in mind, the anti-American government of Myanmar and the Taliban in the mountains of Pakistan both forbade humanitarian outreach from America in the face of killer floods, claiming that the United States was really attempting to infiltrate the region with spies. In Nigeria Muslim populations were told by their clerics to avoid polio shots because the Americans were trying to kill their children in an anti-Muslim plot. These sorts of reactions by adversaries testify to the effectiveness of massive acts of compassion in affecting predispositions toward America. Conversely, as the dominant power with a global reach, the United States' failure to appear at disaster sites promptly and effectively would invite blame for the entire catastrophe.

To make compassionate intervention work, the nation must not be shy in claiming credit—but only to the extent it is deserved. Packages of food should be marked as "A Gift from the USA." News of the work being accomplished should be broadly circulated. In the business of persuasion, there is no benefit to misplaced modesty. Besides, the display of American efforts spurs on greater gifts by other countries that wish to share the limelight.

The attention to natural disasters and disease highlight a basic fact about human existence: people care most deeply about personal safety for them and their families. This pertains to the images of America in war zones. As the United States uses lethal force in pursuit of its interests or principles or for the benefit of others, it destroys lives and shatters the sense of personal safety of many whose lives are not directly touched. Military action will always disrupt personal security. It kills people. It closes schools, disrupts water and electricity, and wrecks buildings and roads. Plans for children's futures are set aside. Businesses are shut and family wealth obliterated. The American government sees higher stakes. The American government might see the benefits of a more responsive, less brutal regime to be created in the country. The American government might see the greater safety to be gained in the region by the removal of a tyrant who is a threat to broader peace. Often, the local population sees little of that.

The counterinsurgency strategy of the United States military acknowledges that limiting collateral damage to the lives of people in war zones is critical to the image of America. More than ever in the past, it has taken on the tasks of building schools where they were destroyed or where they never existed, making water and electricity available to the civilians, and policing communities to assure personal safety. Their enemies confirm the importance of this issue by sabotaging these activities. They attack their countrymen (and coreligionists) in Iraq, Afghanistan, and Pakistan to demonstrate the failure of the Americans and the American-supported central government to deliver personal security. Most people are apolitical. They care deeply about their own safety and futures and those of their children. Satisfying these concerns in the midst of a destructive conflict is a struggle that is central to both winning these wars and establishing the image of compassion that is inseparable from world leadership. As a result, the United States military has become its most important tool of public diplomacy.

The final critical subject to target is the widespread image of American hypocrisy. If the United States is to maintain its leadership position in a world where it must rally other nations and people to its side, it must be seen to tell the truth. As discussed earlier, the United States is constituted in ways that invite the accusation of hypocrisy. It is a nation founded on broad statements of principle. Its people identify as Americans not by their genealogy but by their acceptance of the liberal democratic principles of the Constitution. Over the years the principles have grown in number. In application they often conflict. Moreover, there are many times when national security dictates that principles be abandoned. In this fashion, the United States has backed numerous dictators over the years. Were it a normal nation and not founded on oft-proclaimed principles, no one would care. But it is not a normal nation, and the accusation stings. It is at the heart of the predisposition of disappointment.

Advancing these five ideas globally would create a much greater receptivity to American foreign policy initiatives in this increasingly collaborative world. To do so, the United States will have to implement a modern and reinvigorated outreach program. All the tools of public diplomacy must be used. Historically, the United States had been effective in speaking to foreign publics. Through the Cold War, it used the CIA and the United States Information Agency (USIA) to reach across the Iron Curtain and inform populations that were starved for real news. In the 1990s, with the Soviet confrontation over and with news freely available in most of the world, the USIA was dismantled, its global system of facilities closed, and its radio stations transferred to the Broadcasting Board of Governors. Radio Free Europe, the Voice of America, and the other stations stayed on the air, but the other public diplomacy functions languished. After September 11, the Bush administration sought to rejuvenate this effort with renewed funding and attention. It tried, unsuccessfully, to broadcast advertisements on existing Middle Eastern media. It started its own radio and television broadcast networks in the Middle East, Radio Sawa and Al-hurra. The State Department resumed sponsoring goodwill trips by entertainers and other cultural figures. There have been calls for it to reopen the American libraries that used to be common features in third-world capitals,[11] as well as various suggestions that a public/private partnership like the Corporation for Public Broadcasting be set up to fund and direct such activities.[12] The Obama administration's Public Diplomacy and Public Affairs Office has declared its intention to open American Centers and American Corners in foreign cities to showcase American culture and technology and fill the gap left by closing the libraries.[13] With these and all other tools of the public relations profession, the United States can explain why and how it acts abroad.

To be effective, an information campaign in any medium has to be well conceived and audience tested. It cannot be patronizing or unbelievable. It is best when telling the truth plainly. A well-executed broadcast and Internet public diplomacy program focused on the five messages outlined above would be aimed at mitigating the predispositions borne of frustration and disappointment in people's minds. It would spread popular American culture, and transmit word of American political and social programs, give straightforward news of events in and about America, and offer a friendly outlet for the dissemination of the messages that the American government wants to convey. Moreover, it would operate interactively and listen to people abroad. It would speak in their languages; use local spokespeople rather than Americans; offer non-political programming as well as news; offer choices rather than dictate what can be seen and heard. Most importantly, it would build a reputation for honesty. Its credibility would set it apart from the other sources of information. There is no escape from the need to do this robustly. World opinion cannot be surrendered to foreign governments, the press corps, or the bloggers of the World Wide Web.

There are still limits to what can be achieved in influencing the minds of others. Whatever the United States does, there are some people who harbor antagonistic predispositions and who will not accept new imagery or opinions. Enlightened American policies and communication will not help with the people in the West and the developing world who are hoping for the failure of America and Western bourgeois society. Such people are irreconcilable, and Americans need to live with that. Americans will have to live in the same world with Pakistani journalist Ansar Abbasi, who told Judith A. McHale, President Obama's undersecretary of state for public diplomacy, "You should know that we hate all Americans. From the bottom of our souls, we hate you."[14] Dedicated xenophobes, romantics, and those in traditional societies whose positions are threatened by change shun reconciliation with the United States. At a given moment they might express hatred only of a particular American president or policy, but they hated the predecessor and will hate the successor too. As in the case of most fears and prejudices, the problem is within them rather than with the object of their fixation. For someone who despises all things foreign, the United States will always be an outsider. For a devotee of the romantic worldview centered on Wagnerian heroism, mysticism, lyricism, decline, and irrationality, the United States is a foil. To his mind it represents the contrast with all that he values. As such, nothing the United States does can be accepted. For the person whose life is defined by opposition to real or imagined oppression by the establishment, the leading power, whoever it is, becomes and remains the target of his ire. All its acts are despised. To a member of the elite in ancient societies such as a shaman, an imam, or a warlord, whose way of life will be threatened by change, the American position as leader of the new way, the Western way, makes America a permanent enemy. The practical concern these people have for the loss of their status and well-being may be magnified by traditional and religious modes of thinking that attribute bad events to the connivance of the devil. For them, romanticism and traditionalism merge. The United States becomes the personification of the devil. It cannot better its image in their minds by good policies, good deeds, or good words.

These are people whose attitudes are not subject to persuasion and who will ascribe the worst images to the United States regardless of its demonstrated intentions and actions and regardless of any artful programs of public diplomacy. Only by falling from its top spot as the leading world power and as the avatar of liberal democracy can the United States avoid their contempt. The nineteenth-century European powers, who invented the Western system and who ruled so many colonial peoples, have now escaped opprobrium by the expedient of continually declining in power and influence. The anticolonial America that succeeded them is called upon to pay a price for their imperialist pasts. The Europeans, with their minuscule defense budgets and self-abasing language, do not mind having America bear the burden of imagery for the entire West. It is the price for occupying the seat of primacy in the world.

Those holding the irreconcilable predispositions of romanticism, traditionalism, and the like are adversaries. America must treat them as such. It does not need to wring its hands over each unfair accusation, obsessively examining the mirror to see if its face is really as ugly as they say. Often, accusations hurled at the United States by its adversaries are words used as weapons rather than words that convey meaning.

America can take comfort that the implacable standard-bearers of autocracy and nostalgia are fighting losing, rear-guard actions. That accounts, in part, for the bitterness of their attacks. Antiestablishment ideas are, by definition, the views of those in the minority and out of power. Romanticism is the specialty of European and other Western elites who resent the dominance of the middle class. Except in the days of fascism in Europe, romanticism has always been a minority view and only appears to be otherwise because of the strategic placement of its disciples in the arts, the media, and academia. The Western middle class shows no signs of adopting their worldview or of surrendering political power to the intelligentsia. Extreme voices decrying secular moral corruption, and repressing normal human enjoyments such as dancing, singing, and flirting have had their moments of ascendency, from Girolamo Savonarola to Oliver Cromwell to Mullah Omar and the Taliban. But those moments prove to be brief, as humans need little persuasion to throw off such shackles. Finally, the developing world traditionalists who are unalterably opposed to modernization are a minority because the nature of traditional societies gives valuable positions only to a few. This minority is shrinking because it is clear to most people that a return to a mythical past is impossible. Once changed by outside influences, the old ways are irretrievable. Most of the people in traditional societies who exhibit anti-American predispositions do so out of frustration with the failure of their government and the United States to promptly deliver the new way of life to them, rather than by the possibility that such a new way of life would be undesirable. When a door opens in the wall of frustration and a path appears toward the modern world, anti-American rhetoric subsides.

America remains the most powerfully attractive symbol of a nation. The great challenge for American public diplomacy is to support and perpetuate the belief in the open minds of a majority of people everywhere that their dream of America is tangible and attainable; that the America they imagine is the America of the real world. To succeed, the United States has to reinforce the particular positive images which support that belief. If it does so, over time, as in the past, the nation will continue to enjoy a world that speaks of it in admiration.

Notes

Preface
1. Jean-Marie Colombani, "We Are All Americans," *Le Monde*, September 12, 2001.
2. Jean-Marie Colombani, "We Are All Un-American," *Le Monde*, May 15, 2004.
3. Pew Research Center, *U.S. Image Up Slightly, But Still Negative* (Washington, DC: The Pew Global Attitudes Project, 2005), 1. [Hereafter cited as *Pew Survey 2005.*]
4. Andrew Roberts, "While America Slept," *American Spectator*, February 2009, 22.
5. Pew Research Center, *Confidence in Obama Lifts U.S. Image Around the World* (Washington, DC: The Pew Global Attitudes Project, 2009). [Hereafter cited as *Pew Survey 2009.*]
6. Pew Research Center, *Obama More Popular Abroad Than at Home, Global Image of U.S. Continues to Benefit* (Washington, DC: The Pew Global Attitudes Project, 2010).
7. Pew Research Center, *U.S. Favorability Ratings Remain Positive: China Seen Overtaking U.S. as Global Superpower* (Washington, DC: The Pew Global Attitudes Project, 2011). [Hereafter cited as *Pew Survey 2011.*]

Chapter 1. Introduction
1. Hans Magnus Enzensberger, "What We Think of America," *Granta* 77, 76 (Spring 2002): 36.
2. The term "America" has been used to describe the entire Western hemisphere. However, in this book it is used to describe the United States of America.
3. See *Pocket World in Figures, 2011 Edition* (London: Economist Newspaper, 2010). [Hereafter cited as *Economist Figures 2011.*]
4. State Department, http://www.usembassy.gov.
5. Anne-Marie Slaughter, "America's Edge," *Foreign Affairs*, 88 (January/February 2009): 104.

6. George Washington, farewell address, September 19, 1796.
7. Bret Stephens, "What Ahmadinejad Knows," *Wall Street Journal*, September 28, 2010.
8. Graham Turner, "Travels in the Muslim World," *Daily Telegraph* (London), September 3, 2002.
9. John Gray, "What We Think of America," *Granta* 77, 76 (Spring 2002): 37.
10. CBS News, "Eyewitness: How Accurate is Visual Memory?" July 12, 2009, http://www.cbsnews.com/stories/2009/03/06/60minutes/main 4848039_page4.shtml?tag=contentMain;contentBody.
11. Bernard-Henri Lévy, *American Vertigo: Traveling America in the Footsteps of Tocqueville* (New York: Random House, 2007).
12. George Berkeley, "A Treatise Concerning the Principles of Human Knowledge," in *Basic Problems of Philosophy*, eds. Daniel J. Bronstein, Yervant H. Krikorian, and Philip P. Weiner, 3rd ed. (New York: Prentice Hall, 1964), 294, 296.
13. Ibid., 294–295.
14. Harold R. Isaacs, *Scratches on Our Minds: American Views of China and India* (White Plains, NY: M. E. Sharpe, 1980).
15. Ibid., 79.
16. Ibid., 83.
17. Ibid., 91.
18. Ibid., 99.
19. Ibid., 408.
20. Ibid., xxviii.
21. F. Scott Fitzgerald, "The Crack-up," *Esquire*, February 1936, http://www .esquire.com/features/the-crack-up.
22. Andy Warhol, *America* (New York: Harper & Row, 1985), 8.

Chapter 2. Imprints from Inside America

1. Alain Minc, "Terrorism of the Spirit," *Council on Foreign Relations Correspondence* 9 (Spring 2002): 10.
2. Louis Hartz, *The Liberal Tradition in America; An Interpretation of American Political Thought Since the Revolution* (New York: Harcourt, Brace, 1955), 62–63.
3. Alan Charles Kors, "Francois-Jean Marquis de Chastellux," in *Abroad in America: Visitors to the New Nation 1776–1914*, eds. Marc Pachter and Frances Stevenson Wein (Washington, DC: Smithsonian Institution, 1976), 3.
4. Matt. 5:14–16 (New Testament, New International Version, 2011), referred to in Winthrop's sermon on the deck of the *Arabella* off the coast of Massachusetts.
5. Ivan Klíma, "What We Think of America," *Granta* 77, 76 (Spring 2002): 52.
6. Mark Lilla, "America the Pop," *Council on Foreign Relations Correspondence* 9 (Spring 2002): 52.
7. Stanley K. Schultz, "Foreign Immigrants in Industrial America," University of Wisconsin, http://us.history.wisc.edu/hist102/lectures/textonly /lecture08.html.
8. Norbert Muhlen, "America and American Occupation in German Eyes," *Annals of the American Academy of Political and Social Science* 295 (September 1954): 53. [Hereafter cited as Muhlen, *German Eyes*.]

9. Richard Ruland, *America in Modern European Literature: From Image to Metaphor* (New York: New York University Press, 1976), 48–49.
10. Geoffrey Wheatcroft, "Smiley's (Anti-American) People," *New York Times*, January 11, 2004.
11. Anné Kulonen, interview by the author, January 28, 2010.
12. Bill Donahue, "The Boys From Brazil," *The Atlantic*, March 2010, 24–25.
13. Alexis de Tocqueville, *Democracy in America*, trans. and eds. Harvey C Mansfield and Delba Winthrop (Chicago: University of Chicago Press, 2000), 59. [Hereafter cited as Tocqueville, *Democracy*.]
14. Ibid., 359.
15. John L. O'Sullivan, "The Great Nation of Futurity," *The United States Democratic Review* 6, 23 (November 1839): 429–30.
16. Woodrow Wilson, speech to Senate, July 10, 1919.
17. Robert F. Kennedy, speech announcing candidacy for president, March 16, 1968.
18. George W. Bush, speech at B'nai B'rith Convention, August 28, 2000.
19. Muhlen, *German Eyes*, 53.
20. Tocqueville, *Democracy*, 274.
21. Ibid.
22. See Francis Fukuyama, *Trust: The Social Virtues and The Creation of Prosperity* (New York: Free Press, 1995).
23. Muhlen, *German Eyes*, 58.
24. Tocqueville, *Democracy*, 506.
25. Albert Gleason, "Pavel Svin'in," in *Abroad in America: Visitors to the New Nation, 1776–1914*, eds. Marc Pachter and Frances Stevenson Wein (Washington, DC: Smithsonian Institution, 1976), 16.
26. Luc Sante, "Abundance," in *The American Effect: Global Perspectives on the United States*, ed. Lawrence Rinder (New York: Whitney Museum of American Art, 2003), 63.
27. Chauncey M. Depew, "American Supremacy: Industrial; Commercial; Financial," in *The Great Republic By the Master Historians*, vol. 1, ed. Hubert H. Bancroft (Whitefish, Montana: Kessinger Publishing: 2004), http://www.publicbookshelf.com/public_html/The_Great_Republic_By_the _Master_Historians_Vol_IV/usindustr_ea.html.
28. Paul Halsall, ed., *Modern History Sourcebook*, Fordham University, http://www.fordham.edu/halsall/mod/indrevtabs1.html.
29. Frances Trollope, *Domestic Manners of the Americans* (London: Penguin Books, 1997), 236. [Hereafter cited as Trollope, *Manners*.]
30. Ibid., 40.
31. Geoffrey Wheatcroft, "Smiley's (Anti-American) People," *New York Times*, January 11, 2004.
32. Tocqueville, *Democracy*, 428.
33. Nikolaus Lenau in Lenau to Emile von Reinbeck, March 5, 1833, from *Nikolaus Lenau: Samtliche Werke und Briefe* (Frankfurt: Insel-Verrl, 1971), as quoted in James W. Ceaser, *Reconstructing America: The Symbol of America in Modern Thought* (New Haven, CT: Yale University Press, 1997), 170. [Hereafter cited as Ceaser, *Reconstructing America*.]
34. http://www.brainyquote.com/quotes/authors/g/georges_clemenceau .html.
35. Tocqueville, *Democracy*, 431.

36. Moiseide Ostrogorski, quoted in Larry Bartels, "Economic Amnesia Buoys Incumbents," *Los Angeles Times*, June 20, 2004.
37. Muhlen, *German Eyes*, 54.
38. Thomas Jefferson, first inaugural address, March 4, 1801.
39. Robert Stone, introduction to *The Quiet American*, by Graham Greene (New York: Penguin Books, 2004), xiii.
40. Peter Schneider, "Across a Great Divide: Europe and America," *New York Times*, March 13, 2004.
41. James Hamilton-Paterson, "What We Think of America," *Granta* 77, 76 (Spring 2002): 46.
42. Tsetsegee Munkhbayar, interview by the author, September 17, 2008.
43. Importation of new slaves was banned effective 1808.
44. Thomas Moore, "Epistle to Lord Viscount Forbes" (1804), quoted in Trollope, *Manners*, 189.
45. Tocqueville, *Democracy*, 346.
46. United Nations Commission on Human Rights, Sub-Commission on the Promotion and Protection of Human Rights, Fifty-Second Session, *Report of the Working Group on Contemporary Forms of Slavery on its Twenty-Fifth Session* (July 2000).
47. Asian immigration essentially was forbidden by law until well into the twentieth century.
48. Stanley K. Schultz, "Foreign Immigrants in Industrial America," University of Wisconsin, http://us.history.wisc.edu/hist102/lectures/textonly lecture08.html.
49. Comments by fictional character Berel Isaac, quoted in Bel Kaufman, "Sholom Aleichem," *Abroad in America: Visitors to the New Nation 1776–1914*, eds. Marc Pachter and Frances Stevenson Wein (Washington, DC: Smithsonian Institution, 1976), 276.
50. Klíma, "What We Think of America," 52.
51. *Economist Figures 2011*, 128, 236, 246.
52. See Pew Research Center, "Summary of Findings," *A Year After Iraqi War* (Washington, DC: The Pew Research Center for the People and the Press, March 16, 2004), 4. [Hereafter cited as *Pew Survey One Year After War.*]
53. Lian Yang, "What We Think of America," *Granta* 77, 76 (Spring 2002): 56.
54. Nathan Gardels and Mike Medavoy, *American Idol After Iraq* (Chichester, West Sussex, UK: Wiley-Blackwell, 2009), 14.
55. Tocqueville, *Democracy*, 310–11.
56. Joshua Kurlant, "Thai Noon," *The Atlantic*, June 2008, 119.
57. Maia De la Baume, "French Festival Is a Little Bit Country, a Little Bit Wine'n'Cheese," *New York Times International*, August 6, 2009.
58. George C. Marshall, statement of May 29, 1942, in *Religion, Conflict and Military Intervention*, eds. Rosemary Durward and Lee Marsden, (Burlington, VT: Ashgate Publishing, 2009), 115.
59. Nichole M. Christian, "Duty Calls, and 'There Goes John Wayne,'" *New York Times*, April 13, 2003; and David M. Halbfinger and John W. Fountain, "In the U.S., Elation Wrestles With Anxiety," *New York Times*, April 13, 2003.
60. "This Country is Truly Open to You," *Los Angeles Times*, September 1, 2004.
61. Lech Walesa, "In Solidarity," *Wall Street Journal*, June 11, 2004.
62. David E. Nye, *America as Second Creation: Technology and Narratives of New Beginnings* (Cambridge: MIT Press, 2003), 119.

63. Fredrika Bremer, *The Homes of the New World: Impressions of America*, trans. Mary Howitt, vol. 1 (New York: Harper & Brothers, 1858), 544–545.
64. Tocqueville, *Democracy*, 21.
65. Charles Dickens, "Letter to John Foster March 28, 1842," in *Dickens on America & The Americans*, ed. Michael Slater (Austin: University of Texas Press, 1978), 94–95.
66. Georges Duhamel, "America The Menace: Scenes from the Life of the Future," in *Broken Image: Foreign Critiques of America*, ed. Gerald Emanuel Stearn (New York: Random House, 1972), 231. [Hereafter cited as *Broken Image*.]

Chapter 3. American Footprints Abroad
1. Philippe Roger in *Conversations françaises: Les Relations transatlantiques* (Nashville, TN: Champs-Elysees, 2003), 17.
2. Giovanna Dell'Orto, *The Hidden Power of the American Dream* (Santa Barbara, CA: Praeger Security International, 2008), 51–53.
3. Victor Davis Hanson, *Ripples of Battle* (New York: Doubleday, 2003), 202.
4. Pramoedya Ananta Toer, "Freedom," in *American Effect: Global Perspectives on the United States, 1990–2003*, ed. Lawrence Rinder (New York: Whitney Museum of American Art, 2003), 47, 48, and 51.
5. George W. Bush, speech to the National Endowment for Democracy, November 6, 2003.
6. George W. Bush, speech at Banqueting House, London, England, November 19, 2003.
7. Barack Obama, speech at Cairo University, June 4, 2009.
8. Barack Obama, speech at United States Military Academy, May 22, 2010. See also, Barack Obama speech on Mideast and North African policy at State Department, May 19, 2011.
9. Babak Dehghanpsheh, "Now We Have America," *Newsweek*, April 7, 2003, 35.
10. Muhlen, *German Eyes*, 55.
11. Ibid., 56.
12. Jacques Freymond, "America in European Eyes," *The Annals of the American Academy of Political and Social Science* 295 (September 1954): 37. [Hereafter cited as Freymond, *European Eyes*.]
13. Barack Obama, Nobel Peace Prize acceptance speech, December 10, 2009.
14. Muhlen, *German Eyes*, 59.
15. Peter Schneider, "Across a Great Divide: Europe and America," *New York Times*, March 13, 2004.
16. Jessica Stern, *Terror in the Name of God: Why Religious Militants Kill* (New York: HarperCollins, 2003), 275.
17. Samuel P. Huntington, *The Clash of Civilizations and the Remaking of World Order* (New York: Simon & Schuster, 1996), 310.
18. Freymond, *European Eyes*, 37.
19. Herbert Passin and John W. Bennett, "The America-educated Japanese, II, Images After Return to Japan," *The Annals of the American Academy of Political and Social Science* 295 (September 1954), 105.
20. "Pakistan: 'A Front-Line Ally' on Terrorism," *Los Angeles Times*, February 2, 2003.
21. See Robert Kagan, *Of Paradise and Power* (New York: Alfred A. Knopf, 2003), 37–41.

22. It is also notable that American strength and reliability are what allow nations under its defense guarantees, such as Taiwan, South Korea, and Japan, to avoid acquiring their own weapons of mass destruction.
23. Tariq Ali, "Hegemony," in *American Effect: Global Perspectives on the United States, 1990–2003*, ed. Lawrence Rinder (New York: Whitney Museum of American Art, 2003), 123, 133.
24. Charles Powell, "Our American Guest," *Wall Street Journal*, November 17, 2003.
25. Richard Bernstein, "Respect for US Falls in a Post-Iraq World," *New York Times*, September 11, 2003.
26. Edward Said, "Global Crisis Over Iraq," in *American Effect: Global Perspectives on the United States, 1990–2003*, ed. Lawrence Rinder (New York: Whitney Museum of American Art, 2003), 159.
27. Fazlur Rahman Khalil (leader of Pakistani terrorist group, Harkat-ul-Mujahideen), quoted by Stern, *Terror in the Name of God*, 199.
28. *Pew Survey One Year After War*, 3.
29. Transcript of "Meet the Press," April 11, 2004, 2.
30. Megan K. Stack, "To Many Arabs, The U.S. And U.N. Are One Entity," *Los Angeles Times*, August 21, 2003.
31. Ibid.
32. Roula Khalaf, "Radicals Ensure Explosive Reaction to Cartoons," *Financial Times*, February 6, 2006.
33. Lawrence Pintak and Syed Javed Nazir, "Inside the Muslim (Journalist's) Mind," *New York Times*, February 13, 2011.
34. Nina Bernstein, "Young Germans Ask: Thanks for What?" *New York Times*, March 9, 2003.

Chapter 4. Images from the Image Machines

1. Samuel P. Huntington, *The Clash of Civilizations and the Remaking of World Order* (New York: Simon & Schuster, 1996), 91.
2. Pew Research Center, *What the World Thinks in 2002* (Washington, DC: The Pew Global Attitudes Project, December 4, 2002), 66. [Hereafter cited as *Pew Survey 2002*.]
3. "In general, people around the world object to the wide diffusion of American ideas and customs. Even those who are attracted to many aspects of American society, including its democratic ideas and free market traditions, object to the export of American ideas and customs. Yet this broad-brush rejection of 'Americanism' obscures the admiration many people have for American culture and particularly U.S. science and technology." *Pew Survey 2002*, 63.
4. Peter Schneider, "Across a Great Divide: Europe and America," *New York Times*, March 13, 2004.
5. Gregory Feifer, "Nixon, Khrushchev And A Story of Cold War Love," National Public Radio, March 30, 2009, http://www.NPR.org/templates/story/story.php?storyId=101430375.
6. ReseAnne Sims, "The United States vs. The World: A Theoretical Look at Cultural Imperialism" (Austin: University of Texas, 1994), 13, http://www.utexas.edu/ftp/depts/eems/cultimp.387.
7. Kristin M. Lord, "Voices of America: U.S. Public Diplomacy for the 21st Century," Brookings Institution, November 2008, 10, http://www.

brookings.edu/~/media/Files/rc/reports/2008/11_public_diploma-cy_lord/11_public_diplomacy_lord.pdf.
8. Lauren A. E. Schuker, "Plot Change: Foreign Forces Transform Holly-wood Films," *Wall Street Journal*, July 31, 2010.
9. Neal M. Rosendorf, "A Cultural Public Diplomacy Strategy," in *Toward a New Public Diplomacy*, ed. Philip Seib (New York: Palgrave Macmillan, 2009), 187.
10. *The Economic Impact of the Motion Picture & Television Industry on the United States* (Los Angeles: Motion Picture Association of America, April 2009), 7, http://www.mnddc.org/asd-employment/pdf/09-TEI-MPAA.pdf.
11. Nathan Gardels and Mike Medavoy, *American Idol After Iraq* (Chichester, West Sussex, UK: Wiley-Blackwell, 2009), 4.
12. David Malouf, "What We Think of America," *Granta* 77, 76 (Spring, 2002): 58.
13. Jenny Diski, *Stranger on a Train: Daydreaming and Smoking Around America with Interruptions* (London: Virago, 2002), 8–9.
14. Stephen J. Whitfield, "Projecting Politics: The Grapes of Wrath," *Revue LISA*, para. 38, http://lisa.revues.org/index802.html.
15. Nick King, interview by author, February 5, 2010.
16. Anné Kulonen, interview by author, January 28, 2010.
17. Nathan Gardels and Mike Medavoy, *American Idol After Iraq* (*World Bank* Chichester, West Sussex, UK: Wiley-Blackwell, 2009), 12.

Chapter 5. The United States Looms: Measuring Reality
1. Joseph S. Nye, Jr., "U.S. Power and Strategy After Iraq," *Foreign Affairs* 82, 4 (July/August 2003): 60.
2. U.S. Department of Commerce, Bureau of Economic Analysis, "National Income and Product Accounts," news release, March 25, 2011, http://www.bea.gov/newsreleases/national/gdp/2011/gdp4q10_3rd.htm.
3. Central Intelligence Agency, *World Factbook*, https://www.cia.gov/library/publications/the-world-factbook/geos/ch.html.
4. *Economist Figures 2011*.
5. Ibid.
6. Ibid.
7. World Bank, *World Development Report 2008* (Washington, DC: The In-ternational Bank for Reconstruction and Development/World Bank, 2008), 1.
8. Niall Ferguson, "Complexity and Collapse," *Foreign Affairs* 89, 2 (March/April 2010): 18, 22. Note that forecasts by the International Monetary Fund published in April 2011 estimating that Chinese GDP would ex-ceed United States GDP by 2016 were based on GDP measured on a "purchasing power parity" basis and not on the market price basis used here and generally accepted as the measure of GDP. See Clyde V. Presto-witz, "China Won't Pass the U.S. Anytime Soon," *Foreign Policy* (July 17, 2011), http://prestowitz.foreignpolicy.com/posts/2011/04/28/china_wont_pass_the_us_anytime_soon.
9. Anna Katona, "Sándor Farkas Boloni and Ágoston Mokcsai Haraszthy," *Abroad in America: Visitors to the New Nation 1776–1914*, eds. Marc Pachter and Frances Stevenson Wein (Washington, DC: Smithsonian Institution, 1976), 43.

10. United States Census Bureau figures for 2009. See Rick Rojas, "Using New Method of Tallying, Census Bureau Says 15.7% Live in Poverty," *Los Angeles Times,* January 5, 2011.
11. *Economist Figures 2011.*
12. World Bank, *The Changing Wealth of Nations* (Washington, D.C.: The International Bank for Reconstruction and Development/World Bank, 2010), 162–169.
13. Ibid., 5.
14. Ceaser, *Reconstructing America,* 163.
15. Ibid.
16. *Economist Figures 2011.*
17. Deborah Solomon and Mark Gongloff, "China Unseated as Top U.S. Debt Holder," *Wall Street Journal,* February 17, 2010.
18. *Economist Figures 2011.*
19. Scott De Carlo, "The World's Biggest Companies," *Forbes,* April 8, 2009, http://www.forbes.com/2011/04/20/biggest-world-business-global -2000-11-intro.html.
20. "WFE 2010 Market Highlights," World Federation of Exchanges, http:// www.world-exchanges.org/statistics.
21. Ziauddin Sardar and Merryl Wyn Davies, *Why Do People Hate America?* (New York: Disinformation Company, 2002), 195–96.
22. *Economist Figures 2011.*
23. Ibid.
24. Robert Reich, "America the Stingy," PBS radio, *Marketplace* broadcast, (July 6, 2000), http://www.ontheissues.org/Governor/Robert_Reich _Foreign_Policy.htm.
25. *Economist Figures 2011,* 56.
26. Ibid., 87.
27. Richard Ruland, *America in Modern European Literature* (New York: New York University Press), 68.
28. *Economist Figures 2011,* 62.
29. Ibid.
30. *Pew Survey 2002,* 5.
31. Trollope, *Manners,* 74.
32. *Pocket World in Figures 2005* (London: Economist Newspaper, 2004), 92.
33. Motion Picture Association of America, http://mpaa.org/research Statistics.asp.
34. Lauren A. E. Schuker, "Plot Change: Foreign Forces Transform Hollywood Films," *Wall Street Journal,* July 31, 2010.
35. Pew Research Center, *Views of a Changing World* (Washington, DC: The Pew Research Center for the People and the Press, June 2003), 78. [Hereafter cited as *Pew Survey 2003.*]
36. Kim Willsher, "French Groups Struggle to Beat Back English," *Los Angeles Times,* February 4, 2011.
37. "SIPRI Military Expenditure Database," Stockholm International Peace Research Institute, 2011, http://www.sipri.org/databases/milex.
38. Adam Segal, Harold Brown, and Joseph W. Prueher, *Chinese Military Power* (New York: Council on Foreign Relations, 2003), 2.
39. The Obama administration's proposed defense budget for fiscal year 2011 was $708 billion, a 3.4 percent increase over the amount of the

2010 budget, as stated in United States Department of Defense, "DOD Releases Defense Reviews, 2011 Budget Proposal, and 2010 War Funding Supplement Request—Update," Release No. 084-10, February 1, 2010.

Chapter 6. Conveying and Distorting Images
1. According to a University of Maryland world public opinion survey, 27 percent of Pakistanis, 15 percent of Italians, and 23 percent of Germans express this view. Stephens, "What Ahmadinejad Knows."
2. Lawrence Wright, "The Kingdom of Silence," *The New Yorker*, January 5, 2004, 48, 71–72.
3. World Bank, *World Development Report 2010* (Washington, DC: The International Bank for Reconstruction and Development/World Bank, 2010), 379.
4. *Arab Human Development Report 2003: Building a Knowledge Society* (New York: United Nations Development Programme, 2003), 62.
5. Lawrence Wright, "The Kingdom of Silence," *The New Yorker*, January 5, 2004, 48, 72.
6. Bruce Walker, "There is No Pravda in Izvestiya," *American Daily*, February 19, 2010.
7. International Federation of Journalists, *Live News—A Survival Guide for Journalists*, appendix 2, November 4, 2003, 124, http://www.hnd.hr/uploads/Journalism_survival_guide2003.pdf.
8. Eason Jordan, "The News We Kept to Ourselves," *New York Times*, April 11, 2003.
9. Nicholas D. Kristof, "The World Capital of Killing," *New York Times*, February 7, 2010.
10. Georges Duhamel, "America the Menace: Scenes from the Life of the Future," in *Broken* Image, 234–35.
11. Joseph Braude, "Reelpolitik," *Los Angeles Times Magazine*, November 20, 2005, 10.

Chapter 7. Predispositions
1. Nathan Gardels and Mike Medavoy, *American Idol After Iraq* (Chichester, West Sussex, UK: Wiley-Blackwell, 2009), 56.
2. *Pew Survey One Year After War*, 24, 28.
3. Simon Anholt and Jeremy Hildreth, *Brand America: The Making, Unmaking and Remaking of the Greatest National Image of All Time* (London: Marshall Cavendish Business, 2010), 8.
4. *Pew Survey 2009*, 1.
5. David Zucchino, "Libyan Rebels Embrace U.S. and its Flag," *Los Angeles Times*, August 5, 2011.
6. Luke Harding, "I Will Always Hate You People," *Guardian* (Manchester), May 24, 2004.
7. Abigail Hauslohner, "Postcard: Yemen. An Evening with the Villagers of Al-Qaeda," *Time*, February 1, 2010, 6.
8. *Pew Survey 2003*, 19.
9. Chicago Council on Foreign Relations and German Marshall Fund, *Worldviews 2002*, 8.
10. *Pew Survey One Year After War*, 6, 8.
11. Amelie Mummendey, Andreas Klink, and Rupert Brown, "Nationalism

and Patriotism: National Identification and Out-group Rejection," *British Journal of Social Psychology* 40, no. 2 (June 2001), 159.

12. Christopher Hitchens, *Hitch-22* (New York: Hatchette, 2010), 206.
13. Michaela Hogg and Dominic Abrams, *Social Identifications—A Social Psychology of Intergroup Relations and Group Processes* (New York: Routledge, 1988), 157 et seq.
14. James W. Ceaser, "A Genealogy of Anti-Americanism," *The Public Interest* (Summer 2003): 4.
15. Alexander Stille, "French Philosophy and The Spirit of Terrorism," *Council on Foreign Relations Correspondence* 9 (Spring 2002): 8.
16. Richard Bernstein, "Foreign Views of U.S. Darken After Sept. 11," *New York Times*, September 11, 2003.
17. Maxim Gorky, "The City of Mammon: My Impressions of America," *Appleton's Magazine* (1906), in *Broken Image*, 175.
18. Ned Parker and Rahim Salman, "Iraqi Voter Turnout Estimated at 62%," *Los Angeles Times*, March 9, 2010.
19. Giovanna Dell'Orto, *The Hidden Power of the American Dream: Why Europe's Shaken Confidence in the United States Threatens the Future of U.S. Influence* (Westport, CT: Praeger Security International, 2008), 141.
20. Ethan Bronner, "For Many Abroad, an Ideal Renewed," *New York Times*, November 7, 2008.
21. Richard Bernstein, "The Germans Who Toppled Communism Resent the U.S.," *New York Times*, February 22, 2003.
22. Richard Ruland, *America in Modern European Literature* (New York: New York University Press), 87.

Chapter 8. Romanticism versus Democratic Liberalism
1. The word "liberalism" and the phrases "liberal democracy" and "democratic liberalism" are used in this book to refer to the philosophical theories of the Enlightenment, rather than to the partisan political alignments or philosophies such as conservative and liberal that characterize modern American politics.
2. Michael Mandelbaum, "The Inadequacy of American Power," *Foreign Affairs* 81, 5 (September/October 2002): 62.
3. Ceaser, *Reconstructing America*, 28–29.
4. Ibid., 24–26.
5. Ibid., 67. "Those on the Left initially hailed the American Revolution as a precursor of the French Revolution. Indeed, in the first phases of the French Revolution, the group that pushed the process forward was sometimes referred to as the *americanistes* . . . "
6. William Wordsworth, *The Prelude*, bk. 11, lines 108 and 113.
7. Joyce Appleby, *Thomas Jefferson* (New York, Henry Holt, 2003), 154.
8. James Fenimore Cooper, *The Last of the Mohicans* (New York: Bantam Books, 1981), 47–48.
9. James Bryce observed in 1888, "So far, then, as regards American literature generally, there may be discovered in it something that is distinctive yet little (if anything) specifically democratic. . . . For the purposes of thought and art the United States is a part of England, and England is a part of America. Many English books are more widely read and strike deeper to the heart in America than in England. Some American books

have a like fortune in England. Differences there are, but differences how trivial compared with the resemblances in temper, in feeling, in susceptibility to certain forms of moral and physical beauty, in the general view of life and nature, in the disposition to revere and be swayed by the same matchless models of that elder literature which both branches of the English race can equally claim. American literature does not to-day differ more from English literature than the Scottish writers of the later eighteenth century. . . . But they were English as well as Scottish writers: they belong to English literature and make part of its glory to the world beyond. So Franklin, Fenimore Cooper, Hawthorne, Emerson, Longfellow, Lowell, and those on whom their mantle has fallen, belong to England as well as to America." James Bryce, *The American Commonwealth*, vol. 2 (New York: Macmillan, 1898), 830–31.

10. Henry Wadsworth Longfellow, *The Song of Hiawatha*, chap. 22, lines 62–79.
11. James Hagengruber, "Sitting Bull uber alles," Salon.com, Nov. 27, 2002, http://www.salon.com/mwt/feature/2002/11/27/indians/print.html.
12. Karl Marx and Frederick Engels, *The Communist Manifesto* (1848), trans. Samuel Moore in cooperation with Frederick Engels (1888), http:/www.marxists.org/archive/marx/works/1848/communist-manifesto/index.htm.
13. See Arthur Herman, *The Idea of Decline in Western History* (New York: Free Press, 1997), 46–68. [Hereafter cited as Herman, *Idea of Decline*.]
14. Ibid., 62.
15. Ibid., 90.
16. Ibid., 107.
17. *Knut Hamsun Remembers America: Essays and Stories 1885–1949*, ed. and trans. Richard Nelson Current (Columbia, MO: University of Missouri Press, 2003), 17–18.
18. Ibid., 19.
19. Ibid., 20.
20. Trollope, *Domestic Manners*, 234–35.
21. Ibid., 256.
22. Ibid., 314.
23. Simon Schama, "The Unloved American," *The New Yorker*, March 10, 2003, 35–36. "One of the sights to stare at in America is that of houses moving from place to place. We were often amused by watching this exhibition of mechanical skill in the streets. They make no difficulty of moving dwellings from one part of the town to another."—Trollope, *Domestic Manners*, 70.
24. James Bryce, *The American Commonwealth*, vol. 2 (New York: Macmillan, 1898), 870.
25. Maxim Gorky, "The City of Mammon: My Impressions of America," *Appleton's Magazine* (1906), in *Broken Image*, 173, 175.
26. Ibid., 187.
27. Rudyard Kipling, *American Notes* (Norman: University of Oklahoma Press, 1981), 87.
28. James Bryce, *The American Commonwealth*, vol. 2 (New York: Macmillan, 1898), 932.
29. Max Weber, "The Protestant Sects and the Spirit of Capitalism," in *From Max Weber: Essays in Sociology*, eds. H. H. Gerth and C. Wright Mills (New York: Routledge, 2007), 310.

30. Stanley K., Schultz, "Foreign Immigrants in Industrial America," University of Wisconsin, http://us.history.wisc.edu/hist102/lectures/textonly/lecture08.html.
31. James Joll, *Three Intellectuals in Politics* (New York: Pantheon Books, 1960), 140.
32. See Herman, *Idea of Decline*, 236–245.
33. V. I. Lenin, "Letter to American Workers," in *Broken Image*, 213.
34. Maxim Gorky, "The City of Mammon: My Impressions of America," *Appleton's Magazine* (1906), in *Broken Image*, 179.
35. Rudyard Kipling, *American Notes* (Norman: University of Oklahoma Press, 1981), 144.
36. Georges Duhamel, *America the Menace: Scenes from the Life of the Future*, in *Broken Image*, 230.
37. Ibid., 233.
38. Ceaser, *Reconstructing America*, 192.
39. James W. Ceaser, "A Genealogy of Anti-Americanism," *The Public Interest* (Summer 2003): 14.
40. Ceaser, *Reconstructing America*, 189.
41. Adolf Hitler, *Mein Kampf* (Boston: Houghton Mifflin, 1972), 289, 296.
42. Alfred Rosenberg, *The Myth of the Twentieth Century* (Newport Beach, CA: Noontide Press, 1982), 440.
43. Christopher Hitchens, "The Old Man," *The Atlantic*, July/August 2004, 152, 155.
44. Jean-Paul Sartre, *Nausea* (New York: New Directions, 1964), 158.
45. Ceaser, *Reconstructing America*, 235.
46. Ibid., 237–238.
47. Bernard-Henri Lévy, *Left in Dark Times: A Stand Against the New Barbarism* (New York: Random House, 2008), 113, 128.
48. Ian Buruma and Avishai Margalit, *Occidentalism* (New York: Penguin Press, 2004), 72.
49. Frantz Fanon, *The Wretched of the Earth*, trans. Richard Philcox (New York: Grove Press, 2004), 236–237.
50. Max Colchester, "The French Get Lost in the Clouds Over a New Term in the Internet Age," *Wall Street Journal*, October 14, 2009.
51. Christian Sylt, "Magic Results: Euro Disney Plans New Hotels," *Independent* (London), August 17, 2008.
52. Glenn Whipp, "Is 'Avatar' A Message Movie? Absolutely, Says James Cameron," *Los Angeles Times*, February 10, 2010.
53. "Israel Begins Rerouting Barrier in West Bank," *Los Angeles Times*, February 13, 2010.
54. Jared M. Diamond, *Collapse: How Societies Choose to Fail or Succeed* (New York: Viking Adult, 2004).
55. Harold Pinter, "What We Think of America," *Granta* 77, 76 (Spring 2002): 68.
56. Harold Pinter, "Art, Truth & Politics" (Nobel Lecture, December 7, 2005), http://nobelprize.org/nobel_prizes/literature/laureates/2005/pinter-lecture-e.html.
57. Anthee Carassava, "A Nation at War: Protest, Anti-Americanism in Greece Is Reinvigorated by War, *New York Times*, April 7, 2003.
58. Klíma, "What We Think of America."

Chapter 9. Traditional Societies

1. Stern, *Terror in the Name of God*, 228.
2. Amin Maalouf, *In the Name of Identity: Violence and the Need to Belong* (New York: Arcade, 2001), 74–75.
3. Mohammed Bin Rashid Al Maktoum, "Education vs. Extremism," *Wall Street Journal*, June 3, 2009.
4. Ibid., 71–72.
5. Henry Fairlie, "Anti-Americanism at Home and Abroad," *Commentary*, December 1975, 29, 39.
6. Tariq Ali, "Hegemony," in *American Effect: Global Perspectives on the United States, 1990–2003*, ed. Lawrence Rinder (New York: Whitney Museum of American Art, 2003), 123, 129.
7. Maria Rosa Menocal, *The Ornament of the World: How Muslims, Jews, and Christians Created a Culture of Tolerance in Medieval Spain* (New Haven, CT: Yale University Press, 2002), 12.
8. Prime Minister Dato Seri Mahathir bin Mohamad of Malaysia, speech at Tenth Session of the Islamic Summit Conference, October 16, 2003, http://www.bernama.com/oicsummit.
9. "Arabs and Democracy," *Wall Street Journal*, July 8, 2002.
10. United Nations, *Arab Human Development Report 2003: Building a Knowledge Society* (New York: United Nations Development Programme, 2003), 67.
11. United Nations, *Arab Human Development Report 2002* (New York: United Nations Development Programme, 2002), 3.
12. United Nations, *Arab Human Development Report 2009: Challenges to Human Security in the Arab Countries* (New York: United Nations Development Programme, 2009), 1.
13. Albert Hourani, *A History of the Arab Peoples* (Cambridge, MA: Harvard University Press, 1991), 84.
14. Ibid., 85.
15. Bernard Lewis, *What Went Wrong?* (Oxford, UK: Oxford University Press, 2002), 4, 6.
16. Ibid., 16.
17. Ibid., 114–15.
18. Irshad Manji, *The Trouble With Islam* (New York: St. Martin's, 2003), 145.
19. Ibid.
20. Samuel P. Huntington, "The Clash of Civilizations," *Foreign Affairs* 72, 3 (Summer 1993), 22.
21. Koran, 3:140.
22. Koran, 42:10.
23. Koran, 2:163.
24. Koran, 18:101.
25. Bernard Lewis, *What Went Wrong?* (Oxford: Oxford University Press, 2002), 104.
26. Irshad Manji, *The Trouble With Islam* (New York: St. Martin's, 2003), 133.
27. Sheik Muhammad Fartousi and Sheik Abbas al-Zubaidi quoted in Craig S. Smith, "Iraqi Shiites, Jockeying for Power, Preach an Anti-American Sermon," *New York Times*, April 20, 2003.
28. Koran, 4:14.
29. Koran, 3:185.

30. Paul Hollander, "The Politics of Envy," *The New Criterion*, November 2002, 14, 15–16.
31. Quoted in Jonathan Raban, "Truly, Madly, Deeply Devout," *Guardian* (Manchester), March 2, 2002.
32. Koran, 109:1.
33. Quoted in Jefferson Morley, "Arab Media Confront the 'New Rules of the Game,'" *Washington Post*, April 9, 2003.
34. Raban, "Truly, Madly, Deeply Devout."
35. See *Pew Survey 2003.*
36. Salim Jihad, quoted in "3 Americans Slain in Blast in Gaza Strip," *New York Times*, October 16, 2003.
37. Zaki Badawi, quoted in Graham Turner, "Travels in the Muslim World," *Daily Telegraph* (London), September 3, 2002.
38. John Bradley, quoted in Jefferson Morley, "Arab Media Confront the 'New Rules of the Game'," *Washington Post*, April 9, 2003.
39. Andrea Elliott, "Bombing Suspect's Long Path to Times Square," *New York Times*, May 16, 2010.
40. United Nations, *Arab Human Development Report 2003: Building a Knowledge Society* (New York: United Nations Development Programme, 2003), 4.
41. Adam Davidson, "Loves Microsoft, Hates America," *New York Times Sunday Magazine*, March 9, 2003, 18.
42. Adam Shatz, "An Arab Poet Who Dares to Differ," *New York Times*, July 13, 2002.
43. Khalid S. Al-Khater, "Thinking About Arab-American Relations: A New Perspective," *Middle East Review of International Affairs* 7, 2, (June 2003), 79, 88.
44. Thomas L. Friedman, "Look Who's Talking," *New York Times*, February 19, 2004.
45. *Pew Survey 2003*, 6.

Chapter 10. Disappointment: Envy and the American Dream

1. *Pew Survey 2011*, 20.
2. William L. Hamilton, "For Bantu Refugees, Hard-Won American Dreams," *New York Times*, July 5, 2004.
3. James B. Davies, Susanna Sandstrom, Anthony Shorrocks, and Edwin N. Wolff, *The World Distribution of Household Wealth* (Santa Cruz, CA: UC Santa Cruz: Center for Global, International and Regional Studies, 2007), 7.
4. World Bank, *Development Report 2010*, 379.
5. "1.02 Billion People Hungry," Food and Agriculture Organization of the United Nations, June 19, 2009, http://www.fao.org/news/story/en/item/20568/icode/.
6. World Bank, *Development Report 2010*, 379.
7. Ibid.
8. United Nations, *Millennium Development Goals Report 2007* (New York: United Nations, 2007), 14.
9. Ibid., 11.
10. World Bank, *Development Report 2010*, 383.
11. Ibid.

12. "The State of the World's Children 1999," United Nations Children's Fund, 1999, http://www.unicef.org/sowc99/index.html.
13. United Nations, *Millennium Development Goals Report 2007* (New York: United Nations, 2007), 20.
14. Mark Magnier, "India Lags Far behind in Sanitation Facilities," *Los Angeles Times*, March 22, 2010.
15. Ibid.
16. *Economist Figures 2011*, 59.
17. World Bank, *Development Report 2010*, 379.
18. *Economist Figures 2011*, 18.
19. Juan de Recacoechea, *American Visa*, trans. Adrian Althoff (New York: Akashic Books, 2007).
20. Jenny Diski, *Stranger on a Train: Daydreaming and Smoking Around America with Interruptions* (London: Virago, 2002), 8.
21. Ian Buruma, "What We Think of America," *Granta* 77, 76 (Spring 2002): 20.
22. Adam Davidson, "Loves Microsoft, Hates America," *New York Times Sunday Magazine*, March 9, 2003, 18.
23. Michael Slackman, "Jordanian Students Rebel, Embracing Conservative Arm of Islam," *New York Times*, December 24, 2008.
24. Envy should be distinguished from jealousy. Envy is resentment of a person who has what you want and cannot get. Jealousy is resentment driven by fear of losing to another person that which you already have. Thus, a husband is said to be jealous of his wife if he fears she is in love with another man. A person is said to guard his privacy jealously. Envy and jealousy come closer to being opposites than to being synonymous.
25. Trollope, *Manners*, 235.
26. *Knut Hamsun Remembers America: Essays and Stories 1885–1949*, ed. and trans. Richard Nelson Current (Columbia, MO: University of Missouri Press, 2003), 17.
27. Georges Duhamel, *America the Menace: Scenes from the Life of the Future*, in *Broken Image*, 214.
28. Nathan Gardels and Mike Medavoy, *American Idol After Iraq* (Chichester, West Sussex, UK: Wiley-Blackwell, 2009), 6.
29. *Pew Survey 2002*, 56.
30. Lawrence Rinder, "The American Effect," in *The American Effect*, ed. Lawrence Rinder (New York: Whitney Museum of American Art, 2003), 15, 16.
31. Anna Katona, "Sándor Farkas Boloni and Ágoston Mokcsai Haraszthy," in *Abroad in America: Visitors to the New Nation 1776–1914*, eds. Marc Pachter and Frances Stevenson Wein (Washington, DC: Smithsonian Institution, 1976), 43, 51.
32. World Bank, *Development Report 2010*, 387.
33. Rinder, "The American Effect," in *The American Effect*, 25.
34. Dell'Orto, *The Hidden Power of the American Dream*, 2.
35. Philip Collins, "Charles Dickens," in *Abroad in America: Visitors to the New Nation, 1776–1914*, eds. Marc Pachter and Frances Stevenson Wein (Washington, DC: Smithsonian Institution, 1976), 83, 89.
36. Gamil Mattar, quoted in Graham Turner, "Travels in the Muslim World," *Daily Telegraph* (London), September 3, 2002.
37. Jan Morris, "Down, Down on America," *New York Times*, November 13, 1983.
38. Dell'Orto, *The Hidden Power of the American Dream*, 159.

Chapter 11. Enhancing the Image of America Strategically

1. James Bryce, *The American Commonwealth*, vol. 2 (New York: Macmillan, 1898), 846.
2. Bertrand Russell, *War Crimes in Vietnam* (London: Allen & Unwin, 1967), 112, 117–118.
3. *Pew Survey 2003*, 19.
4. In April 2003 Indian novelist Arundhati Roy, who had called the U.S. invasion of Iraq a "racist war" bringing on "starvation" and "mass murder," wrote that, "At the end of it all, it remains to be said that dictators like Saddam Hussein, and all the other despots in the Middle East, in the Central Asian republics, in Africa and Latin America, many of them installed, supported and financed by the US government, are a menace to their own people. Other than strengthening the hand of civil society (instead of weakening it as has been done in the case of Iraq), there is no easy, pristine way of dealing with them." (Quoted in Ian Buruma, "Wielding a Mighty Moral Club," *Financial Times*, September 13, 2003.)
5. Laura King, "In Afghanistan, Doubts Grow, Weariness Deepens," *Los Angeles Times*, June 24, 2010.
6. See Kristin M. Lord, "Voices of America: U.S. Public Diplomacy for the 21st Century," Brookings Institution, November 2008, 11, http://www.brookings.edu/~/media/Files/rc/reports/2008/11_public_diplomacy_lord/11_public_diplomacy_lord.pdf.
7. Sonni Efron, "Reaching Arabs Via Airwaves," *Los Angeles Times*, August 26, 2002.
8. Ibid.
9. Office of the Under Secretary of State for Public Diplomacy and Public Affairs, *Public Diplomacy: Strengthening U.S. Engagement with the World*, February 2010, 13, http://mountainrunner.us/files/dos/PD_US_World_Engagement.pdf.
10. Barack Obama, speech at Cairo University, June 4, 2009.
11. Thomas Friedman, "Shoulda, Woulda, Can," *New York Times*, May 27, 2004.
12. See, e.g., Lord, "Voices of America: U.S. Public Diplomacy for the 21st Century."
13. Office of the Under Secretary of State for Public Diplomacy and Public Affairs, *Public Diplomacy: Strengthening U.S. Engagement with the World* (February 2010), 14, http://mountainrunner.us/files/dos/PD_US_World_Engagement.pdf.
14. Helene Cooper, "U.S. Officials Get a Taste of Pakistanis' Anger at America," *New York Times*, August 20, 2009.

Selected Bibliography

Al-Shaykh, Hanan, Amit Chaudhuri, Ariel Dorfman, et al. "What We Think of America." *Granta* 77 (Spring 2002): 9–81.

Anholt, Simon and Jeremy Hildreth. *Brand America: The Making, Unmaking and Remaking of the Greatest National Image of All Time.* London: Marshall Cavendish Business, 2010.

Armitage, Richard L., and Joseph S. Nye Jr., cochairs. *CSIS Commission on Smart Power.* Washington, D.C.: Center for Strategic & International Studies, 2007.

Aslan, Reza. *No god but God: The Origins, Evolution, and Future of Islam.* New York: Random House Trade Paperbacks, 2006.

Baudrillard, Jean. *America.* London: Verso, 2010.

Bryce, James. *The American Commonwealth.* 2 vols. New York: Macmillan, 1899.

Buruma, Ian, and Avishai Margalit. *Occidentalism: The West in the Eyes of Its Enemies.* New York: Penguin, 2004.

Ceaser, James W. *Reconstructing America: The Symbol of America in Modern Thought.* New Haven, CT: Yale University Press, 1997.

Chiozza, Giacomo. *Anti-Americanism and the American World Order.* Baltimore, MD: Johns Hopkins University Press, 2009.

Cooke, Alistair. *Alistair Cooke's American Journey: Life on the Home Front in the Second World War.* London: Allen Lane, 2006.

Crèvecoeur, J. Hector St. John de. *Letters from an American Farmer and Sketches of Eighteenth-Century America.* New York: Penguin Classics, 1986.

Dell'Orto, Giovanna. *The Hidden Power of the American Dream: Why Europe's Shaken Confidence in the United States Threatens the Future of U.S. Influence.* Westport, CT: Praeger Security International, 2008.

D'Souza, Dinesh. *What's So Great About America.* Washington, DC: Regnery, 2002.

Diski, Jenny. *Stranger on a Train: Daydreaming and Smoking Around America with Interruptions.* London: Virago Press, 2002.

215

Ferguson, Niall. *Colossus: The Price of America's Empire.* New York: Penguin, 2004.

Friedman, Thomas L. *The World Is Flat: A Brief History of the Twenty-first Century.* New York: Farrar, Straus and Giroux, 2005.

Gardels, Nathan, and Mike Medavoy. *American Idol After Iraq: Competing for Hearts and Minds in the Global Media Age.* Chichester, West Sussex, UK: Wiley-Blackwell, 2009.

Gelb, Leslie H. *Power Rules: How Common Sense Can Rescue American Foreign Policy.* New York: Harper, 2009.

Gulddal, Jesper. "The Most Hateful Land: Romanticism and the Birth of Modern Anti-Americanism." *Journal of European Studies* 39: 419 (2009), http://jes.sagepub.com/content/39/4/419.

Hamsun, Knut. *Knut Hamsun Remembers America: Essays and Stories 1885–1949.* Edited and translated by Richard Nelson Current. Columbia, MO: University of Missouri Press, 2003.

Harris, Lee. *Civilization and its Enemies: The Next Stage of History.* New York: Free Press, 2004.

Hartz, Louis. *The Liberal Tradition in America.* 2nd ed. New York: Harcourt Brace Jovanovich, 1991.

Herman, Arthur. *The Idea of Decline in Western History.* New York: Free Press, 1997.

Hertsgaard, Mark. *The Eagle's Shadow: Why America Fascinates and Infuriates the World.* New York: Farrar, Straus and Giroux, 2002.

Hollander, Paul. *Anti-Americanism: Irrational & Rational.* New Brunswick, NJ: Transaction Publishers, 1995.

Hourani, Albert. *A History of the Arab Peoples.* Cambridge, MA: Belknap Press of Harvard University Press, 1991.

Huntington, Samuel P. *The Clash of Civilizations and the Remaking of World Order.* New York: Simon & Schuster, 1996.

Isaacs, Harold R. *Scratches on Our Minds: American Views of China and India.* White Plains, NY: M. E. Sharpe, 1980.

Kagan, Robert. *Paradise and Power: America and Europe in the New World Order.* New York: Alfred A. Knopf, 2003.

———. *The Return of History and the End of Dreams.* New York: Vintage Books, 2009.

Katzenstein, Peter J. and Robert O. Keohane, eds. *Anti-Americanisms in World Politics.* Ithaca, NY: Cornell University Press, 2007.

Lévy, Bernard-Henri. *American Vertigo: Traveling America in the Footsteps of Tocqueville.* New York: Random House Trade Paperbacks, 2007.

———. *Left in Dark Times: A Stand against the New Barbarism.* Translated by Benjamin Moser. New York: Random House, 2008.

Lewis, Bernard. *What Went Wrong? Western Impact and Middle Eastern Response.* New York: Oxford University Press, 2002.

Maalouf, Amin. *In the Name of Identity: Violence and the Need to Belong.* Translated by Barbara Bray. New York: Arcade, 2001.

Martin, Dick. *Rebuilding Brand America: What We Must Do to Restore Our Reputation and Safeguard the Future of American Business Abroad.* New York: American Management Association, 2007.

Menocal, María Rosa. *The Ornament of the World: How Muslims, Jews, and Christians Created a Culture of Tolerance in Medieval Spain.* Boston: Little, Brown, 2002.

Patcher, Marc, and Frances Wein, eds. *Abroad in America: Visitors to the New Nation 1776-1914.* Reading, MA: Addison-Wesley, 1976.

Plate, Thomas Gordon. *Doctor M: Operation Malaysia—Conversations with Mahathir Mohamad.* Singapore: Marshall Cavendish, 2011.

Rather, Dan. *The American Dream: Stories from the Heart of Our Nation.* New York: William Morrow, 2001.

Rinder, Lawrence et al. *The American Effect: Global Perspectives on the United States, 1990–2003.* New York: Whitney Museum of American Art, 2003.

Rubin, Barry and Judith Colp Rubin. *Hating America: A History.* New York: Oxford University Press, 2004.

Sardar, Ziauddin and Merryl Wyn Davies. *Why Do People Hate America?* New York: Disinformation, 2002.

Seib, Philip, ed. *Toward a New Public Diplomacy: Redirecting U.S. Foreign Policy.* New York: Palgrave Macmillan, 2009.

Servan-Schreiber, Jean-Jacques. *The American Challenge.* Translated by Ronald Steel. New York: Atheneum, 1968.

Schoeck, Helmut. *Envy: A Theory of Social Behaviour.* Translated by Michael Glenny and Betty Ross. Indianapolis: Liberty Fund, 1987.

Slater, Michael, ed. *Dickens on America & the Americans.* Austin: University of Texas Press, 1978.

Tocqueville, Alexis de. *Democracy in America.* Translated and edited by Harvey Mansfield and Delba Winthrop. Chicago: University of Chicago Press, 2000.

Trollope, Frances. *Domestic Manners of the Americans.* New York: Penguin Classics, 1997.

Whybrow, Peter C. *American Mania: When More Is Not Enough.* New York: W. W. Norton, 2005.

Index

Note: *Italicized* page numbers refer to illustrations and their captions.

About the Author

Barry A. Sanders is an adjunct professor of communications studies at the University of California, Los Angeles. He is deeply involved in the foreign affairs community as a member of the Council on Foreign Relations and the Pacific Council on International Policy. He honed his international credentials in a career of extensive travel and cross-border negotiations as a well-known international business lawyer for the global law firm Latham & Watkins. He chaired both the State of California and Los Angeles County Bar Associations' international law sections. Sanders was the principal lawyer for the 1984 Los Angeles Olympic Games and remains deeply involved in the Olympic movement as Chair of the Southern California Committee for the Olympic Games. He lectures and writes often on topics of international law and civic affairs.

In Los Angeles, Sanders is a civic leader. He is president of the Board of Commissioners of the City of Los Angeles Department of Recreation and Parks, and immediate past president of the Board of Commissioners of the Los Angeles Memorial Coliseum. He is a member of the Executive Committee of the Los Angeles Opera. He has served as chairman of the Los Angeles Philharmonic Orchestra, the Los Angeles Public Library Foundation, Rebuild LA (the public-private organization created after the 1992 Los Angeles riots), and several other charitable organizations. Sanders has a BA from the University of Pennsylvania and a JD from Yale Law School.

For more information about this book, or if you have questions, comments, or would like to contact the author, please visit www.american avatar.com.